D0336820

CENTRE STAGE
Jamie Roberts

with Ross Harries

HODDER &
STOUGHTON

First published in Great Britain in 2021 by Hodder & Stoughton
An Hachette UK company

1

Hardback ISBN 978 1 529 36883 3
eBook ISBN 978 1 529 36884 0

Typeset in Fresco by Hewer Text UK Ltd, Edinburgh
Printed and bound in Great Britain by Clays Ltd, Elcograf S.p.A.

Hodder & Stoughton policy is to use papers that are natural, renewable and recyclable products and made from wood grown in sustainable forests. The logging and manufacturing processes are expected to conform to the environmental regulations of the country of origin.

Hodder & Stoughton Ltd
Carmelite House
50 Victoria Embankment
London EC4Y 0DZ

www.hodder.co.uk

Tomos, this book is dedicated to you. I hope you get to stand on the touchline and watch me play before I hang up my boots, and that you find as much joy in sport as I have.

CONTENTS

PROLOGUE

My mood is as dark as the inky black sky, as the road unfurls beneath me. I hurtle eastwards, chewing up the miles between Cardiff and London, feeling like I no longer belong to either. The car is quiet, the radio silent. There is enough noise inside my head. I loosen the grip on the steering wheel, noticing my knuckles have turned white. I've never been so angry. The needle on the speedometer flickers into the red.

For ten years, I've been a gladiator. An international rugby player with a reputation forged through strength, fortitude and physical dominance. My battles have been fought in stadiums across the globe, under lights, against some of the most feared warriors in my sport. I bow to no one, and fear nothing. I've experienced unadulterated joy and crippling heartache. I've broken bones, torn ligaments, lost consciousness and seen stars. I've toured the world, climbed podiums and lifted trophies. I've shed tears singing my anthem, and felt my heart thudding in my ribcage as, time and again, I pulled those three feathers over my chest.

I play for Wales.

I played for Wales.

It was all being ripped away from me. Not because of injury, infirmity or poor form. I was being denied the right to play for my country by petty bureaucrats. Men in suits who had no idea what it meant, what it felt like and why it defined who I was.

Anger and sorrow are natural bedfellows, and when I wasn't trembling with rage, I was crying softly. The road swept by, ghostly wind-blown trees and road signs visible through a tear-stained glaze. I saw the junctions come and go, the service stations pass me by – Leigh Delamere, Reading – each one a chance to stop, to reassess, to turn around. But I kept going, every passing mile feeling like a swelling ocean between me and the thing I cherished most.

I'd been recalled to the Wales squad for the autumn internationals, after originally being overlooked for selection. That was the euphemistic way of looking at it. A more prosaic interpretation was that I'd been dropped like a stone. After ten years as the fulcrum of the Wales midfield, a decade as one of the first names on the team sheet, I was deemed surplus to requirements. It had been a devastating moment, but my recall was a reprieve. A chance to reclaim my shirt, my status and my identity. The circumstances were unfortunate – an injury to my mate Jonathan Davies had opened the door for my return – but it was an opportunity I was going to embrace. Until it was whipped away from under my nose.

I'd been picked to face South Africa at the Millennium Stadium. The powerful, intimidating, granite-hard Springboks against whom I'd enjoyed my first start in the number 12 shirt, the shirt that became an extra layer of skin. The match fell outside the official Test-playing window, which meant clubs weren't obliged to release their players. Those who played club rugby in Wales were free to play, thanks to an agreement between the Welsh Rugby Union and the clubs. Those, like myself, who played in England weren't, unless they'd made their own arrangements. When I'd signed for the English aristocrats Harlequins, it was on the explicit understanding that I had full release to play for Wales, wherever and whenever the matches were scheduled. So what happened next caught me as unawares as a below-the-belt sucker punch.

They issued an ultimatum: report back to Harlequins for training on Thursday, or don't bother coming back at all. It was couched in slightly more diplomatic language, but the crux was clear: play for Wales and you're sacked. Imagine being offered the chance to do something you cherish more than anything else, but by accepting it you'll be holding a flaming torch to the rest: your job, your livelihood, the place you've chosen to settle, the life you've carved out for yourself. All up in smoke. It was an impossible, emotionally overwhelming decision, but one I was forced to make as though I was ticking a box on an application form.

The farewell of my dreams had been denied to me. No ovation in front of a capacity crowd, no hundredth cap. No final chance to breathe in the exhilarating air of international day in Wales, to feel my quickening pulse as I stand in the tunnel, before being transported by the intoxicating churn of emotions as I run into the swirling cacophony that reverberates around the greatest stadium on earth.

1
THE ROBERTS CLAN

Monday, 22 April 1985

It's approaching ten o'clock at night, and my sensible, law-abiding father is speeding down the M4 at 90 mph. The doors are rattling in the frame of his Ford Cortina as my heavily pregnant mother shifts uncomfortably in the back seat. My father groans inwardly as the flashing blue lights of a police car illuminate the road behind. The one time in his life he's broken the speed limit. Mercifully, the driver overtakes him and continues on his way, leaving the road clear to the Royal Gwent Hospital.

Half an hour earlier, they had been standing on a footbridge overlooking the wood-chipping plant at Sudbrook Paper Mill. It had been juddering and vibrating, and as the guide was explaining how the logs were being sliced, my mother's waters broke dramatically. Cue the mad dash from Chepstow to the hospital where, within moments of their arrival, my brother David was born five weeks ahead of schedule.

I arrived eighteen months later, and rather than learn their lesson from their fraught first experience, my parents took a holiday to Jersey the week I was due. During their stay an industrial strike was called by the union of ferry workers, and they very nearly got stranded on the island before the ports closed. Had it not been for a mad dash for the final boat to leave, I'd have been born a Channel Islander and would have been eligible to represent any of the home nations.

As it was, I was born, like my brother, in the Royal Gwent, making me a Newportonian by birth, though I've long considered myself a Cardiff boy. Ironic, given that in rugby terms Newport and Cardiff were mutually despised rivals. I was 8 lb 2 oz, nearly three pounds heavier than my brother, but by no means a big baby. My transformation into a giant would come later.

It was my arrival that prompted the move from Newport to Cardiff. The presence of a second child made my parents' modest maisonette in Allt-yr-yn seem cramped and claustrophobic, and after seven months coping with two rambunctious young boys, the eldest of whom seemed determined to destroy the fixtures and fittings, my parents decided the time was right to upscale. In July of 1987, we moved west to a new-build on the northern fringes of Cardiff. 'North Cardiff' hadn't existed a few years earlier, but as the capital was expanding, the suburbs were encroaching further into the meadowlands that had once encircled the city, and we found ourselves in a little detached house on an estate in Thornhill. My parents are still there to this day.

Hidden away in a drawer in my Auntie Pam's house in Newport is a corner of Adolf Hitler's desk. It lies alongside some pieces of war memorabilia, including a dagger and a few medals. It's been a source of fascination for me ever since I held its smooth marbled surface in my hand as a young boy, but I still know very little about how it came to be there. That's because my paternal grandfather, Percy Roberts, was a quiet man. He'd fought as a Regimental Sergeant Major in the Second World War, and found himself in the Chancellery in Berlin during the dramatic final days when the Nazis were defeated. Sensing that he was standing at the heart of history, he picked up the corner of the desk lying among the wreckage of the bombed-out room and stuffed it into his pocket.

He told my father next to nothing about what went on during the war, and me even less. As with most soldiers who'd experienced such horrors, he was reluctant to relive them, and probably thought nobody but those who'd been there would ever understand. My father said that whenever he'd tried to dig deep into my grandfather's memories, it would be like a pick sparking off solid rock. He'd only ever scratch the surface. Families didn't talk to one another the way we do today, but his influence has loomed large in my life through a phrase my dad coined when I was growing up: 'Percy-verance'. Percy was a stoic, determined sort of bloke, and my dad was keen to inculcate those qualities in Dave and me.

Percy was Newport born and bred, and after the war he worked at the site that manufactured steel tubes for Stewarts & Lloyds. During the war years, the company had built the so-called 'Pipeline Under the Ocean' after the D-Day landings to supply fuel for the Allied forces. Steelwork was his trade, but rugby was his passion. Every Saturday he'd walk from his house in St Julians down Christchurch Hill, and across to Rodney Parade, with his colleagues from the factory. On the same terraces I now play in front of, they'd stand and swig their pints of mild, while lustily shouting their support for the Black and Ambers. When he was old enough, my dad would accompany them. As soon as the final whistle blew, they'd file out of the ground and amble over the town bridge to wait for the football papers to roll off the presses. The *Football Argus* and the *Football Echo*, or the 'pink 'un' as it was colloquially known, were still warm to the touch when they were published within an hour of the final whistle. An avowed scholar of the game, it wasn't enough for Percy to have watched the action from the terraces. He had to digest and analyse what was written about it; to get the correspondent's perspective. He was the only grandparent I really knew. Dad's mum, Dorothy, died of cancer ten years before I was born.

Auntie Pam inherited the house on St Julian's Road when Percy died, so it remained in the family. I spent a lot of time there as a boy, watching Disney movies in the front room and playing Monopoly and Cluedo around the kitchen table. Grandad was always a jovial presence around the house, and brought a real sense of warmth and fun to those games sessions. I vividly remember breaking down in tears when he appeared in the kitchen doorway one evening with a severely bloodshot eye. It was genuinely frightening and I thought there was something seriously wrong. It turned out to be nothing, but his health started to fail him soon after. I'll never forget the image of my dad crumpled on the bed, sobbing uncontrollably, when Grandad eventually passed away. Dad was holding a Get Well Soon card that David and I had written to Grandad and were due to deliver to hospital the following day.

As a confused eight-year-old boy, I was incredibly sad and desperate for hugs and reassurance, whereas David seemed to process it more easily. He was far more emotionally detached than me, asking questions and trying to make sense of it. It was a pattern that would repeat itself throughout our lives. David's the pragmatic older brother and I'm the emotional younger one, incapable of holding my feelings in check. For a bloke with an outwardly tough exterior, I have a very soft centre. Years later, when I was celebrating the end of my GCSEs in a Newquay nightclub, Dad called to say that our cat had died. I was so bereft that I left the club, slumped onto a bench outside and cried my eyes out. When the lads came to find me, they couldn't believe I was so emotional over a family pet and, rather than offering sympathy, chose instead to take the mick.

My mum's mum, Margaret, was more of a spectral presence in my life. She lived in Risca, a town a few miles north-west of Newport, in a strange house that lacked the warmth and conviviality of Percy's place. Her relationship with my mum was strained, and there wasn't much affection between them. She had an aloof, eccentric air about her, amplified by the presence of squawking parrots in her front room. She was a heavy smoker, and there was always a fug of cigarette smoke hanging in the air. Mum's demeanour changed in Margaret's presence. She became a little less warm, a little more impatient. The atmosphere between them was often as oppressive as the smoke in the room. As a result I never felt particularly close to her. My mother never met her natural father, so when Margaret died in 2005, all my grandparents were gone. To this day, it breaks my heart that I had so little to do with them all.

My mother Jackie's upbringing was fractured and itinerant. Though she was born in Bristol, there was no one place she considered 'home'. Growing up, she rarely spoke about her childhood, but when David and I left home, she wrote a seventy-page memoir reflecting on all of our lives up to that point, in which she spoke really candidly about her formative years. It was the first time we had an insight into what she'd been through. It was a jumble of vague and unsettling memories involving domestic violence, grinding poverty and being constantly on the move. A particularly upsetting passage described a memory of being carried into a car by a strange man on a gloomy night while another man sobbed and begged them not to leave. My mother thinks the crying man was her natural father, but she never asked the question and remains haunted by the episode. As a fearful, confused child, she was discouraged from asking too many questions.

Not long after, she has a strong memory of sitting at a table and being taught to write her new surname. She was struggling to spell 'Proudfoot', writing 'fwt' in the Welsh phonetic way, and was berated by her mother and new father for being slow and incompetent. For five years, she lived with her Auntie Val and Uncle Ted near Monmouth, referring to them as 'Mum and Dad'. It's not clear where Margaret was during this time, and Mum only has a single faded photograph of this period. It's of her and an older boy painting a dog's toenails. She discovered years later that the boy was her brother, Patrick.

When her mother reclaimed her, they moved to a flat on Cardiff's City Road with another man, and a new sister, Heather. One night, tempers flared, objects were thrown and the man broke his arm. Details are hazy, but it led to Margaret moving into sheltered accommodation with the two girls. There was a brief reconciliation when they all moved to a place near Barry Docks, but this was short-lived and another sudden move followed, under cover of darkness, to a flat on Barry Island. The man would routinely come and bang on the door, and Heather and my mum would hide behind the bed. It must have been an incongruous scene. Two terrified girls cowering in silence while people were laughing, joking and careering about on the funfair rides below.

Several moves later, after her younger brother Peter had been born, the three children and Margaret settled in a caravan site in Newport, braving the freezing winter weather by wearing multiple layers and huddling together. When it rained, the reen next to the site would flood, making a loud gushing noise which kept them awake for hours. Food was scarce, and personal hygiene hard to maintain. Mum had to have her long locks cut off after persistent problems with nits. They ended up in Bettws, a notoriously rough housing estate in Newport. When Mum was living there, the threat of violence was a constant malignant presence. A police car was once set on fire, and a man was stabbed to death in the infamous Nightingale pub. At one point, the bin men were so frightened to come onto the estate, the rubbish lay piled up, uncollected, for weeks. The stress, anxiety and permanent sense of dislocation took its toll, and after completing her O levels, Mum made an attempt on her own life.

It was only when she applied for a job at the Passport Office in Newport that she discovered the identity of her real father. Needing a birth certificate to accompany her application, her mother reluctantly dug it out and the name in the box marked 'father' was one she didn't recognise. Margaret told her he'd died years earlier, and any further questions were heartlessly deflected. She was told that what happened in the past was best forgotten.

Desperate to break free of her increasingly claustrophobic existence, Mum accepted a marriage proposal from the brother of a friend and left Newport to start a new life in Manchester, where she soon began to feel restless and unfulfilled. Losing herself in American literature, she hatched a plan to escape to the US for a road trip. Her career-minded husband declined to accompany her, and the eventual cross-country voyage with a bunch of Australian and Kiwi backpackers proved a defining experience. It led, inevitably, to the breakdown of her marriage and, after arriving home, she returned to Newport to start afresh.

Most of my mum's school friends had left, so in a bid to meet new people, she signed up to the Newport Outdoor Group. A long-distance trek in the Grand Canyon had awakened a love for hiking, and while South Wales didn't provide quite the same epic backdrop, rambling offered a sense of freedom and escapism. On a fateful Monday night in April of 1982, when she introduced herself to the group, she was struck by the alluring presence of a certain Norman Roberts. Not your conventional hunk, with his knobbly knees poking out of his camouflage shorts and his laminated Ordnance Survey map around his neck, he nevertheless charmed young Jackie.

Discovering their mutual love of the outdoors, they agreed to meet for a drink the following evening. It was a smooth move from Norman, but any credit evaporated when he was forced to postpone, having forgotten that Newport were playing that night. Fortunately, Jackie wasn't too offended and they convened at the Newbridge-on-Usk country inn on the Wednesday instead. Norman's chat-up line about owning every OS map ever published worked like a dream, and he persuaded Jackie to accompany him on a 26-mile 'marathon' trek that Saturday. She wore the wrong socks and developed painful blisters before the first checkpoint, but through a combination of stubbornness on her part and gentle encouragement on Norman's, she completed it. The flame of romance had flickered into life.

Given Mum's own experience, she was determined to raise us as independent and curious-minded boys. We weren't going to endure the same suffocating control that she had. Our upbringing was to be a 'social experiment'. Dad was rarely home from work before eight in the evening, so Mum had free rein. The house was always a glorious mess, with toys, games, books and dressing-up clothes permanently scattered all over the place. In those early years we took advantage of the long leash and drew extravagant, colourful murals all over the walls. Mum had been a mature student at Newport Art College, so the bohemian within her encouraged it. She also emphasised the importance of hearty, home-cooked meals, a position no doubt forged by her own experience of poverty and a frugal diet. There wasn't a microwave in the house, and ready meals were banned.

We saw less of Dad, as he was the breadwinner in those early years, but he doted on us. If Mum was the nonconformist, arty influence, Dad was the strict, regimented one. Inheriting his own father's disciplinarian approach to life, for forty years he followed the same ordered routine. Up with the lark, he'd get out the electric razor for a daily shave, don a crisp pressed shirt and head out of the door before eight. He'd climb into his shiny Toyota – itself a symbol of Japanese efficiency – and drive the same route from Thornhill to the ArvinMeritor factory in Cwmbran, where he worked as an IT manager. He was resolutely old-school: never sick, never late. Norman. His name couldn't be more appropriate. It defines him. He'd always arrive home early on Fridays with liquorice and a bunch of flowers for my mum.

Norman kept a notebook in his glove compartment, and every time he filled the car with petrol, he'd note how many litres he'd put in and how much it had cost. He had records going back decades. To what end, I've no idea. Whenever my brother and I questioned it, he'd simply say, 'It's nice to keep a record.' This obsession with detail has led him to meticulously document my entire career. The archive of newspaper clippings, TV recordings and collectibles he's assembled could fill a museum. There are chests full of old jerseys and boots scattered about their house and garage.

Norman is the most sensible, practical man you'll ever meet. On family holidays, he'd take us to the airport hours before we really needed to be there, just in case there was a crash or an unexpected delay. He's always been very diligent with his finances and his record-keeping. His music collection is carefully catalogued and his paper-work neatly categorised into labelled binders. All his records and CDs have stickers on them so they can be easily found.

There's no doubt I've inherited some of these habits. I've always had a laser-sharp clarity and sense of single-mindedness about my life. I too have everything neatly stored in filing cabinets and despise clutter. I'm a bit more spontaneous than my dad, who plans things years in advance, but I definitely have some of his traits. By Sunday evening of every week, I like to ensure my affairs are in order and my emails up to date. My brother is the polar opposite. He's inherited Mum's maverick spirit. He's the kind of guy that will work his nuts off for months on end and never get round to invoicing for it. Growing up, he was always that bit more mischievous and accident-prone. We once had to cut short a family holiday in Pembrokeshire because he tumbled into a bed of nettles and was stung so badly that his neck and throat swelled up and he had to be rushed to hospital. Despite his more chaotic approach to life, David almost always lands on his feet. As part of his sociology A level, he wrote an essay the night before it was due, having done little to no research. Years later, it was still being cited by his teachers as the perfect example of how to write an essay.

Neither of my parents are Welsh speakers, but they decided to send us both to a Welsh-medium school. A common concern among non-Welsh-speaking parents is that their children's English might suffer at Welsh school, but the headmistress, Mrs Whettelton, convinced Mum that the opposite was the case: that learning two languages at a young age improved your facility in both, and that's before mentioning the cultural benefits that came with learning your native tongue. So it was that in September of 1991 I trotted through the gates at Ysgol y Wern, with my oversized backpack, to join my brother in the world of Welsh-medium education.

Mum enrolled on a Welsh language course at Cardiff University so that she'd be able to help and support us, but our progress soon overtook hers, and it became a convenient way of communicating with each other away from the prying ears of our parents, much to their exasperation. Welsh became our secret code. Mum's Welsh has completely faded now. She likes singing Welsh songs but considers herself an English person in Wales. She's even threatened to buy an England rugby top once I've stopped playing, and I'm not entirely convinced she's joking.

It couldn't have been an easy decision to send us to a Welsh-medium school, but they saw the benefits of us being bilingual, and Dad – as a proud Welshman – didn't want us to miss out on an opportunity that had been denied him. The school was super strict, and you'd be told off if you were caught speaking English. I was once admonished for wearing an 'English Heritage' T-shirt during PE. Because I didn't speak Welsh at home, I was the kind of kid who would rebel, speak English and get myself into trouble. It seems bizarre that this was happening only a couple of generations on from the 'Welsh Not', which was a punishment used to stigmatise pupils caught speaking Welsh. Looking back, it's obvious that the Welsh language had been on the point of dying out and some kind of positive discrimination was needed for it to survive. Amazingly, it's worked and the language is alive and flourishing once again.

I've always felt proud to be Welsh, and I'm proud to speak the language. I'll speak Welsh to my children and encourage them to learn, but in the same breath, I don't subscribe to the pseudo-nationalist notion that you're less Welsh if you can't speak Welsh. It's a beautiful language, but I don't use it much in day-to-day life. I have a few friends with whom I converse in Welsh, but by and large I live my life through the medium of English.

The school year was divided into two classes of thirty. You had the 'Welshy Welsh' – the kids whose parents spoke Welsh; and you had the kids who didn't have Welsh-speaking parents – the not-so-Welshy-Welsh. It didn't occur to me at the time, but I guess it was a form of social engineering.

Growing up in Cardiff is different from growing up in a Welsh-speaking heartland, where the language plays a much bigger role in shaping your life, your outlook and potentially your politics. It's a cosmopolitan city, and virtually all my mates from North Cardiff – places like Thornhill, Llanishen and Lisvane – came from English-speaking families. The other kids, whose families had moved to Cardiff a generation before from places like Carmarthenshire and Gwynedd, inhabited a different world even within the city. They'd watch S4C and hang out in places like Clwb Ifor Bach, and their cultural references would all be Welsh. Me and my mates would be listening to the Top 40, and watching *Neighbours*, whereas they'd be listening almost exclusively to Welsh-language acts like Gorky's Zygotic Mynci and the Super Furry Animals. So there was a subtle divide between those 'pure' Welsh families and the mongrel Welsh like me. I was hanging out almost exclusively with English-speaking kids and would only hear Welsh within the school's four walls.

The school was on Newborough Avenue in Llanishen. We'd walk down Garrick Drive, round the field, taking a right onto Templeton Avenue before going through the lane to the schoolyard. If you were feeling adventurous you could go the long way and take in the sweet shop. When I started getting pocket money, I'd take this route more and more and blow my money on Fruit Salads, Millions and Coconut Mushrooms. My first major transgression came when I was ten, and I stole some sweets from the newsagent's in Thornhill. When I walked in through our front door sucking on a Cola Bottle, my mum asked how I'd paid for it and I burst into tears. She turned me on my heel, marched me back and forced me to confess. With a trembling hand, I handed over what remained of my pilfered stash. I was mortified and continued to sob all the way home.

Pocket money became a running joke. My brother and I were always fighting, bickering and swearing at each other. My parents never smacked us and didn't believe in grounding, so their only option was to withhold pocket money. We were so badly behaved at times that we racked up bans stretching for months into the future. Our only way of reducing them was through bribery and manipulation. We would play cricket in the yard, and Dad, like the character from *The Fast Show*, would get pretty competitive, often slugging the ball into the next-door neighbour's garden. As the responsible adult, he'd be way too embarrassed to ask for it back, so he'd bribe one of us to do it by offering to reduce our pocket-money bans. Either that or he'd agree to buy us a couple of packs of football stickers. I've got completed albums from 1992–93, the first year of the Premier League, all the way through to 2002–03. David and I were avid collectors of the Merlin stickers and as a result, my knowledge of English football during that era is virtually encyclopaedic. I could tell you in an instant who played right back for Aston Villa in the 1997–98 season. Those footballers are heroes of mine in the way those of the present day never could be. Carlton Palmer retweeted me recently, and I was over the moon.

I used to tear my school clothes to shreds, coming home most days with holes in my trousers and stains on my jumpers. Money was tight, and my parents weren't the type to shell out repeatedly on new things, so Mum would patch everything up, or repurpose one of my dad's old jumpers that was vaguely the same colour as my torn, threadbare school one. There are myriad photos of me in my dad's baggy old YHA or Slimbridge jumpers and wearing trousers with random mismatched patches like some rogue character from the Bash Street Kids. That's not to say my parents were frugal; they just didn't see the value in forking out for new stuff that would be ripped, stretched and ruined within days.

My dad had a goal to visit every youth hostel in the UK before he retired, and would tick them off methodically every weekend. He finally completed his mission in 2012, finishing, appropriately enough, in Cardiff. Every weekend, we'd set off with the scent of adventure ripe in the air. Their love for the outdoors made the world seem much bigger to our eyes. We went everywhere: Cornwall, Pembrokeshire, Snowdonia, the Lake District, the Yorkshire Dales, the Norfolk Broads. We travelled the length and breadth of the United Kingdom. My brother and I would tease Dad, regularly pointing out that the Y in YHA stood for 'youth', but it didn't remotely dampen his enthusiasm. The original movement was about encouraging young people to enjoy the outdoors, and my parents saw it as a great opportunity to travel. To this day, you'll find them scrambling up Welsh mountainsides and trekking through valleys most weekends, still stretching the notion of 'youth-hostelling' to its absolute limit.

Those trips brought us close as a family. We'd cook together, and talk for hours, huddled around the camping stove under a blanket of stars. It taught me what to value in life. My parents wouldn't spend money on things like school uniforms and fancy meals out, but they would happily splash out on experiences for us. We'd often prove useful accomplices on their weekend jaunts as well. Once, after a particularly arduous hike in the Quantock Hills, we returned to find the hostel locked and bolted. At that age I was lean and skinny enough to slide through a narrow letterbox-shaped window to let everyone in from the inside. The youngest member of the Newport Outdoor Group earned his Ovaltine and marshmallows that night.

As a teenager, the idea of spending weekends hostelling with your parents when your mates were out discovering booze and girls felt a bit nerdy, but looking back, it was a brilliant experience. Staying in dorms, mixing with people of all ages and backgrounds, getting wet and muddy while climbing the jagged peaks of Scafell Pike and Snowdon – it beat playing computer games from behind the closed curtains of your bedroom, and importantly, through the tutelage of my dad's eccentric mate Richard Weeks, I built up an impressive vocabulary of swear words. On another occasion, my innocent four-year-old eyes witnessed a grown man sprint butt-naked through our group and dive-bomb into an icy swimming pool. It offered an early insight into the rugby initiations I'd later endure. Nudity and swear words. It was like having a temporary pass into an illicit adult world.

Camping was another passion, and we'd scramble together last-minute trips down the Gower Peninsula to make the most of any fine weather. We once arrived at Port Eynon in pitch dark, hurriedly erected the tent and, barely being able to see beyond the end of our noses, brushed our teeth with sun cream. I could still taste it days later. Every summer, we'd embark on an annual pilgrimage to Babbacombe in Torquay. My dad had bought into a fifteen-year time-share in the Babbacombe Cliff Hotel, a lovely ornate old building perched on the cliffs above the beach. They'd obviously advertised quite aggressively in South Wales as virtually everyone who stayed there was from Cardiff and the Valleys: a little Welsh colony in Devon. Shockingly, in the fifteenth year, when everyone was due to get their deposit back, the hotel burnt dramatically to the ground.

The week in Babbacombe was dominated by sport. David and I would be in the pool before breakfast, desperately trying to beat one another swimming lengths, while Dad would stand timing us on his digital watch. Mum would be stretched out on a recliner, rolling her eyes behind her latest novel. Once we'd showered and changed, we'd head up to the local cricket ground to knock a few balls about, before continuing to the beach for a spot of crabbing. Even that was competitive. I *had* to catch more than David and would get pretty tetchy if I didn't. From there, it was into Torquay for a round of pitch-and-putt and a few sets of tennis, before a detour back via the snooker hall.

It was no different back home. Every waking moment was spent outdoors, running, jumping and climbing trees. Dad would take us to Roath Park for kick-abouts with a rugby ball, encouraging us to work on our passing, dodging and sidestepping. He used to pit us against one another, timing us running in straight lines or around a track. For many years there was nothing between us. I'd win one race, David the next, and we'd spur each other on. We had so much energy, Dad would barely get a second to relax, so he hatched a plan to put rocks in our rucksacks so it would take us longer to do laps. That would allow him to have a quick coffee before we burdened him with our next set of demands.

As I got bigger and stronger, my victories against my brother started mounting up. When I was around thirteen or fourteen, the tables began to turn. Our wrestling bouts would end with me pinning David rather than the other way around, and he hated it. It rarely boiled over, but we used to fight really aggressively in the back seat of the car, and occasionally Mum would completely lose it. For the most part, she was calm and patient, but when the fuse was lit, she could explode and her language would get pretty industrial. Dad always took Mum's side, but some of her tirades would have undoubtedly been a shock to his middle-class sensibilities.

The older we got, the less enthusiastic we were about joining our parents on their weekend jaunts. As young teenagers, we were allowed to stay in the house on our own. We promised to be responsible, but the minute their Toyota puttered off down Garrick Drive, we'd be on the phone inviting our friends over for parties. It was all pretty innocent – crisps and fizzy pop rather than drugs and booze – but things got a bit boisterous once and we totally wrecked the sofa. It turned out that it wasn't robust enough to withstand six or seven rowdy teenagers jumping all over it like a trampoline, and it collapsed in on itself. David and I spent an hour trying to repair it with Sellotape and drawing pins, and we thought we'd pulled it off until Dad slumped into it that night, collapsing onto the floor in a flurry of splintered wood, flying cushions and spilt beer. The trip to Bath the next day to shell out for a new one was undertaken largely in silence.

2
GREAT TRY, YOUNG MAN

There is nothing more evocative than the smell of frying onions on the terraces of an old-fashioned rugby stadium. And there are few better stadiums than Rodney Parade. My childhood heroes weren't Wales internationals; they were Newport players. Newport was a successful club with a rich history – they had once beaten the All Blacks – but it lacked the glamour of a Cardiff or a Bath. Its image was one of a working-class underdog. It didn't have the allure of those clubs when it came to enticing players from outside the city or its surrounding valleys. That all changed when an English businessman by the name of Tony Brown decided to pour some of his considerable fortune into the club.

The dawn of professionalism in 1995 led to an active transfer market, and global stars, once considered mythical beings from the other side of the world, started appearing in British and Irish clubs. Brown's enthusiasm and largesse saw the likes of Springbok legends Gary Teichmann and Percy Montgomery lured to the Parade. They were joined by Simon Raiwalui, Shane Howarth and the Canadian cult hero Rod Snow. I can't tell you how much I looked up to those guys. It was like watching comic-book superheroes made flesh, and they were wearing *my* shirt. The fabled 'black and amber'.

Following in the family tradition, my brother and I would head to the terraces every Saturday and cheer on 'the Port'. Dad was a season-ticket holder for close to thirty years, and still has them all labelled, laminated and stored in one of his innumerable folders. The match-day tickets are tucked inside the programmes and filed away in chronological order.

As young boys we were intoxicated by the sounds and smells of the place. Warm, malty beer, frying hot dogs, stale urine, the raucous chanting of the crowd, and the fuzzy yellow floodlights bathing everything in an ethereal glow. The smell of Vicks the players had rubbed on themselves when they stood close to you, the steam rising from the scrums in the winter, the gruff voices raining down abuse one minute and barking encouragement the next. It was an authentic, warts-and-all rugby ground.

The toilets weren't even toilets, just bare brick walls and a gutter that led directly to the drains. Standing with a load of wheezing drunk blokes amid a cloud of rising steam was a rite of passage. It absolutely stank. I loved it.

This is still what it's all about for me. I may have experienced the sharpest end of professionalism, and enjoyed all the benefits of modern coaching, but rugby at its purest is about standing on the terraces, pint in hand, with your mates.

The banter was brilliant at Rodney Parade. If a home player shanked a kick, missed touch or fell off a tackle, the crowd would get stuck right in. Whenever an away player was lining up a kick you'd give it the old 'wooooooaaahhhh', and there was nothing wrong with that. That's how you'd exploit your home advantage. The reverence we show towards place-kickers these days has made it all a bit sterile. The Rodney Parade faithful has a reputation as one of the most vociferous and aggressive in British rugby, and it's what makes the experience what it is. I was one of those kids shouting abuse at the players, albeit an octave higher than most of the grizzled factory workers standing around me. I have really fond memories of swinging on the barriers with my brother, lunging to catch the ball whenever a touch-finder came my way.

When the final whistle blew, we'd race onto the pitch, hoping for a fleeting interaction with one of our heroes. I'd chase down players like Ian Gough and Ceri Sweeney and beg for their autographs. I had no idea I'd end up being team-mates of theirs. It all seems so innocent in the age of the mobile phone and selfies, but my autograph book was my holy grail. I had one for every season, and you can guarantee my dad has them somewhere, numbered, labelled and stored away for posterity.

The blond-haired, swashbuckling Percy Montgomery was my idol. I bumped into him in Cape Town recently and regressed to the teenage version of myself, gushing about how much I'd worshipped him.

I loved that closeness to the players, the opportunity to run onto the pitch and literally rub shoulders with them, and I fear that those threads binding the clubs to their communities are beginning to fray. We'd routinely take a ball down with us, but you'd always hope to nick one as well, racing out of the ground when one was booted over the stand to comb the streets for it and tuck it under your jumper. A proper Welsh match ball, handled by your heroes, was a real treasure; a collector's item. Once our autograph books were filled, we'd spend another twenty minutes running ourselves ragged on the churned-up pitch, kicking spirals and up-and-unders back and forth to one another until it was time to go home.

You'll most likely have heard of Newport RFC. You won't necessarily have heard of Clwb Rygbi Ieuenctid Caerdydd. That was where my personal rugby journey began at the age of six. A mouthful for non-Welsh speakers, it's become colloquially known as 'CRICC'. The club was founded on the idea of junior-level rugby through the Welsh language. Back then, it was primarily a social affair. We only went up to Under-12s, and all the teams were run by the dads of the kids.

It was September of 1992 when I took my first tentative steps onto the rugby field. My brother was already in the Under-8s, so I went along too – to chuck the ball around with a bunch of kids a year or two older than me on the playing fields of Ysgol Plasmawr in Fairwater. Soon after, it became a regular Saturday-morning ritual. It wasn't even rugby per se, just lobbing the ball about, playing touch and having fun.

Our fixture list didn't follow much of a pattern, but we did enter a team in an Under-8s tournament at London Welsh's ground, Old Deer Park. I scored a length-of-the-field try, weaving in and out of would-be tacklers before touching down under the posts. As I left the field grinning from ear to ear, an old man in a sheepskin coat and flat cap ruffled my hair and, in a voice that sounded vaguely familiar, said, 'Great try, young man.' My dad, hovering in the background, seemed far more animated about this than he'd been about my try. 'Do you know who that was?' he asked breathlessly, as he appeared alongside me. 'It was only Cliff bloody Morgan.' I had no idea.

I was voted CRICC's Under-8 player of the year at the end of the season, and I knew full well who the guy presenting the award was. It was Jonathan 'Jiffy' Davies, one of the finest players Wales has ever produced, and one of Cliff Morgan's successors in the ten jersey. So in the space of a season, I'd been praised by two of Wales's best ever fly-halves. My dad interpreted this as a sign. He'd not played much rugby himself other than a few outings for St Julian's High School, and the odd appearance for Norwich University, where a certain Andy Ripley was the star player. He was beginning to think he could live his rugby dreams vicariously through me.

I'll never forget the day I was handed the trophy by Jiffy, and he gave me a proper manly handshake. It made me realise that perhaps I could do this. That you didn't necessarily have to breathe rarefied air or be anointed by some higher power. Perhaps I could just practise, work hard and become a rugby player myself. Many years later I was invited back to CRICC to present the end-of-season awards, and they had a young kid called Rhys Patchell in their youth side. It wasn't long before he was running out at the Principality Stadium. There's a lovely sense that the baton is being passed on through the generations.

3

WELCOME TO RUMNEY

The referee blew his whistle decisively as the scrum collapsed, awarding a penalty to the opposition. Within seconds the ref was staggering backwards, clutching his ribs and gasping for air. He'd been punched square in the stomach. Standing in the backfield with my hands on my hips, I had to blink to process what I'd just seen. Did that actually just happen? Our scrum-half, Craig, unhappy with the decision, had responded with his own form of justice: an angry, swinging haymaker. Welcome to Rumney RFC.

Craig was a chopsy kid, and a genuine hard bastard. He was a great player, but his ability was often overshadowed by his fiery temperament. Aggression oozed from his every pore, and he wasn't the type to defer to authority. After the ref had given the penalty, he'd got right up in his face, snarling and gnashing his teeth. There was a bit of pushing and shoving, and then, *bang*, he unleashed the punch. It was a decent shot and the ref did well to stay on his feet. There was a gasp of disbelief from the sidelines, before the scene descended into chaos. While some of the parents would have been inured to the sight of casual violence, most would have been shocked. The match was abandoned, the incident investigated and our team was banned for six months.

Rumney RFC was about as far away from the warm bosom of CRICC as you could imagine. A run-down suburb in the east of Cardiff, Rumney is one of the less salubrious parts of my home city. Just last year, there was a machete attack on one of its estates that caused life-changing injuries to the victim. I don't want to denigrate the entire area, but it was rough, menacing and edgy in a way that North Cardiff wasn't. My parents' reaction to the Craig incident was revealing. Dad was genuinely horrified, Mum far more sanguine. As she liked to remind us, she was a Bettws girl. In her more confrontational moments, she'd smack a clenched fist into her open palm and say,

'You don't mess with a Bettws girl.' Growing up on one of Europe's most deprived housing estates, she'd seen enough to put a punch on a rugby field into perspective. You can't say I hadn't been warned. At one of the youth training sessions, we were casually going through our warm-up when a police car rolled up, with its blue light flashing silently. I heard a whispered swear word and, like a bullet from a gun, one of the lads bolted across the field. It wasn't his first run-in with the law, and he's spent a good deal of time in prison since. As I say, edgy.

I'd gone to Rumney because CRICC wasn't giving me the kind of competitive rugby I'd begun to crave. They didn't have a proper youth or senior side, and we were lucky if we played three or four meaningful games a year. We'd play against other Welsh-speaking teams like Llandovery and Newcastle Emlyn, and maybe one or two other games in Cardiff, but it wasn't a proper league. We were just there for the fun of it.

I was at secondary school by now, Ysgol Gyfun Gymraeg Glantaf, and my passion for rugby had ratcheted up a few notches. My school-friend Andrew Carlson was a Rumney boy and he had enticed me and a few of the other lads down to his local club. My mum approved wholeheartedly because she thought it would toughen me up. A part of her enjoyed the fact I was moving to a rough-and-ready club and would be going through adolescence in that sort of environment. It was in stark contrast to my home and school life. When I turned up at Riverside Park for my first session, I felt like a fish out of water. I wouldn't say I was a posh kid from Thornhill, not by any stretch of the imagination, but that's how I felt. The accents in Rumney were different and the language much coarser. Twelve- to thirteen-year-old kids were using language I'd never dare to, and their parents were even worse.

The other boys were also far more aggressive than me. I may have had size on my side, but some of these raw-boned, snarling youths were nasty pieces of work: always scrapping, swinging and stamping on each other in training. I'd learned all about skill, balance and dexterity at CRICC. At Rumney I was to learn about smashing people, about no-holds-barred collisions, about pretending I wasn't hurt when I was and, for want of a better word, combat. At one point, the coaches announced that all rugby training was to be cancelled and replaced by full-contact boxing sessions. For three weeks, we slugged it out with punchbags and sparred with one another until our lungs were ready to burst and our arms felt like jelly. We didn't touch a ball the whole time, but we were much better fighters by the end of it.

There was peer pressure, as in any other rugby club. As a self-conscious, insecure twelve-year-old, I was wary of getting in the showers naked, and was ridiculed when I tiptoed in wearing my pants. From that point, I made a habit of showering at home. Mum would collect me, and I'd clamber into the car still in my kit, caked in mud, while she rolled her eyes in despair. I'm pretty sure she thought I'd been subjected to some humiliating ritual and scarred for life. The showers proved the least of my worries when I was exposed to the initiation ritual on my first away trip. There was no drinking of urine or downing of shots; you simply had to fight your way to the back of the bus. Literally. The challenge was to walk down that narrow exposed aisle while every member of the squad punched, kicked and whipped you with impunity. You just had to tense your muscles, grit your teeth and stride forward while pretending it was all a bit of fun.

I was a sensitive kid and struggled to embrace this raw machismo that seemed to characterise the club and youth rugby in general. I struggled not to cry at anything that triggered me emotionally, including pain. I broke my collarbone once at Riverside Park and immediately started bawling my eyes out. As you can imagine, there wasn't much sympathy from the Rumney crowd. A few years later, on a youth tour to Butlins, the alcohol started flowing and things got ugly. One of the dads punched his wife in the face during a night out. I was horrified, naturally, but listening to some of the boys afterwards, I got the impression they thought it was fairly normal.

It was at Rumney where I learned to tackle. We'd experimented with it at CRICC, but there wasn't much technique involved. Because I was bigger than average, I could grab kids by the shirt and chuck them to the deck, but it wasn't proper tackling. Early on in my Rumney adventure, one damp Wednesday night, the coach introduced us to the 'man-up' drill. We lined up in a grid, with four corners. One of us had to stand in the middle for a minute, while each of the guys in the corners would take turns to run diagonally to the opposite corner. Sidestepping, dummying, shimmying or any kind of footwork were banned. The sole aim of the ball-carrier was to run into and over the poor sod in the middle. It was a man test: front up and tackle, or be humiliated. In the space of a minute, you'd be expected to make six or seven tackles.

Gareth Cutler was a big lump. One of those kids that relished contact. All he wanted to do was hurt people, and he'd regularly bowl people over, leaving a trail of flailing arms and crumpled bodies in his wake. It was my turn in the middle, and I looked up to see his menacing frame tensed and ready for action. I was nervous. As he thundered towards me, with the ground appearing to shake, I set myself, got down low and absolutely *melted* him. In one fluid movement, I picked him up, drove him back and dropped him on his backside, absorbing all his power and using it against him. It didn't even hurt. It was like a nonchalant stroke of the cricket bat sending the ball over extra cover for six. Something about the timing, the execution and the outcome made it seem effortless, yet ludicrously satisfying. It was my first real tackle, and something of an epiphany. I can *do* this. It's about courage, yes, but it's more about technique. Like a sorcerer's trick. You need the bravery to go for it, but beyond that, it's all about the mechanics. I'd felt the sweet spot, the crucial shift in momentum, and it was magical.

If I could distil my entire experience at Rumney down to one moment, it would be that. It's stayed with me to this day. They wouldn't have put you in that situation at CRICC; they'd have been afraid of injury, or of someone getting embarrassed or shown up. The environment at Rumney was 'sink or swim'.

Glantaf was a rugby institution. Former pupils like Huw Harries and the Robinson brothers, Jamie and Nicky, had all gone on to play for Wales, and I'd begun to fantasise about following in their footsteps. You got the vibe straight away that it was a rugby school. There were balls everywhere, boots in the old store cupboards, pictures of players all over the walls, and a rusting, creaking multigym covered in peeling paint. I may have been a tall kid, but I was pretty rangy and skinny – all elbows and knees, with little in the way of chest and shoulders – so I was drawn to this multigym as a means of bulking up. From year 8 onwards, a group of us would congregate there whenever we had a spare half an hour and devise little competitions. Who could bench-press the most? Who could lat-pull the most?

I threw myself into everything at this stage: cross country, athletics, football, cricket. We'd have regular inter-school athletics meetings down at Leckwith, and I'd want to enter every event. Sprinting, jump-ing, throwing, whatever it was, I couldn't get enough, and I'd be devastated unless I came first. I dabbled a fair bit with cricket, playing for several years for Cardiff Cricket Club and the county under some excellent coaches like Kevin Lyons and Phil Harrington. My gangly physique was ideal for opening the bowling. Fast and wide was my speciality, and what I lacked in accuracy, I made up for in speed and aggression.

I wanted to be the best academically as well. I was on the maths team and the road-safety quiz team, and I took piano lessons. It all came easily to me. I was that annoying kid with my hand constantly in the air, straining to get the teacher's attention. I'd race through a test before sitting smugly with my arms folded while everyone else was chewing their pencils and looking confused. I must have been insufferable.

The late Keri Evans was my head of year, and he was one of life's characters, brimming with effervescence: a Robin Williams-in-*Dead-Poets-Society* type. He taught art, but his passion was PE and he had a whistle permanently hanging from his neck and a pencil behind his ear. He loved his rugby and appreciated its values of honesty, hard work and discipline. Dai Williams and Huw Llewelyn, known simply as 'Gat', were his two accomplices. Together, they were the three amigos, and easily among the most influential characters in my career. Keri, who virtually lived in his tracksuit, would famously award penalties for 'dull play'. If you butchered a two-on-one, ignored a support runner or made a poor decision, you'd hear a loud blast, followed by the words 'penalty against Roberts, dull play', spoken in his sing-song Trebanos accent.

Huw Llewelyn was another character. He had a neatly trimmed goatee and ran the tuck shop, regularly entrusting us boys to take charge, knowing full well we were scoffing as many chocolates as we were selling. He was more of a forwards coach, whereas Dai Williams looked after the backs. Dai had played in the centre for Pontypool, so was a tidy player with a hard edge. In the finest tradition of Welsh nicknames, he was known as 'Dent-head Dai' because his skull had been caved in during a nasty collision back in the day. He was a tough bloke and would resort to a bit of old-school discipline when necessary. As we got older, he wouldn't hesitate to get involved on the field, rucking and mauling as if he was still wearing the red-white-and-black hoops of Pontypool, often getting cut up and bloodied in the process.

As inspirational as Dai was, I couldn't forgive him for later defecting to our big rivals Whitchurch High School, where a certain Sam Warburton would be tearing up trees a few years later. That match became something of a local derby, but we also developed rivalries with the strong teams down west, like Bro Myrddin in Carmarthen and Ysgol Gyfun Gŵyr in Swansea. Both were breeding grounds for future Welsh internationals like Ken Owens and Rhys Priestland. Glantaf were a mid-table kind of team. We'd win some and we'd lose some, but that Saturday-morning buzz was always awesome.

I got picked for Cardiff Schools at the age of fifteen, when my increasing size and power was becoming an asset. I had no fear when it came to collisions and the more physical side of the game. Tactics often revolved around giving me the ball and seeing what I could do. My Cardiff Schools debut was in the centre against Swansea Schools at St Helens, and half an hour before kick-off the coach casually announced I'd be captain for the day. I'd had no prior warning, but I was expected to deliver an address to the best players in the region. My mate Will Jones sniggered throughout my rather awkward, fumbling speech, which did little to inspire the lads as we fell to a crushing defeat. Swansea were a very good side, with a genuine talent in Leigh Bevan at full-back, but losing my first representative game as captain felt like the end of the world.

That first step on the ladder of representative rugby was when my ambition crystallised. I wanted to play for Wales, and didn't see any reason why I couldn't. Test rugby was no longer the mist-shrouded summit of a soaring mountain; it was something within reach. If I played my cards right, and continued to work hard, I could be pulling on a senior Wales jersey in five years. Call it confidence, arrogance or blind faith, but I knew I was going to run out at the Millennium Stadium one day.

Cardiff Rugby had an open day around this time, and I went and had my photo taken with Hemi Taylor and Jonathan Humphreys. That connection to these larger-than-life heroes helped foster my ambition. Being close to them and realising they were just human convinced me that what they'd achieved was attainable. That connection continues to span the generations. Arwel Robson, our young fly-half at the Dragons, was recently showing me photos on his phone of him and me when he was a ballboy at Cardiff and I was an international.

To my dad's eternal disappointment, when I started playing for Cardiff Schools, I suddenly and callously renounced my loyalty to Newport RFC. Mere months before, as part of a school project, I'd declared my Newport shirt my most treasured possession, and put it in a Millennium time capsule. Now, I was ready to trade it for a Cardiff one. In my mind, I was a Cardiff boy, and that's where my loyalties would now lie. That said, Nicky Robinson likes to remind me of a televised Newport–Cardiff match he played in, in which the cameraman cuts to the crowd for a shot of the baying mob underneath the East Stand. Among those hurling abuse at the Cardiff players is a skinny, baby-faced Jamie Roberts, clad in the black-and-amber stripes of Newport RFC.

Dai Williams approached me in training one day and said, 'Jamie, you've got a good kick, you're quick, you cover space well and can read the game. We think you'd make a good full-back.' They switched me there and then, and I loved the new-found freedom it gave me. I loved the up-and-unders, loved kicking the ball as far as I could, and relished being the last line of defence. Whenever anyone broke through, I'd think, *Right, this is my responsibility*. Some baulked at the thought of being so exposed, but I took pleasure in knowing that the spotlight of scrutiny was being shone brightly on me. Most school-age kids just love scoring tries and the glory that goes with it, but for me there was something addictive about stopping someone dead in their tracks. Rugby's a team game, but I loved those moments when the lens is narrowed and it's one on one. You against the guy running towards you. That's what I came to relish. Between the ages of sixteen and twenty-one, other than a few games in the centre, I was exclusively a full-back, for the school, for the county and for Rumney Youth. The one game when I realised it was definitely the position for me was a county game against Monmouthshire. In addition to my defensive duties, I launched three high, hanging up-and-unders and chased and caught every one. Running off the field that day, I thought, *I'm pretty good at this full-back lark.*

The next step was playing for Wales Under-16s, but I couldn't dislodge Leigh Bevan from the first team, so I only ever got picked for the A team. It was the same Leigh Bevan who'd bested me in that Swansea Schools v Cardiff Schools game, and I worried I'd be stuck behind him for the rest of my teenage years. Meanwhile, my performances for Rumney Youth had been noted by the coach of the men's team, Danny Wilson, and he threw me into the cauldron of senior rugby a few times to test my mettle. I must have done all right, because in early 2002, I was asked to train with the Cardiff RFC academy. Danny was also destined for bigger things, eventually becoming coach of the Cardiff Blues and leading them to Challenge Cup glory.

The hours I spent on the multigym were helping develop my strength, as was the paper round I took on. I was doing two rounds at once, carrying two heavy sacks criss-crossed over my shoulders through Lisvane and Llanishen before and after school. I came to resent *Sunday Times* readers because the amount of supplements it came with made it ludicrously heavy. My companion on the round was a tough, streetwise kid called Lloyd Jones, the type of lad who'd started smoking when he was thirteen. I was happy enough with my paltry weekly wage but he was always hustling to make extra money.

Once he'd emptied his bags of papers, he'd fill them with stolen dust caps off cars to sell on to one of his dodgy contacts. One Christmas he came up with a plan to guilt-trip punters into tipping us. He knocked on every door to personally hand over the paper with a card and wish people a Merry Christmas. That would usually yield an extra fiver, and by the time we'd finished, our pockets were stuffed with cash.

My progress accelerated rapidly, and Andrew Carlson and I were soon considered the two best players in our year. As a result, we were invited on a school tour to Australia in 2002 with the year above. I ran home to tell my mum, unsure how she'd feel about sending her fifteen-year-old to the other side of the world, let alone paying for it. Her response was 'Whatever it takes, you're going. Don't worry about the money; even if we have to go into debt, you're going.' Dad agreed, but encouraged me to raise funds for the trip. I set up my own 'lottery'. It was twenty quid to enter, and the prize was £100, so if I got twenty quid from thirty people, I'd make a £500 profit. I packed bags in the supermarket for a bit too, taking donations to raise money for the tour. I was beyond excited about the adventure that lay ahead.

Australia more than lived up to my expectations. Seeing the iconic Sydney Harbour Bridge in real life, hanging out in Melbourne's funky bars and snorkelling on the Great Barrier Reef – that was an unbeliev- able experience, so much so that one of my mates pinched a piece of coral, wrapped it in a towel and smuggled it home on the plane. I won't mention his name in case anyone from the Australian govern- ment is reading this.

As part of the touring tradition, you get hosted by local families. Our bus would pull into a car park in some nondescript town and, like the testosterone-fuelled teenagers we were, we'd be scanning the families lined up to greet us, searching for the most attractive girls. One of the teachers would stand at the front and read out the list of who had been matched with whom. On this occasion, in Townsville in Queensland, there was a family with two unbelievably hot sisters standing with their parents. They were tanned, blonde and athletic- looking: the classic Australian fantasy honed in our imaginations from years of watching *Neighbours* and *Home and Away*. They looked unspeakably exotic to a coachload of pasty, hormonal Welsh teenagers, and everyone was silently praying they'd be paired with them.

Most of the lads were a year older – sixteen and seventeen – so I was one of the young bucks, as was another lad called, coincidentally enough, James Roberts. The teacher called our names together: 'Jamie and James Roberts, you're with . . .' There was a pregnant pause as his finger ran down the list. '. . . the McKays.' The two sisters stepped forward and the coach erupted. You can imagine the scene: a load of boorish Welsh teenagers whooping and hollering with a mixture of excitement and envy. In the interests of discretion, I'll be brief about what followed, but that night one of the sisters sneaked into my room after dark. I'll let you draw your own conclusions about what happened.

If that nocturnal encounter had swollen my ego, it was soon punctured during a boat trip to the Outer Reef the following morning. Rumours of my midnight fumblings had spread, and the rest of the boys, consumed with jealousy and a desire to bring me crashing back to earth, unleashed a barrage of piss-taking and abuse. Amid a relentless stream of tasteless jokes, I burst into tears. I'd become a man the night before, but had now been reduced to a blubbering mess by a bunch of leering schoolboys.

4

MORE CARL LEWIS
THAN EMYR LEWIS

My dad had had enough. With an uncharacteristic rush of blood, he hurled his empty plate at me. I jumped to my feet and swung at him clumsily with an open palm. To my horror, blood started gushing from his nose. Panicking, I scampered up the stairs, collapsing on my bedroom floor in floods of tears. I'd never felt so ashamed. What on earth had possessed me? We'd been arguing about something utterly trivial, but I'd seen red. During the past year, I'd been getting a bit cocky, a bit sure of myself. I was beating my brother at everything and my ego had started to swell. All of a sudden, being the biggest, strongest bloke in the house, I thought I was the alpha male. I'd had scraps with mates before, but I'd never hit anyone in the face like that. I cried for hours, and my parents left me to it, knowing it was the best way for me to learn my lesson. I couldn't look Dad in the eye for weeks afterwards, and no amount of apologising was sufficient. It was a formative moment. I never disrespected him like that again. Dad was my hero. I'd always looked up to him, and in one senseless act of petulance, I'd risked driving a wedge between us. I was getting above my station, and I'd massively overstepped the mark.

It was the last year of my GCSEs, and my size had been getting me into trouble. I was suspended from school following an 'altercation' in the corridor, when a friend of mine was being bullied by a gang of rough kids. I'd stepped in to cool things down, but they were clearly spoiling for a fight and one of them took a swing at me. Instinctively, I hit back, and a few shots were landed before the teachers waded in and hauled us apart. My mother was summoned from work to take me home, where I was to remain until the GCSEs formally began. The official line was that the school was worried about repercussions because these other boys were renowned troublemakers and would be out for revenge. I was essentially suspended for my own safety, but it was apparent I was becoming a bit of a hothead, and my PE teachers had started to notice. Their coaching philosophy was as much about developing good people as it was good players. They had a knack of letting you know what was the right way to behave and what wasn't. Fighting in the corridors and hitting my dad was definitely not the right way to behave.

While I was in the sixth form, my involvement with the Cardiff RFC academy became formalised, and the former Wales international Mike Rayer became my unofficial mentor. I saw a bit of myself in him. He was a full-back, a Cardiff boy, and he enjoyed a pint. Booze was something I was starting to discover, and by the time I celebrated my eighteenth birthday, I was fully conversant with the tradition of getting leathered in the bar after a game. I marked the occasion at Llanishen Rugby Club, where I was made to drink a shot of every spirit from the top shelf. Predictably, I was violently sick, and the nearest receptacle when the urge arrived was an empty pint glass. Less predictably, a mate declared he'd drink the contents if enough people donated a quid. He did a circuit of the bar and, deciding that thirty pounds was sufficient reward, made good on his promise. I'm disgusted to report that he did it with relative ease, and treated himself to a new pair of jeans with the takings.

The day after, I had a kicking session with Mike Rayer at Hailey Park and I was all over the shop. He was launching huge spiral kicks into the air, and whenever I tried to focus on the ball, there appeared to be at least four of them descending from the skies. I was suffering – or 'hanging', as they say in Wales – and Mike knew it. He was a bit of a party boy and understood exactly what I was going through. He'd been there and done it, and wasn't about to judge me too harshly for turning up with a crippling hangover. On another occasion, he saw me crossing the high street in Llandaff North dressed as a woman while on a team social. The full works: dress, wig, lipstick and heels. I stumbled over the zebra crossing, glancing inside the car that had let me pass, only to see Mike tapping the wheel impatiently. He gave me the most withering of looks, but I could tell he was laughing inside.

The priority during those early academy years was to get bigger. The rugby I was playing with Glantaf and Rumney was keeping me fit and game-sharp, but if I was going to turn professional, my lean, lanky physique would need to fill out. I was more Carl Lewis than Emyr Lewis at this stage. Every day, I'd be up at the crack of dawn, wolfing down four sugar-coated Weetabix, before heading to the Welsh Institute of Sport in my P-reg Rover 10, where Trystan Bevan and Chris Tombs would be waiting for our little group. There, they'd put us though a strict 'hypertrophy' session or, to use a less scientific expression, they'd make us lift weights. Heavy weights. The sessions were designed to stress our muscles to the point of exhaustion, whereupon they'd repair themselves and get bigger in the process. Once we'd finished, Trystan would kick us out of the door with the order to 'go and eat'. It didn't matter what; we just had to get the calories down our necks. So, dipping into the £55 monthly allowance provided by the academy, we'd troop into the centre of town and have a full English at Cardiff Market alongside all the tradesmen fortifying themselves for a day of hard labour. It was the only place open at 7.30 in the morning. Suitably sated, I'd wander back through Bute Park to pick up my car and drive straight to school.

I was doing that every other day. We were a little gang: me, Chris Czekaj, Will Jones, Dafydd Hewitt, David Walsh and Matt McLean. A hand-picked bunch of promising youngsters that Cardiff saw as the next generation. In time we'd be joined by the likes of Sam Warburton, Dai Flanagan, Leigh Halfpenny and Bradley Davies. At school, I'd snack constantly and neck two or three Mammoth shakes every day, each of which contained 2,500 calories and an inordinate amount of protein. That was on top of my regular meals. We felt like guinea pigs: the first generation of professional academy kids. It was all incredibly advanced and scientific, with a dietary expert called Jon Williams telling us exactly what to eat and when. He went on to become the WRU's head nutritionist, so he obviously knew what he was talking about. In the space of two years, I went from 86 kg to 106 kg. I could feel myself metamorphosing from a skinny kid into a muscle-bound warrior.

When Welsh rugby went regional, Cardiff and Pontypridd merged to form the Cardiff Blues, and the two academies became one. As a result, our training base switched from the Welsh Institute of Sport to Treforest, where the weights sessions were augmented by an intense cardiovascular programme. Those sessions were significantly less enjoyable. They were brutal and unrelenting, and our fitness trainer, Stephen 'Rittaz' Richards, accepted nothing less than 100 per cent. His notorious treadmill workouts weeded out some of the less committed. They were torturous: repeated minute-long sprints, flat out on level 20. I once pretended to faint to get out of finishing it. I didn't want to admit defeat, but I couldn't carry on. There were times during those sessions when I genuinely questioned whether it was worth it. Rugby was meant to be fun, and this most certainly wasn't.

During my time in the sixth form, my teenage aggression was channelled into real progress on the rugby field, and in my last year, I did something that had never been done before: I played for Wales Under-18s, Under-19s and Under-21s in the same season. While I was captaining the Under-18s in Foix in France, I was summoned as injury cover for the Under-19s in South Africa, flying straight to Durban for a whirlwind few days. When I arrived, Ken Owens was in isolation, having contracted mumps, and during our first training session our hotel was robbed and my digital camera containing all my pictures of France was stolen. I was devastated. Before the days of cloud storage, that was my most treasured possession. What was even more sickening was the fact it was an inside job. All the safes had been left wide open and empty.

In June, I got a message saying the Wales Under-21s' first-choice full-back was injured, and did I fancy joining the squad for the Junior World Cup in Argentina? It was a golden opportunity. The Under-18s and Under-19s were significant rungs on the ladder, but the Under-21s side was essentially one step away from the real deal. Make the right impression there, and you're going places. It felt like a pivotal moment, coinciding as it did with the end of my school years. It also presented a massive problem. My A levels were scheduled to take place at the same time. By then I'd already decided to study medicine. I'd developed a fascination with science at school, and loved problem-solving, so medicine seemed the perfect avenue to explore, but I needed good grades to get into university. Being selected for the Under-21s at the age of eighteen was mind-blowing, but accepting the offer might jeopardise the outcome of my exams. It was the very definition of a blessing and a curse. My schoolteachers were dead against the idea. I was genuinely torn.

At my first Under-21s training session, I approached the coaches, Dai Rees and Chris Davey, to tell them about my dilemma. They looked me in the eye and told me not to worry. They'd get it sorted. For several years Chris had been a lecturer at the University of Wales Institute, Cardiff (UWIC) and he was a qualified invigilator. He told me, 'Keep studying, keep training and I'll worry about the rest.' There would be a number of occasions in the future when my twin worlds of sport and academia would collide, but this was the first. It was a crazy time, and it took a lot of discipline and organisation to stop my brain from getting fried.

We had a really strong squad in Argentina, including Alun Wyn Jones, Andrew Bishop, Aled Brew, Dominic Day – all great players who'd go on to represent Wales at senior level – and, at hooker, Gerwyn Price, who years later would become world darts champion. Unfortunately, most of my interaction with these guys was confined to the training paddock, as every other waking moment was spent hunched over my laptop in my spartan hotel room. The spindly desk would be groaning under the weight of maths, chemistry and biology textbooks, and my table lamp would continue to burn long into the night.

Days off were the worst. After breakfast, I'd watch forlornly as the boys skipped out of the hotel without a care in the world, before tramping up to my room and knuckling down to yet more revision. After an hour or so, my mind would wander and I'd picture them sitting on some sun-soaked terrace in Mendoza, sipping Argentinian coffee and flirting with the latino ladies. During those moments, a devil would alight on my shoulder and ask what the hell I was doing. *The lads are all out bonding, taking in the sights and sounds, experiencing all the thrills that come with touring an exotic country, and I'm holed up in my room trying to cram all manner of complex information into my brain.* Whenever I was about to waver, a more strident inner voice would interrupt, telling me this was more important. *You can do all that other stuff another time.* I tried to persuade myself that it would be worth it, that the feelings I'd experience when I got into medical school would outweigh these feelings of disappointment. But when you're a teenager on tour, it's tough. The nights were even worse. I'd hear the boys coming back from a night out, and I'd be all bleary-eyed and exhausted, thumbing through textbooks while they loudly recounted their tales of debauchery and excess.

The deal Chris Davey had struck was that we had to sit the exams at the same time as they did so in the UK. Argentina is four hours behind the UK in June, so I had to start in the middle of the night. If there was a 9 a.m. exam back home, I had to start at 5 a.m. The papers would get faxed the day before, Chris would print them off and I'd meet him in the hotel conference room. It was the size of an exam hall, but instead of being thronged with anxious, fidgety students behind rows of desks, it was almost entirely empty. There were the two of us, in the middle of a cavernous room, with the weak early-morning sun just about spilling in through the open windows. Chris was the ultimate professional and there was no preferential treatment. My reward for completing my exams was to join the end-of-tour celebrations, which were cut short when the strip club we found ourselves in turned out to be a brothel. You've never seen a bunch of blokes skedaddle out of a place with such haste.

When we got back to Wales, I donned my best baggy suit and Cardiff RFC tie and attended my interview for Cardiff Medical School. It went swimmingly, and the man who interviewed me, Peter Winterburn, was a keen rugby fan, which ensured even the small talk was good. It was a stark contrast to my interview at Manchester University. For that, I set off from Cardiff at four in the morning in my wheezing old banger and arrived looking knackered and dishevelled, then tried, unconvincingly, to blag it. It was a *Sliding Doors* moment. I'd really wanted to go to Manchester, and had I not spectacularly flunked the interview, I probably would have done so, giving up my place in the Cardiff Rugby academy. Perhaps I would have joined a decent rugby side in Manchester, but it's equally possible I might have let my rugby ambitions wither and I wouldn't have had anywhere near the career I've enjoyed.

My grades came through – straight As – and I passed the Cardiff interview. My destiny was sealed. I was going to stay in my home city and continue my twin pursuits of rugby and medicine. My parents had given me an Interrail ticket for my eighteenth birthday, and that summer I took off with four of my best mates – Tom, Rhys, Owain and Gruff – with a thousand quid in my bank account and a guidebook in my rucksack. We had no concrete plan other than to follow our noses. We traversed much of France, Spain, Germany, Italy and Austria, sleeping in hostels or campsites, and occasionally on park benches. We lived on bread rolls, blocks of cheese and sliced baloney. My hostelling experience was put to good use, although the morning we woke up beneath a phalanx of commuters on a train into Budapest having missed our connection to Vienna would have disappointed my father, who prized his schedules and itineraries above all else. It was a wonderful trip, and a chance to embrace my hippy ideals away from the rigour and demands of the Cardiff academy. I swapped my rugby boots for a pair of sandals and dropped the routine for a month of spontaneity and adventure.

5
THREE PERFECT THIRDS

Dai Young and Bob Norster were sitting opposite me in a hospitality suite overlooking the sun-drenched Arms Park, which was looking every inch the field of dreams. On the table between us was a senior contract promising untold riches, and a blank space awaiting my signature. There was a hitch, though. The reason I hadn't scribbled my name on the dotted line was something Dai had just said: 'You can't be a full-time professional at the Blues and carry on studying. It's one or the other.'

I tried my hardest to stay composed, but I was furious. For the last couple of years I'd combined the two perfectly well, priding myself on my all-out commitment to both. My hackles were raised, but I knew diplomacy was the best route out of this. I had to persuade them that I could do this; that it needn't be one or the other.

Dai could be intimidating, whereas Bob was the ultimate charmer. He was always impeccably turned out, with the finest-cut suit hugging his bulky frame, and his hair neatly slicked into place. As a young lad, I was in danger of being either bullied or charmed into making a decision I'd regret. There is no doubt they had my best interests at heart, but their perspective couldn't have been more different from mine. It took a bit of cajoling, but I managed to convince them I could keep these trains on parallel tracks.

The facts were these. I was three years into my studies and had signed an initial contract at the age of nineteen. I was still technically in the academy, but they'd offered me a three-year deal starting on £40,000 and rising by £10,000 each season. I was a student, so this was an astonishing amount of money. While my colleagues in med school were accumulating debt, living on Pot Noodles and cheap lager, and taking out loans to cover the cost of their studies, I would be drawing a substantial salary. In typical 'Norman' fashion, though, I resisted the urge to splash the cash, using a chunk for a deposit on a

Victorian townhouse in Pontcanna and tucking the rest away for the future. It was a veritable fortune for a student, and there was an expectation that I'd treat the lads to some drinks now and again. We'd occasionally go to London for a weekend, get hammered and splash the cash in some swanky nightclub, but that was a rare indulgence.

When I started university, Justin Burnell was head of the Cardiff Blues academy, and he made it clear I'd not be receiving any special treatment. That was fine by me; I wasn't looking to cut corners. He was resolutely old-school. As a player he'd been a fearsome, uncompromising back-rower for Cardiff, Pontypridd and Neath, and he brought that no-nonsense attitude to his coaching. Insisting I submit a weekly plan to him every Monday at 8 a.m. on the dot, I'd barely have my foot through the door before he'd bark, 'Where's the schedule?' It was always chock-full. Monday to Friday, 7 a.m. to 8 p.m. Thirteen-hour days mapped out on a spreadsheet with no gaps and no down time. Strength and conditioning, skills sessions, university lectures, semi-pro training with Cardiff RFC on Tuesday and Thursday evenings, cricket at Cardiff Cricket Club on Mondays, matches on Saturdays, recovery and study on Sunday. That degree of organisation was going to be necessary to see me through university. I got into those habits early and vowed to maintain them.

Some aspects of Burnell's personality that others found intimidating actually helped keep me focused. He wasn't into the idea of 'positive affirmation', preferring to rain down insults in a way that sometimes felt a bit nasty and condescending. He could be loud, brash and demanding, and that was exactly what I needed, although we did clash over Freshers' Week. He insisted I had to train, but Freshers' is a once-in-a-lifetime thing – the start of your university experience – and there was no way I was going into it half-heartedly. It was one of the few times I stood up to him and won.

I owe a huge debt of gratitude to my fitness coaches, Trystan Bevan and Chris Tombs. They knew my circumstances were unique and went above and beyond to help me. Every Sunday night I'd email them my lecture schedule, and they'd tailor my training around it. If I couldn't make the group sessions, they'd arrange to meet me at a gym at 6 a.m. for a bespoke one-on-one session. They weren't obliged to do it, and most people in their position would have told me to get stuffed. The fact they didn't has earned them my eternal gratitude. There were around fifteen boys in the academy, but more often than not, I'd be training solo with Trystan and Tombsy.

This was all evidence that I was finding solutions to the problems the double commitment was presenting. I was doing exactly the same as the other academy boys were, just at different times. When Dai Young and Bob Norster issued their ultimatum a few years down the line, I was able to make a compelling case that not only could I combine medicine and rugby, I was already doing so. It was wrong of them to apply that pressure. What do you want in a rugby player? Someone who's compliant and rolls over, or someone who shows initiative and fights their corner?

My mum had been sceptical too, to be fair. When I moved out, she'd said, 'You know you're not going to have time for a social life, don't you?' Playing professional rugby and studying for a medical degree represents a huge demand on anyone's time, but the notion that it would stop me going out drinking and socialising wasn't something I was prepared to accept. I wasn't about to become a recluse to achieve my goals. I wanted to be the life and soul of the party, to play pro rugby *and* to ace all my exams. I wanted to be the best at everything. I had this idea about my life being a pie chart of three perfect thirds. I wanted my rugby life, my academic life and my social life to share equal billing, and I wasn't willing to sacrifice one for either of the others.

I arrived in the Talybont halls of residence at the start of university with my arm in a sling, following surgery on the shoulder I'd damaged at the Under-21s World Cup. Back then it was a six-month process from going under the knife to playing again. My first game back after all the intensive rehab was for Cardiff University, playing up at Llanrumney. Some idiot who didn't understand the laws took me out in the air and I landed square on my head. I made a decision there and then that I wouldn't play for the university side again.

By the following season, 2006–07, during my second year of uni, I was pulling on the fabled blue-and-black jersey of Cardiff RFC. Ever since I'd switched allegiance from Newport (sorry, Dad), this was the jersey I'd coveted. The same iconic shirt worn by Gareth Edwards, Barry John, Gerald Davies, Bleddyn Williams and countless other bona fide legends. That year, a side containing Leigh Halfpenny, Tommy Isaacs, Rhys Gill, Andy Powell and myself went on a run in the domestic cup competition, making it all the way to the final. It had only been six years earlier that I'd accompanied my father to the Millennium Stadium to watch Newport and Neath compete for the same trophy. Llandovery were our unfancied opponents, a team from rural West Wales who'd reached the final despite winning only six league games all season. We were 18-13 ahead when the clock ticked into the red, but their prop Endaf Howells scored an injury-time try to deny us victory. Although the cup had lost some of its magic since the advent of regional rugby, it still went down as one of the biggest shocks in the competition's history.

It wasn't just the cup I lost that day. I heard afterwards that Nigel Davies, the Wales caretaker coach, had pencilled me into his squad for the summer tour to Argentina. My name had evidently been rubbed out after my underwhelming performance in the final. I mistakenly wore boots with moulded studs on a pitch that was rock hard, causing me to slip and slide around for eighty minutes, contributing virtually nothing to a losing cause.

My time with Cardiff remains the only period in my career when I experienced a proper rugby club environment, and I look back on it with enduring fondness. It just felt more authentic, sitting with the lads around a big table, wearing my club shirt and tie, sharing buffet food, playing drinking games and singing songs before heading into town en masse. That sense of innocence and brotherhood became more and more difficult to recreate later in my professional career. There was a really good bunch there, the likes of Owen Ruttley, Chrissy Anderson, Richard Jones and Nick Hampson – lads who represented Cardiff for a long time. My pathway into professional rugby may have been preordained, but this was an essential rite of passage. You can't go straight from the academy to pro rugby. Part of the learning process is playing against grizzled old blokes who want to hurt you on the pitch, then buy you a beer in the bar afterwards.

It dovetailed perfectly with my life as a student, and at times I felt like a bit of a rock star. Representing the city I was studying in was a great buzz. My life was careering forwards at 100 mph, but I was always full of energy. Other kids in the academy would be genuinely bemused, asking me, 'How on earth have you got time to do that? Are you serious? Why are you bothering?', but as long as I had seven hours' kip a night, I could function. And I enjoyed proving all the doubters wrong. The litmus test for me was always my exams, and over the course of my studies I passed every one.

I was out every Tuesday, Wednesday and Saturday night without fail, and more often than not, I'd head down to the Philharmonic nightclub for the famed Thursday Healthcare night, where all the consultants, surgeons, nurses and medical students would congregate. It developed a reputation as one of the wildest nights in Cardiff. I was leading parallel lives, mixing and matching my Saturdays with the Cardiff RFC lads and my student mates, and feeling like a square peg in a round hole in both environments. I was never 100 per cent a student, because I had this rugby career blossoming in the background and would usually have to rein in the hedonism. The lads would be drinking until stupid o'clock, and I'd be surreptitiously tipping my pint into a plant pot because I knew I had training in the morning.

It may sound weird, but I was able to discriminate between physical and mental fatigue, and compartmentalise them. Is rugby mentally demanding? Not really. It's physically demanding, but as long as you've got half a brain, you know your plays and can problem-solve on the field, you'll be fine. Is sitting in lectures physically demanding? No, but it is mentally demanding, and that's a different sort of tired. When I was physically tired after training, my brain was still alert, so I was happy to slump in a lecture while my muscles healed and absorb all the medical stuff. My body would be chilling, but I was exercising my brain. The opposite was true during rugby training: I could switch my brain off and allow it to recharge while my body got a workout.

I'm obsessive. Not obsessive-compulsive necessarily, but definitely at the extreme end of the scale. I've always had a strong desire to maximise life and to drain every drop out of every experience, which sometimes makes it hard to relax. I can't relate to those who drift through life. I'm a deep diver rather than a surface dweller, always looking for the next thing to tick off or the next target to reach, and I see being weary or tired as an obstacle to reaching those goals. I've been the same since childhood. I was never one to vegetate in front of the TV or waste hours playing computer games. That hyperactive drive to fill every moment has been with me since birth.

The smell of formaldehyde will forever evoke memories of my first year of university. As you approached the Biosciences building on Park Place, the acrid scent would drift over from the labs, assailing your nostrils. It absolutely stank. Early in the course, all 250 medical students were ushered into an enormous aircraft hangar of a room containing thirty dead bodies. Lifeless cadavers, drained of blood and laid out on slabs like something from a horror movie. Dissection class: no place for the squeamish. I'd had an op on my shoulder, so I'd been in that surgical environment, but this was my first experience of real medicine, with me wielding the instruments. We wouldn't see live patients until our third year, but there I was, eighteen years of age, young and naive, and slicing into dead flesh with a scalpel. I didn't appreciate the magnitude of it at the time. At that age you're just absorbing scientific facts in order to pass an exam, barely pausing to consider the beauty and complexity of the human body. It's a much bigger source of fascination to me now than it was then.

A few years down the line, I was back in that room sawing the top of a guy's head off. I can't imagine too many people reading this will have done that, and I can tell you from experience that it's a tough job. I was chosen on the grounds I'd have the strength to pull it off. Or saw it off, to be more precise. You needed to put a bit of weight into it. The lecture was about neuroscience, and we were removing the top of his head to examine the most delicate and complex organ in the human body. But there I was slicing into his skull with a hacksaw like a carpenter sawing strips of MDF on a workbench.

There was no blood, just tissue and fluid, but he still had eyes, ears and teeth, and the organs were still moist because they'd been preserved. He was a recognisable human, just very dead. As surreal as it felt, in a weird way it was my escape from rugby, allowing me to leave those pressures in their own box. Some of the students were into their rugby and knew who I was, but the majority didn't, so it was liberating to escape into this parallel universe. I'm not saying rugby's boring, but training can be monotonous. The uni stuff not only kept me mentally stimulated, but gave me a far more rounded perspective on the real world.

That said, my concept of the real world had become a little distorted with all the high jinks and nonsense I was being exposed to as a rugby-playing medic. During a second-year tour of Edinburgh, I watched as the new guys were put through the ritual humiliation of a Freshers' initiation. This one involved lying face up on the floor while a naked team member squatted over your head. A third person would pour a full can of beer down the back of the squatter, into the mouth of the initiate. The following year, I watched a group initiation on Llandaff fields. Thirty lads, completely naked, playing rugby with a frozen chicken instead of a ball. Every ten minutes, a whistle was blown and everyone had to run to the corner of the pitch to down whatever drink had been served up – vodka shots, whisky shots, pints of lager, pints of cider, whatever it may have been – before returning to the game. Needless to say, most of what went in eventually found its way back out as the afternoon progressed. To those of you who've never played amateur rugby, I realise this may sound depraved. To those who have, I imagine you've seen and taken part in much worse.

People think it's incongruous that I managed to simultaneously inhabit the very different worlds of elite sport and university. My response has always been that they have far more in common than you'd imagine. For all the serious application, they're essentially both environments where mickey-taking is rife and adolescence is prolonged. No one is allowed to get above their station, and you're only ever one misstep away from ritual humiliation.

One of the boys in med school, Steff, was annoyingly good-looking and a bit of a ladies' man. Spying an opportunity to make a bit of money on the side, he registered with a modelling agency and made the crucial mistake of telling us. After a few days, I got one of my uni mates, Adam, to call him up and offer him a modelling assignment. He laid on the charm, telling Steff the photos he'd sent had been exceptional, and that his chiselled features could land him some plum, well-paid gigs. We fabricated a story about a Cowbridge-based paintball company having a rebrand, and needing a muscle-bound hunk to front the campaign. Adam explained that the shoot would be topless, and that Steff would need to turn up looking lean and rugged, preferably with a bit of stubble. We could hear Steff's excitement through the phone as Adam casually referenced a £100 fee. The deal was struck and Adam told Steff to meet them in three weeks' time at 3 p.m. in the grounds of Cardiff Castle.

For the next three weeks, Steff skipped the Medics' rugby training, spending every free hour in the gym buffing up his physique. His housemate claimed he was doing a hundred sit-ups every morning before breakfast. On the assigned day, a bunch of us arrived before the rendezvous, settling into a café opposite the castle. It unfolded beautifully. At five to three, we spotted Steff sashaying down Castle Street, checking himself out in the shop windows. He strode up to the main gates and struck up a conversation with the guard. The guard looked down his list and shook his head. Steff started gesticulating and pointing inside, but even from a distance, we could see his shoulders starting to slump. He turned and pulled out his phone. Seconds later, Adam's phone started buzzing. I answered it, telling Steff to look across the road, at which point we all collapsed in stitches. He was utterly crestfallen. I bought him lunch by way of apology, but I don't think he ever truly forgave me.

As proof of just how similar the rugby fraternity is, the Cardiff Blues lads played virtually the same prank on Xavier Rush during my first year at the Blues. Rushy was the ultimate alpha male. He'd come over from New Zealand with all the swagger and bravado you'd associate with an All Black, and also fancied himself a bit of a ladies' man. He'd met this gorgeous girl on a night out, and had spent the following week banging on about her. We sensed a weakness. One of the Blues lads started texting Rushy, pretending to be this girl. The messages were racy and flirtatious, and after a few had been exchanged, we set up a date at Salt Bar in Cardiff Bay. Rushy was delighted, telling us how this stunning girl had pursued him and that they were going on a hot date. On the night in question, his flatmate Jamie Robinson started filming Rushy's pre-date routine: emerging from the shower, having a shave and ironing his shirt, all while delivering seductive asides to the camera about what an amazing lothario he was.

The filming continued from the upstairs balcony in Salt Bar, where half the squad were assembled in silence when Rushy strode confidently through the doors. The waiter directed him to his table as we watched on from above. After half an hour had passed, and Rushy had polished off an entire bottle of wine on his own, he rose sheepishly to his feet and slunk off.

Two days later, we were assembled in the Blues' meeting room, ready for a video session on our next opponents, when our analyst, Rhod Manning, wandered in and stuck a DVD on. He'd lovingly crafted a five-minute film of Rushy's date night, starting with the braggadocious scenes in his flat, and culminating with his humiliating exit from Salt Bar, all to the swooshing accompaniment of Celine Dion's 'All by Myself'. Rushy turned beetroot-red and sank so low in his chair that all you could see were a few strands of wispy hair. It was genius. We'd shot the alpha down.

6

I WAS DAVID MAY

31 August 2007, Cardiff Blues v Ospreys, round one of the Magners League

The clock is ticking towards the end of the match, and I'm reflecting on how my senior debut for the Cardiff Blues has gone pretty well. My parents and mates are in the crowd, and I'm determined to get through to the final whistle without embarrassing myself. I've made a few telling tackles, had a few nice touches and generally felt comfortable with the pace of the game. It's been a scrappy affair, dominated by kicking, but with thirty seconds left, we're 17–15 up against our arch-rivals, the Ospreys. They're in possession and work it towards Stefan Terblanche, their Springbok winger. A fraction before he catches the ball, I launch myself purposefully at him, determined to kill the attack dead. The whistle blows. Not for full time, as I'd assumed, but for a penalty against me. Early tackle. I've taken the man without the ball. An amateur mistake.

It happened right by the dugout, where all my mates were standing. They'd been vocal throughout, hollering their support from the stand, but I'd been studiously ignoring them, wanting to project an air of professional detachment. Now they fell completely silent, as did the rest of the crowd. The silence was far worse. I felt so exposed. Ten thousand pairs of eyes were boring into me, all thinking, *You muppet.* I was convinced I'd lost us the game.

Shaun Connor stepped up to take the kick. It was 35 metres out and at an angle, but he hadn't missed all night, even knocking one over from his own half. I could barely look as he swung his leg confidently towards the ball. There was a collective gasp and then a cheer as he skewed it horribly wide. I looked up at my mates, wiped the sweat theatrically from my brow and mouthed the word 'phew'. They looked as relieved as I did.

Terblanche followed me down the tunnel, shook my hand and said, 'You lucky f***er.' Dai Young wasn't quite so blunt, but he didn't need to be. His expression said it all. Dai can communicate more with a raised eyebrow or curl of his lip than most can with a two-minute diatribe. We were from opposite ends of the spectrum. He was a dyed-in-the-wool valley boy who'd spent his playing career in the dark recesses of the front row. I was a middle-class city boy who preferred the open spaces of the back field. In that moment, I felt like the apprentice I was. His look may have been fleeting but its meaning was clear. *You're playing with the big boys now. Don't f*** it up.*

It was a World Cup year. I'd had a good pre-season and my chance with the Blues had come earlier than expected. Tom Shanklin, Jamie Robinson and Gareth Thomas were all in the World Cup squad, and Chris Czekaj had been sidelined with a horrific leg injury, a spiral fracture to his femur, to be precise. With those stalwarts missing, Dai had chucked me in, and I'd been determined to embrace it. But it wasn't long before I'd incur his wrath again. A few weeks later, I was playing on the wing against the Dragons in Newport, my first experience of playing on the hallowed Rodney Parade turf, when Nicky Robinson launched one of his deft cross-field kicks. Rushy caught it and offloaded to me in a bit of space. I set off towards the try line, and with 10 metres to go and nothing in front of me but thin air, I slowed down, raising my right arm to celebrate. I was blindsided by Martyn Thomas, who appeared from nowhere and very nearly tackled me into touch. I grounded the ball, and we won handsomely, but I knew I'd made another schoolboy error.

The following Monday, as I was walking down the corridor at our training base, Dai approached from the opposite direction. Blocking my path with his trademark power stance, he declared, 'Do that again, and it will be the last time you wear a Cardiff Blues shirt.' The raised eyebrow softened it slightly, but there was no doubt he meant it. Celebrating early was a real bugbear of his. It undermined his whole creed of humility and respect for the opposition.

One person you don't want running downhill at you is Andy Powell. The burly, powerful back-rower packs a real punch, and once his knees are pumping, it's like trying to tackle a bull. Wanting to impress during a tackle drill, I set myself firm as Andy charged towards me, determined to prove my worth. My right shoulder smashed into his hip bone and I slumped to the floor in agony. It continued to hurt for weeks and no amount of rehab seemed to improve things. I was gutted. It had been my chance to cement a place in the Blues side while the big guns were away, and I was spending most of it on a physio bench.

On the morning of my twenty-first birthday, I was sitting in my grubby student flat off Richmond Road, affectionately referred to as 'the Crack Den' by my mate Richie Rees, when the phone rang. It was the shoulder surgeon Richard Evans, calling with my scan results. The news wasn't good. I had a large labral tear in the shoulder and it needed surgery. I burst into tears. Less than two years previously, I'd had my other shoulder rebuilt and spent my first six months of university unable to play rugby. How could this be happening again? Both shoulders medically knackered by the age of twenty-one. My first season of pro rugby could have been a write-off barely weeks after it had started. I'd begun to fantasise about getting picked for Wales, and was genuinely thinking it might be about to happen. Happy bloody birthday.

The next day, I spoke to the Cardiff Blues doctor, Geoff Davies, who saw how upset I was and suggested we postpone surgery and continue with the rehab. It was a partial rather than a full dislocation, and he was convinced we could avoid the op and six months on the sidelines. His assessment proved correct, as I was back playing within six weeks. Fifteen years have passed, and I've still not had surgery on that shoulder. It's my dominant tackling shoulder, and I've tackled a fair few people with it over the years.

It was another *Sliding Doors* moment. By January, I was fighting fit and had shown up well in the Christmas derbies, the tribal all-Welsh affairs that were considered unofficial national trial matches. I was nursing a hangover in my flat when the post dropped through the letterbox. In amongst all the pizza menus and takeaway flyers was an official-looking manila envelope with the WRU logo on it. Tearing it open with trembling hands, I pulled out a letter saying I'd been selected in Wales's squad for the Six Nations. Not long afterwards, to confirm it wasn't an elaborate practical joke, I had a call from Wales team manager Alan 'Thumper' Phillips to congratulate me.

It was a serendipitous moment. Had I opted for surgery, it wouldn't have happened, and by the time I'd recovered there might have been a new kid on the block. It may sound melodramatic, but when you're young and desperate, you think that way. If Chris Czekaj hadn't been injured the previous summer, I wouldn't have had my chance with the Blues. Sport is ruthless. There are so many kids hanging around squads who never get a break, then disappear without trace. No matter how confident you are, there's always a scintilla of doubt. I knew when Czeks got injured that it was my chance. If I didn't seize it, or if I played terribly, I'd be dismissed in the minds of the coaches. Just another promising kid who'd had his opportunity and blown it. When that shoulder injury came around, I gambled on my recovery, and it paid off.

There was something gloriously incongruous about leaving my damp, gloomy student flat, climbing into my rusty Ford Focus and driving to the luxurious Vale of Glamorgan Hotel to train with Wales. I was in my third year of uni, living the life of a student – boozing, partying all hours, munching on late-night kebabs and chasing girls – yet now I was reporting for duty at an elite centre of excellence as one of the best thirty-five rugby players in the country.

I was keen – one of those kids I look at now I'm older and think, 'Shut the hell up' – but I did my best to keep a low profile in that first camp. There were some serious alphas on parade: Ryan Jones, Martyn Williams, Gethin Jenkins, Stephen Jones and Tom Shanklin, to name just a few. They weren't the sort to tolerate a young whippersnapper piping up when his thoughts weren't asked for. They were welcoming enough, but there was a definite hierarchy. I wanted to work hard and be conspicuous, but I didn't want to come across as a complete nause. It was a delicate balance to strike.

I'd been selected as a winger, and knew I was a long way behind Shane Williams and Mark Jones. I'd played thirteen games for the Blues, whereas these guys were established internationals. It was the start of a World Cup cycle and the new coach, Warren Gatland, wanted to see if I was made of the right stuff. My first encounter with him was pretty perfunctory. He shook my hand and said, 'Hi, Jamie, welcome aboard, work hard and we'll see what you're about.'

It was an interesting time to be joining the Wales squad. They'd just been dumped out of the 2007 World Cup after a chastening defeat to Fiji, and Gatland's predecessor, Gareth Jenkins, had been ignominiously sacked in the hotel car park. Expectations were low, and Warren's first priority was to restore morale. Within a few days of the start of this new regime, I got the sense that things had radically changed. Eavesdropping on the conversations between the senior lads, it was obvious they considered this a significant step up. I got the impression the previous set-up had been looser and less disciplined, more akin to a club-rugby environment. Warren had arrived with a sterling reputation after a hugely successful stint in English club rugby, and was determined to transform Wales from a team of talented under-achievers to one in the mould of his trophy-winning Wasps side.

Warren's defence coach, Shaun Edwards, also arrived with a reputation. The former rugby league hard man had a glowering presence and could instil fear with a mere look. There had been accusations of player power in previous regimes, and a resistance to the rugby-league style blitz defence. Wales's defensive system had been derisively referred to as 'the Dritz' because it had been a clumsy amalgam of a drift and a blitz. Neither one nor the other. Shaun must have got wind of this, because his first words at his first meeting were, 'From now on, we're a blitzing team. And if you don't like it, you can f*** off.' Other than a few darting eyes, no one moved, let alone spoke. In a room full of strong, opinionated characters, the hierarchy had been swiftly established.

Shaun's manner was brusque and his expressions difficult to read. In those first few weeks, he communicated in short, sharp sentences, rarely calling anyone by their name. During drills, it would just be 'you', 'dark hair, come here', or 'big lad, over there'. It could have been reverse psychology – *I couldn't give a stuff who you are* – but I think it was genuine. On one occasion, he was showing the lads a demo with the pad and shouted at Robin Sowden-Taylor, 'Mark! Get over the ruck!' Robin hesitated, and Shaun got angry. '*Mark*. Are you deaf? Get over the f***ing ruck, lad.' Robin was too frightened to correct him, and we were all too scared to laugh. Shaun's appearance was as much a source of confusion as his manner. For someone who prized discipline as highly as he did, he rarely ever had the right kit. If he wore branded gear, it was almost always the wrong brand or from the wrong era. A Wasps top in Wales training, or Reebok gear when we'd switched to Under Armour. But more often than not, it would be his trademark mishmash of white vest, tracksuit bottoms and, inexplicably, polished black brogues.

He remains the only coach I've played under whose standards were so exacting that I'd feel frightened if I slipped beneath them. If I made a mistake on the pitch, I'd immediately get the fear. If I'd 'bitten in' in defence – committed too early – or over-chased, I'd immediately flash-forward to the rollocking I knew I was going to get, and the absolute shame of public humiliation in the Monday debrief. It became a powerful deterrent, and it was no coincidence that over the next few years our defence became the meanest in world rugby.

The first game of the 2008 Six Nations campaign was the toughest: England at Twickenham. I was barely a year old when Wales had last won there. Warren Gatland picked thirteen Ospreys in the starting side. It was essentially a club side playing against an international one, and the international side in question had just reached the final of the World Cup. Headline-writers couldn't decide whether Gatland was a genius or a lunatic. The reason he gave us was that the Ospreys were the only side in Wales that used the blitz defence, and we needed that level of familiarity to be competitive.

I was named twenty-fourth man for the trip, which means you're next in line if someone goes down injured just before the game, but it's mainly an opportunity to give you a flavour of the experience, to be among the boys and take in the atmosphere. Even when you're not playing you learn a lot; you get an idea of the pressures involved. It's a strange halfway house. Unlike the rest of the non-playing squad, who were in their suits in the stand, I was down on the Twickenham turf in my tracksuit fully taking part in the warm-up. I had to prepare myself emotionally to face England in front of 80,000 baying fans while knowing deep down that the warm-up would be the most I'd exert myself all day. And that was how it unfolded. No one went down, and I jogged to the touchline to take up my duties as water boy.

I couldn't have had a better view as Wales laid their twenty-year hoodoo to rest in dramatic, heart-stopping fashion. The match went by in a blur of jumbled limbs and flashpoints: Lesley Vainikolo smashing Mark Jones into the middle of next week; Huw Bennett denying Paul Sackey a try with a heroic last-ditch tackle; Lee Byrne's try; Mike Phillips's lunging charge-down and dramatic dive for the line. It was pure theatre. Twenty unanswered points in the second half to overturn a 19-6 half-time deficit. Gatland's gamble had paid off, and Wales's World Cup exit had receded to a speck in the rear-view mirror. The coach journey home was a riot of singing, drinking and raucous celebration. I was buzzing to be part of it, but I felt like a passenger. I was in the midst of it, but I felt like a wide-eyed kid who'd sneaked in uninvited. That was all about to change.

There was a big review on Monday. A lot of bum-taps, a lot of high fives, and the newspaper headlines were hyperbolic in the extreme. Wales were back, and Gatland was the new messiah. Everyone was on a high. Everyone apart from Gatland himself. There wasn't a single note of triumphalism in his address. 'We ain't done nothing yet' was the theme. *Concentrate. Don't let this go to your head. Lose to Scotland and it means nothing.* Warren had won at Twickenham many times, having taken Wasps to European and domestic finals there, and it hadn't held any fear for him. His reaction to the victory was subdued to the point of indifference.

The following morning, we were sitting on the pitch in the indoor training barn at the Vale when Gats pulled a crumpled bit of paper from his pocket and said, without fanfare, 'Right, lads, here's the team for Scotland.' He went straight into it: 'Full-back, Lee Byrne. Right wing, Jamie Roberts . . .', and that's the last thing I heard. As he read out the rest of the team, my mind was racing. I was *in*. I glanced over at Mark Jones as his head dropped between his knees. 'Boycie', as he was known, was one of the guys that had welcomed me into the squad, including me in the jokes and making me feel at ease. He was a really good team man. As delighted as I was for myself, I felt awful for him. He was the only one to have lost his place. We'd just beaten England *in* England, for the first time in twenty years, and Gatland had gone and dropped someone. As much as I think he backed me to do a job, I'm convinced he was using Boycie to send a message. It was a prick to the collective ego. A reminder that, win or lose, no one's place was sacred.

The indignity didn't end there for Mark. He got the full treatment in Shaun's defensive review. The incident where Vainikolo bulldozed him and Mark had been a bit sluggish returning to his feet was played several times from different angles. It was barely more than a few seconds, but Shaun was furious, pausing the video and shouting, 'Boycie, what are you doing, lad? Were you unconscious?' Boycie shook his head. 'Had you broken your leg?' 'No,' Mark replied, with as much conviction as he could muster. 'Well you should have got back in the f***ing line then.' Then, as if Mark's discomfort hadn't already reached unbearable levels, Shaun cued up a clip of Ian Gough suffering a stinger while making a tackle. It was clear from the video that he'd lost all feeling in his right arm. It was hanging limply down to one side, but he still got up and sprinted back into the defensive line. '*That's* what I expect of you all,' Shaun bellowed. 'If you're not dead or you haven't broken your leg, get back in the f***ing line.' With that, he stalked out of the room.

After training, I swung by my parents' house to tell them I'd been picked. They were beside themselves with excitement and we had a meal together to celebrate. It was late when I got back to the Crack Den and my housemates had all retired early, so, after an intense couple of days, I thought I'd do the same. I flung open my bedroom door and there on my bed was an enormous stack of dirty dishes, with congealed food rotting on their surfaces. An assortment of household appliances had been stacked in a precarious tower, a vacuum cleaner, an iron and a toilet brush among them. Next to this strange exhibit was a handwritten note signed by my housemates, Tommy, Owain and Adam, which basically said that just because I was a professional rugby player, it didn't mean I could stop pulling my weight around the flat. They had warned me a few times about my habit of leaving dirty crockery in the sink, so I was bang to rights. From a four-star luxury resort, and the promise of a first Wales cap, to this. Talk about coming back down to earth with a thud.

During the anthem, as I stood next to Jughead (Ryan Jones), I was overwhelmed by the whole experience. The band striking up behind us, guys marching to the beat of the drums and the regimental goat trotting obediently by – these were things I'd long associated with an international in Cardiff, but it was surreal seeing it all up close. I was thinking, *I'm part of this now. I'm on the other side of the TV screen.*

It's a cliché to talk about the pace of the international game, but it's true. Everything moves so much faster. My heart was thumping in my chest, I was constantly catching my breath and my adrenaline levels were off the charts. Gavin Henson put me into a gap early with one of his delicate passes, and I looked up to see an ocean of space. I accelerated into it, convinced I was going to score, but in the blink of an eye the cover came across, the space disappeared and I was swamped by defenders on the 22-metre line. It was bewildering. Had that happened in a club game, I'd have been over the line and under the sticks. Space at Test level was at a premium, and despite the vast expanse of the stadium and its towering tiers, I spent much of my debut trying to navigate the tight channels and running into brick walls.

As debutant wingers usually are, I was tested with a succession of high balls, but I had a few inches on my opposite number, Chris Paterson, and was able to pluck most of them safely from the air. On several occasions, I'd glance up at the clock and be astonished to discover how much time had passed. Paterson scored all their points that day, knocking over five penalties, but we had far more in our armoury than them. Shane Williams was in the form of his life, terrorising defences with his pace, sidestep and Houdini-like ability to evade tackles. Shane scored twice and James Hook bagged another, leading us to a 30–15 victory. A first cap, in the world's best rugby stadium, in my home city, and a comfortable win. It was a dream start. My smile was as wide as the Severn Bridge as I swapped jerseys with an understandably gloomier-looking Chris Paterson.

We hadn't had a chance to celebrate the England win, so we were given licence to let off steam. I was presented with my first cap at the Hilton Hotel by the WRU President, Dennis Gethin, after which the night became a feat of endurance. Debutants are toasted by every member of the squad, which rather undermined my efforts to pace myself. I didn't have enough hands to accept all the drinks I was being plied with, and never had fewer than two on the go. You didn't know what was coming next. It could be a pint of Guinness, a glass of Sauvignon Blanc, a double whisky, anything. After a while my ambition for the night narrowed to a pretty singular focus: don't be sick in public, and make sure you leave without falling over.

After the official function, we had an after-party at Revolution Bar. It's a five-minute walk from the Hilton, but we were driven for security reasons. Once we were all on board the bus, Jughead drunkenly declared that I had to serenade the squad with a song. Suitably oiled, I strode to the front and delivered what I thought was a pretty swinging rendition of 'King of the Road'. Once the last note had subsided, I relaxed, my initiation complete. I was one of the big boys now. As that thought was settling, an unimpressed Nugget (Martyn Williams) bellowed from the back, 'Come on, water boy, let's have another.' In my reverie, I hadn't noticed that the bus had barely moved an inch. We were crawling at a snail's pace through the match-day traffic. So I did 'Leaving on a Jet Plane', the only other song in my repertoire that the lads would know. Thankfully, they all joined in after a few bars. There's nothing worse than choosing an obscure B-side that leaves you singing a cappella to a coachload of leering, drunk rugby boys.

I thought I was king of the world in 'Revs'. Propping up the bar in my tailored suit and Wales tie, acting all nonchalant as a succession of girls flirted with me and random strangers offered me drinks. After an absolute skinful, I stumbled over to the Oceana nightclub to meet my schoolmates. My Welsh regalia allowed me to skip the queue, and I was ushered through to a VIP area where I was plied with yet more drinks. I was absolutely steaming by the end of the night, and the lads had to carry me home, gleefully taking pictures all the way. I woke the next day in my crumpled suit with a pounding head and a slowly dawning sensation that my life had changed forever. I was a Welsh international.

Gatland has never had an issue with us celebrating the good times. He used to say he was happy for us to peer over the edge of the cliff, as long as we didn't topple over it. Some of the boys occasionally crossed the line and regretted it. I felt that Mike Phillips was vulnerable in that way: he'd have a few drinks and a different, darker character would sometimes emerge. It was the same with Gavin Henson. Thankfully, I was a friendly drunk: more likely to hug someone than start a fight.

A week later, we were back in the barn, cross-legged on the floor, when Gatland, with similarly little ceremony, drew out a piece of notepaper and announced the team to face Italy. 'Full-back, Lee Byrne. Right wing, Mark Jones . . .' It was my turn to drop my head between my knees. From the elation of being picked to the despair of being dropped in less than a fortnight. There had been no prior warning, no quiet word in my ear. I felt myself welling up, but was determined not to show it. My rational mind was telling me this had always been the plan; that my selection against Scotland was as much a warning to Boycie as it was an affirmation of my talents. But that didn't stop me replaying every minute of the Scotland game in my mind, wondering what I'd done wrong.

I didn't get picked for the rest of the campaign. I just trained and soaked up everything I could. I wanted to show hunger and battle for my position, but I didn't want to overdo it. You have to respect those above you in the pecking order. I didn't want to come across as a cocky kid who thought he knew it all. Mark Jones had been marauding around the training paddock like a man possessed. He was determined to reclaim his place and had responded in exactly the way Gatland had hoped he would. A few years later, Tom James blotted his copybook by claiming he was a better player than Mark in a newspaper interview. That crossed a line and Tom had to apologise. We're all competitive beasts who might believe we're better than our rivals, but it's naive to express that publicly. Unity is essential in team sports.

You train hard and push those in your position to the extreme of their capabilities, so that you both improve. It's a strange dichotomy, in that you're trying to persuade the coaches you're better than the next guy, but you also have to support him and do everything you can to help the team win. Mark remained above me in the hierarchy, but now I'd dined at the top table, I was desperate for a second course.

Wales beat Ireland at Croke Park thanks to another sublime try from Shane, and Tom Shanklin christened me 'David May' when I jostled my way into the photo when we hoisted the Triple Crown. David May was the guy who barely ever played for Man United but always seemed to be front-and-centre in the trophy photos, gurning next to the likes of Roy Keane and Eric Cantona. Martyn Williams enthusiastically picked up on it, and I couldn't walk into a room for months without either him or Shanks piping up, 'Here he is: David May.'

Shanks had had a taste of his own medicine before the Italy game. He was given the honour of leading the team out on his fiftieth cap, and before the match, Warren gathered the lads in a huddle to mark the occasion. Shanks was expecting a warm tribute, maybe even a showreel of his highlights. Instead, a deadpan Gatland said, 'When Wasps used to play Saracens, I always singled Shanks out as their weak link. If you'd told me then he'd go on to win fifty caps for his country, I'd have thought you were insane.' Then, with the timing of a stand-up comedian, he said, 'Right, lads, on the bus.' Shanks was crushed. He recovered well enough, though, scoring one of five tries as Wales thrashed Italy to remain on course for a Grand Slam decider against France.

Mark Jones nearly scored a try for the ages in that game. Receiving the ball deep in his own 22, he set off on an arcing run, burning off French defenders as they grasped at thin air. He was tackled agonisingly short of the line and denied what would have been one of the tournament's greatest ever solo tries. It didn't matter in the end, as Wales romped to a 29–12 victory after tries from Shane and Martyn Williams, and secured the Grand Slam in style.

I was present in the official squad photo, grinning in my dinner jacket on the churned-up Millennium Stadium turf, but I felt strangely detached. I had a medal with 'Grand Slam 2008' engraved on it, but I didn't feel like a Grand Slam winner. I'd played one game out of five. Does that count? I'd seen the delight on the faces of those who'd played every game, those guys who'd suffered the humiliation of defeat to Fiji only a few months earlier. *They* had earned this; I was just a wide-eyed kid along for the ride. I could claim to be a Grand Slam winner, I had the medal to prove it, but I felt like an imposter. I was David May.

A month or so later, seventeen grand dropped into my bank account. My Grand Slam winner's bonus. It was pro rata, so I got a fifth of what the other guys got. You'd get a fifth if you played one minute of one game off the bench. Four years earlier, I had been earning £55 a month in the Blues academy, and supplementing it with minimum-wage shifts as a pot-washer at a local hotel and barman at the Mochyn Du pub. Now, I was awash with cash. It was almost inconceivable that I'd earned that amount for doing something I'd happily have done for nothing. Not everyone was so fortunate. Robin Sowden-Taylor was the only member of the squad who didn't get a game, and he ended up owing the WRU money. The cost of tickets he'd been given for friends and family exceeded the modest fee he'd been paid for training, so when the lads got their payslips at the end of the tournament, he received an invoice. And I'm still not sure Shaun Edwards knew his name.

7

I FELT INDESTRUCTIBLE

Pretoria, South Africa, 11 June 2008

I was alone in the team room of our lodge hotel surrounded by well-thumbed medical textbooks. The pages were festooned with coloured stickers and scribbled notes. Shaun Edwards ambled in, sank into a chair and, by way of greeting, said, 'Lad, have you ever played twelve?' I replied that I'd once captained Cardiff Schools as an inside centre when I was fifteen, but had been a full-back ever since. 'OK, lad, I've spoken to Gats and Rob, and we're thinking of playing you at twelve at the weekend. Happy with that?' I was surprised but, wanting to appear decisive, replied, 'Yeah, awesome, why not?' 'Good,' he said, and left as swiftly as he'd arrived. With that perfunctory exchange, the course of my career changed completely.

Once he'd gone, the realisation dawned: the world champions, at Loftus Versfeld; going up against Jean de Villiers, one of the greatest centres of his generation. This was the biggest test of my manhood yet. I'd won my second cap four days earlier, allaying my fears I'd be a one-cap wonder. But we'd been soundly beaten in Bloemfontein, failing to live up to our billing in the battle of the Grand Slam champions versus the World Cup winners. The fact I'd scored a try and shared the field with my childhood hero Percy Montgomery did little to ease my disappointment. They were always going to test me as a rookie full-back, especially at altitude, and I'd dropped an early high ball under no pressure. I'd caught thousands like it, but this one had slipped through my fingers. Even the memory of the try was tarnished by the earful I received from my attack coach, Rob Howley, for celebrating early. And I'd compounded the error with a rubbish dive. Concerned about winding myself, I'd collapsed half-heartedly over the line. Luckily, I atoned for those two faux pas with a crunching tackle on their big No 8, Pierre Spies, after he'd breached the front line of our defence. As a full-back, two things are non-negotiable: being safe under the high ball, and being solid as the last line of defence. I'd failed at the first with that dropped ball but passed at the second. As I got to my feet after decking this big lump of a bloke, I thought, *That's why I love playing full-back*, not realising it was the last time I'd ever play in that position.

Craig White was our conditioning coach, an eccentric northerner with some quirky theories on fitness and nutrition. He gave a presentation before the first Test outlining his plan to fly up to the highveld the day before the match rather than spending a week acclimatising there. Whether it worked to our advantage or not I'll never know, but the fact we were well beaten and I'd spent most of the game gasping for air and chasing kicks that travelled 30 metres further than normal suggests it didn't. Before we'd left for South Africa, a colleague of his had given us a talk about water and hydration. The overarching message was not to trust bottled water. His reasoning was that bottled water apparently contains micro-plastics or micro-estrogens which can alter your hormonal balance, affecting your testosterone levels. I was cynical; even if it was true, could such a microscopic amount really make a difference? Some of the impressionable boys were taken in by it, especially when they heard that a surplus of micro-estrogens might lead to them growing boobs. One of the less enlightened squad members wondered aloud whether too much bottled water would 'turn him gay'. Several of the boys took this bloke at his word, and spent hundreds of pounds installing expensive water filters in their homes. We later discovered that he was a salesman with shares in the filter company.

The tour coincided with my third-year medical exams. It was an unpleasant case of déjà vu as I strove to combine elite rugby with full-on academia. These were huge exams: the culmination of all the foundation work I'd done before I advanced to the clinical part of my degree. Cardiff University is notorious for asking fiendishly difficult questions on obscure, little-known diseases, to ensure you revise *everything*. Professor John Williams, the team doctor, became my closest companion on tour. He was a renal specialist, and after enough time in his company I knew I'd ace any questions about kidney failure. He was brilliant; nothing was ever too much trouble. As was the case on the Under-21s tour in Argentina, I had little time to relax and see the sights. When I wasn't training, I had my head in the books, fantasising about climbing Table Mountain or going on safari with the rest of the boys. The only difference this time was that the exams were two weeks after the tour rather than smack bang in the middle of it. When I revise, I have to laboriously hand-write every-thing, before condensing those notes into spider diagrams, which is very time-consuming. It often felt perverse being on tour with Wales but dedicating most of my time to revision. As much as I wanted to pat myself on the back for managing to do both, it felt like my commit-ment to each was diluted. It was a theme I'd wrestle with again and again.

We needed to redeem ourselves in the second Test, and Gatland made a few tweaks to the team. James Hook started at full-back for the first time in his international career, so with me at inside centre, there were two of us playing out of position in the backline. They had some really dangerous runners who'd look to exploit any kinks in our defensive formation. Bryan Habana was on one wing, and a guy called Tonderai Chavhanga, being touted in some circles as the fastest man in world rugby, was on the other.

We'd been outmuscled in the first Test, and Gats told me he wanted to meet fire with fire. My positional switch was a key component of this tactical shift. I was to be, in his words, 'relentless on the gain line'. At that age, I thought I could run through brick walls, and I was itching to get out there. The plan was to run hard, straight lines off our fly-half towards their ten, especially off line-outs, where there'd be an opportunity to get up a head of steam. More often than not, though, I found myself running straight into my opposite number, Jean de Villiers. He was a seriously tough cookie. He didn't look the biggest, but he was easily one of the hardest I've played against. His legs weren't particularly muscular or powerful, but his upper body was solid and compact, like granite. Even if you were running hard at him, with momentum on your side, it still hurt.

In the back three, you're in and out of the game. You play an impor-tant role, fielding high balls, chasing kicks and finishing tries, but for

long periods you feel like you're dancing around the periphery, waiting for the action to come your way. In the midfield you're always
involved. The synapses are constantly firing and you can't switch off
for a second. That second Test was as mentally demanding as it was
physically exhausting. I had my hands on the ball far more than I was
used to at full-back. I experienced more collisions and more contact,
and gobbled up a much bigger slice of the action than I'd enjoyed the
previous week. I felt absolutely battered in the changing room afterwards, far more so than after any other game I'd played in. The bruises
were bigger, the aches went deeper and my tank had been drained of
fuel. We lost again but by a narrower margin, and the consensus was
that we'd restored some pride. Shane stole the headlines with an
outrageous solo try, another stride on the road to becoming World
Player of the Year at the end of the season.

Returning home, as most of the boys escaped on holiday after a long
hard season, I snapped into exam mode. My vitamin D levels plummeted as I spent a fortnight doing eighteen-hour shifts in the dimly lit
surroundings of the hospital library. Between 6 a.m. and midnight
every day, I set about cramming three years' worth of knowledge into
my brain. This was a major crunch point. I'd won three caps for Wales
and secured a contract with the Cardiff Blues. Now I just needed to
make it through these exams. Failures and resits were not part of the
plan. Thankfully, the hard work paid off, and I passed.

The experiment of playing me at inside centre had also paid off,
and Dai Young was persuaded to pick me there for the Blues when the
2008-09 season began. If he objected to being leant on by the national
coaches, he never said. Nicky Robinson was inside me at fly-half, and
his brother Jamie was often outside, so it was a Glantaf trio making
up that 10-12-13 axis. The mercurial Gavin Henson was back for the
autumn internationals, and while he was named as the only specialist
inside centre in the squad, I think my conversion was already complete
in Warren's mind. Gav's Achilles injury flared up before the opening
match, against South Africa, meaning I was picked to renew my
nascent rivalry with de Villiers in the midfield. He picked off a James

Hook pass to score the decisive try, but in the febrile cauldron of the Millennium Stadium we gave a far better account of ourselves and finished within a score. Impressive debuts from Leigh Halfpenny and Andy Powell suggested we were making progress.

It was in the game against New Zealand on 22 November that things began to fall into place. I really began to understand that out-to-in line you run at 12. I did it early on in their 22, running towards the gap between Ma'a Nonu and Dan Carter, beating Nonu's inside shoulder and using my momentum to hand off Carter. It was a simple movement, just one manoeuvre in a game of constantly moving parts, but it was a light-bulb moment: *That is what I do.* It was the first time I'd done what would become my trademark move in a Welsh jersey, and I did it against the best side in the world, getting past Nonu, the dreadlocked, eyeshadow-wearing behemoth I'd so admired growing up. It's difficult to explain it without it sounding basic, but when you get it right it's like diving into a pool without making a splash. Timing is everything: starting your run at precisely the right moment so you catch the ball at full pace without having to check your momentum. And the subtlety of the angle gives an almost imperceptible change in direction that buys you an extra few yards through the tackle.

I had Shanks outside me, and Mike Phillips and Stephen Jones at nine and ten. I was young, inexperienced and out of position, and they undoubtedly had to grit their teeth at times due to my naivety and lack of nous. They had hundreds of caps between them, and were essentially babysitting a rookie in the Test arena. I knew I'd have to listen to every word these guys had to say to help me ride that steep upward curve. Steve was used to having a second distributor outside him. That's the role Henson had played during the Grand Slam campaign. Gav was a very different player from me: a craftsman as opposed to a bludgeon. He would use cunning and guile to unlock defences; I would try to smash the doors off their hinges. It was a different way of playing, and these guys were being asked to adapt, to make allowances for me. There have been times in my career when I've been tearing my hair out over some of the naive things young players do – wrong options, dropped balls, mistimed tackles, needless penalties – and there's no doubt some of those lads must have been thinking the same thing about me at that time. They didn't crow about it, but a look from Shanks or Phillsy was enough to know you'd screwed up. No one mastered the look of withering disdain as effectively as Gethin Jenkins. Many's the time I've emerged from a ruck having been penalised to find Melon, as he was known, staring at me with murder in his eyes.

We led New Zealand at half-time but a similar narrative unfolded in the second period as they pulled away to win by 20 points. I was relaxing in the Vale golf club after the game when Shaun sidled up to me and said, 'Lad, you became a Test player today.' It was a typically pithy exchange, but it meant the world to me. I'd been something of a rabbit in the headlights during my first four Tests, a bit wet behind the ears, but I'd felt more comfortable that day. My tackles were sticking, my carrying was increasingly forceful, my breakdown work was precise and my positional awareness more acute. It had been a big gamble for him and Gats to switch me to the midfield, and in that game they'd seen the evidence it had paid off. It was a departure from their policy of having a second five-eighth like Gavin Henson, a conscious decision to recalibrate their game plan, and they were essentially placing faith in my ability to alter their approach. If there was ever an ego boost for me, that was it: an international side changing its shape and putting me at the heart of the game plan.

It was a model they'd used at Wasps, where it was all about gain-line dominance and speed of ball. Since its origins in the nineteenth century, rugby has always been about those things. Without big carriers who can get you across the line and create space out wide, you're going nowhere. Flooding those channels with big ball-carriers at speed will inevitably cause cracks to appear in the opposition defence. Under stress and fatigue a constantly realigning defence will eventually end up short on numbers, or with a mismatch to be exploited. That kind of game plan was tailor-made for me. It was exciting, fast and full of collisions, and I loved it just as much without the ball. I was an enthusiastic convert to the blitz defence. That predatory way of closing in on players from the outside and levelling them was immensely satisfying. Drifting teams don't get the chance to put those big hits in: the drift is all about making passive leg tackles with your outside shoulder. Dominant, head-on hits were the drug I wanted more and more of. There are many players in the game that are a bit soft, especially at club level. They don't run into collisions flat out or chuck their full weight into it. I pledged never to be one of those. Test rugby is a kind of physical warfare and it requires a 'no retreat, no surrender' approach. That was my mentality going into the final game of the autumn against Australia, and it led to the most frightening injury of my career.

Two minutes in, we were awarded a free kick off a scrum on their 10-metre line. Refs were giving loads of scrum free kicks at the time because of the law changes which meant front rows were still getting to grips with a new method of engaging, and Rob Howley had devised a move specifically to take advantage. Australia had been defending tightly, leaving big gaps on the edge of the field, and we knew they were vulnerable if we got the ball wide quickly. The move was simple: Andy Powell would take a quick tap, hit Gareth Cooper at nine and I'd run a hard line towards my opposite number, Stirling Mortlock. Mortlock was a big unit, whose reputation was built on a no-frills, abrasive approach to the game. We were two peas in a pod. Rob knew he'd want to put an early hit on me to try to seize a psychological advantage. He saw me running the line off Gareth and, as anticipated, he swivelled his hips inwards to take me head on, sniffing an intercept. Like a poker player facing a bluff, he'd fallen for it. I was just a decoy. By jamming in and committing to me, he'd narrowed their defence, allowing Gareth to play it 'out the back' to Steve and exploit the space. For those unfamiliar with such terminology, 'out the back' simply means passing to a player standing deeper and *behind* the first line of offence.

So while the ball was heading towards the left-hand touchline, Mortlock and I were careering towards one another. Two 6 foot 4, rippling, 17-stone blokes, pumping their knees into an inevitable thunderous collision. BANG! Unlike a car that smoothly decelerates before coming to a halt, I'd gone from maximum velocity to a complete standstill in a nanosecond. I didn't feel any pain or lose conscious-ness, but I was suddenly spreadeagled on the deck wondering what the hell had just happened. *Then* the pain hit. An intense, throbbing sensation that quickly extended through my entire body. My head was pulsating and I felt a little woozy, but I was still compos mentis, still aware of what was going on around me.

Mortlock was completely gone. His lights were out. He was lying motionless, face down on the turf. The doc came on and asked if I'd been knocked out. I told him my head was really hurting but insisted I was all right. In that moment, the replay was rolling on the big screen, and the entire stadium let out a collective groan. Seventy-five thousand people winced in unison. I watched it back as I lay there and felt strangely empowered. In that febrile, gladiatorial arena I felt like a victorious warrior in the Colosseum. Mortlock was returning to his senses, but his jelly legs wouldn't support his weight. He had to be dragged to his feet and carried off. Over the past decade the game has made enormous advances in concussion awareness, so it feels irresponsible to admit this, but watching him go off made me feel proud. In that turbocharged, adrenalised environment where the blood is coursing through your veins, your sinews are stretched, your heart is pumping and your senses are heightened, you revert to a more primal mode of being. Your actions are less cerebral, more elemental, your thoughts less considered, more instinctive. In that moment, I'd knocked my opponent to the deck and forced him off the field. I was invincible.

Had it happened in this decade, I'd have been taken off for a mandatory Head Injury Assessment, but such things didn't exist back then. Instead Prof conducted a basic cognitive-ability test right there on the pitch. 'Who are we playing against?' I could see gold jerseys, so I said, 'Australia.' 'What minute are we in?' I could see the stadium clock, so I said, 'The third minute.' 'What's the score?' 'Nil-nil.' That was proof I was, according to the vernacular, 'orientated in time, space and location'. He then tested my eye movement and peripheral vision using the time-honoured 'how many fingers am I holding up?' method, and reassured me that despite the presence of a tender egg-shaped lump on my forehead, my looks were intact. After this fairly perfunctory exchange, I was declared fit to continue. I would have contested any alternative diagnosis.

It may seem surprising in the modern context, but it didn't even occur to me to go off. I'd always been a clumsy kid. My nickname was 'Lump-head' because of the number of times I walked into lamp-posts, ran into people or fell off my bike, banging my head. My skull has thickened over time because of all the knocks I've taken. It was very early in my medical training and I didn't have a clue about the dangers of concussion. It was only much later I learned that you can suffer a serious brain injury without being knocked out. The fact I hadn't lost consciousness emboldened me to carry on. Shaun's mantra was echoing in my mind. *If you're not dead or you haven't broken your leg, get back in the f***ing line.* When I got up, the crowd rose to its feet to applaud me back into the action.

I felt indestructible. But I wasn't. The next few minutes wobbled by in a dreamlike blur. Quade Cooper is one of world rugby's more elusive runners, but my missed tackle on him was inexcusable. It began to feel like the game was happening at warp speed and I was running through treacle. Around fifteen minutes after the collision, I was standing beneath the posts as Matt Giteau lined up a penalty kick and I felt a stream of warm blood trickling from my nose. *Strange,* I thought. I'd hit my forehead, not my nose. Seconds later I almost gagged as a stream of salty fluid began to dribble down the back of my throat. My mind flashed back to those lonely hours in the hospital library and I remembered something I'd read about cerebrospinal fluid having a salty taste. In an instant, my air of invulnerability deserted me and was replaced by blind panic.

I gestured frantically to Prof, and he beckoned me to the touchline to ask what was wrong. His expression darkened when I told him I could taste salty fluid in my mouth. He didn't want to alarm me, but he knew. There was an urgency in his step as we strode towards the tunnel. The crowd were shouting, 'Well done, Jamie,' but despite how close they were, they felt strangely remote, as if they were hollering at me across a distant plain. I was worried. What had I done? Was this brain damage? Cerebrospinal fluid surrounds your brain and spinal cord, and it was pouring into my mouth. That can't be good. With every step I took, my head was squeaking. It was a weird, disconcerting sound, like a creaky hinge that needed oil. In the cauldron of the stadium amid the din of 70,000 voices, it was the loudest thing I could hear.

My mum was up in the stand crying her eyes out. A stranger next to her, noting her distress, had offered her a hand to hold. She had no idea the player being rushed to hospital was this woman's son. Mum maintains to this day that the next hour was the worst of her life, as her mind conjured up all kinds of awful scenarios. My dad was apparently more composed, reassuring her that I was in the hands of the medics and that there was nothing they could do. I don't think he wanted to miss the game, to be honest.

Mortlock came into the medical room with his pristine, sparkling clean jersey and said, 'F*** me, mate, that's the cheapest cap I've ever had.' We swapped shirts and wished each other luck, then I jumped into an ambulance. A CT scan confirmed that I'd fractured my skull. Not just the bit behind my forehead as you'd expect, but the base of the skull too, which should give you some idea of the sheer force of the impact. If you imagine your brain as a lump of haggis, the base of the skull is the plate it sits on. The fracture began above my eye socket and extended through the base of the skull, creating a crack big enough for the cerebrospinal fluid to drip through. If I'd had another knock in the same place, the fracture would have deepened and the consequences of that are not worth contemplating. The thought of exposing my brain to another collision without the protection of my skull makes me shudder to this day. I could have had a life-changing brain injury, or worse. Thinking about it makes me feel sick. I'd wanted to battle on, and as senseless as it sounds now, it didn't feel reckless at the time. It wasn't that old-school attitude of having to play through the pain barrier to prove your manhood; I genuinely felt fine. But I wasn't. It was a salutary lesson.

I followed the rest of the game on the BBC website on a doctor's phone. We won 21–18. Our first scalp against one of the 'big three' in eleven attempts. I couldn't take much credit for it, other than the fact I'd wiped out their skipper in the second minute. I messaged Rob Howley to congratulate him and the lads, and tell him I was doing OK. When my parents arrived at the hospital they were bemused to find me sitting up, smiling and flirting with the nurses. They'd steeled themselves for a more sombre scenario involving me lying flat out with tubes and pipes everywhere. That validated the old man's decision to stay at the game, as he got to witness a historic victory. I'm not sure my mum's ever forgiven him, though.

The fracture wasn't displaced, which meant surgery wasn't necessary. It's the same as any bone: if it's not displaced, it usually heals within six weeks. I didn't even have an overnight stay, nor a battle scar to boast about. The lump subsided quickly, and didn't leave a mark. A TV programme later conducted an experiment which calculated that a ton of force had passed through my skull, and that the collision was the equivalent of a major car crash. And all I had to show for that were a few sleepless nights and a headache.

8

AN INSUFFICIENT BREEZE

I could count the number of forwards who take goal kicks on the fingers of one hand. John Taylor, Allan Martin, John Eales . . . that's about it. So when Martyn Williams was lining up a penalty shot in the Heineken Cup semi-final it felt wrong. Our European fate shouldn't be decided by the kicking prowess of a bloke whose job it is to bury his head in rucks. He stepped up, hooked it to the left of the uprights and the Cardiff Blues went tumbling out of Europe. It was the first, last and only penalty shoot-out in the history of the sport, and the cruellest way to lose. I was discovering that 2009 was becoming the year of spirit-crushing defeats.

Rewind to two months earlier, and we were in the same stadium, in the final round of the Six Nations, moments away from Triple Crown glory. We'd gone into the game against Ireland with a chance of defending our title, but the margin of victory required was out of reach by the seventy-fifth minute. No matter: finishing with a win and denying Ireland their first Grand Slam in sixty-one years was sufficient motivation. Stephen Jones's clutch drop goal had given us a 15–14 lead, and we had five minutes to defend it. Moments later, Ronan O'Gara had responded in kind, reclaiming the lead for Ireland. It must have been agonising for both sets of supporters. Victory proffered and snatched away in an instant.

The drama didn't end there. As the clock ticked into the red, we were given a penalty in our half, on the outer edge of Steve's range. If the two drop goals had been shots in a tense rally, this was Steve's chance for the smash. After going through his usual, un-showy routine, he glanced briefly at the posts before beginning his run-up. He struck the ball beautifully and it sailed in a graceful upward arc towards the posts. Even as its downward trajectory began, it seemed to have the distance, but as it descended it dipped agonisingly short of the crossbar. The same crossbar Martyn Williams would aim towards two months later. Two huge games in front of two huge crowds at the cathedral of Welsh rugby. Two sickening defeats. It didn't take a clairvoyant to tell me that these things tend to happen in threes, and by the end of the summer, I'd experience the most heartbreaking of them all.

But I'm getting ahead of myself. The 2009 Six Nations campaign was a big one for me. After my cameo appearance on the wing the previous year, I'd become a first-choice centre, and was ready for a proper assault on the world's greatest rugby tournament. Our opening fixture was away to Scotland, where I actually ran out with '13' on my back, but Shanks and I had instructions to swap places regularly to keep the Scots guessing. I continued to settle into my groove, running hard lines and clattering into defenders, and we were too powerful for them. I didn't get on the scoresheet, but I was named Man of the Match. The day after, my dad called to say he'd seen an article mentioning me as a candidate for the Lions tour to South Africa that summer. My heart skipped a beat. Although I was a capped international, the Lions felt way beyond my reach. I associated it with craggy-faced icons like Willie John McBride, Gareth Edwards and Graham Price. I was just a baby-faced student learning my trade. Being spoken of as a contender was surreal, especially when I was playing in the same position as people like Brian O'Driscoll, Gordon D'Arcy and Mike Tindall.

The next game, against England, was the most physically demanding I've ever experienced in my career, before or since. They had clearly identified me as our most potent attacking weapon because they devised a strategy specifically to contain me. Half an hour in I was sick of the sight of Joe Worsley, their teak-tough flanker. I hit the deck hard about five times, and every time I got to my feet, I'd discover it was him who'd levelled me. He wasn't my opposite number, but I seemed to be permanently running into his solid, unyielding shoulder. It was happening too much to be a coincidence.

We had a scrum and I looked up to scan their backfield, assessing my options. Where were the weak links, the soft shoulders? *Where's Andy Goode?* Running at the opposition fly-half was always a safe bet, but I couldn't see him. *Where the hell has he gone? Where are they hiding him? Has he been subbed off?* My eyes drifted back to the scrum, where I saw him attempting, self-consciously, to pack down on the blind-side flank. My gaze returned to the backline and, sure enough, there in the ten channel was the granite-boned man mountain Joe Worsley. Tensed, poised, flexing his muscles and glowering at me. It dawned on me in that moment: his sole mission, at the expense of anything else, was to hunt me down.

Marking me off set piece was one thing, but even in phase play, when their defensive line would be realigning and filling the space, he'd always be in front of me, blocking my path or looming into my peripheral vision like a bloody berserker. A shadow I couldn't shake. An old-fashioned, no-frills, rough-hewn hard bastard. There were no verbals or sledging; he's a silent assassin who lets his actions do the talking. The most he did was look at me splayed on the deck and laugh, which was arguably worse.

We were told to change nothing at half-time. Gats said if they thought this one-man demolition attempt was going to force us off course, they could think again. 'Keep running those lines' was his message: keep charging into the teeth of their defence, because that's exactly what they didn't want us to do. It wasn't sexy or glamorous, but it was brutally effective. Gatland wanted to imprint his DNA on this team, and England knew we weren't intruders hoping to sneak through and burgle them: we were the type of team that announced we were coming, then kicked the bloody doors in.

I made a few inroads in the second half, but we're talking inches rather than metres. Dents rather than line-breaks. The official statistics showed that Joe Worsley tackled me ten times. Ten is a decent tackle count in total; to tackle one bloke ten times is virtually unheard of. I couldn't find a way through, so while our personal duel ended in a tie, the result that mattered was the one on the scoreboard. We won 23–15. Gats and I shared a drink afterwards, and he seemed both bewildered and intrigued that England had changed their entire defensive pattern to cope with one player. The morning after, I had to grab on to the roof of my car to haul myself out of the seat. I had two dead legs, front and back. My quads were throbbing, my hamstrings were aching and my legs were covered in angry welts and bruises. I couldn't train for four days.

I had another man mountain to contend with in the next match, against France. Mathieu Bastareaud was making his debut and the French press was talking him up. He was big, powerful and hungry. It was one of those games where you strap up your shoulders and prepare to muscle up. He was their midfield missile, and the responsibility to shoot him down lay with me. He proved early on he was as capable as anyone of dishing it out in defence. The whistle blew as I was thrown a high, looping miss-pass. You relax when you hear the whistle, no longer needing to brace for impact. Bastareaud either didn't hear it or chose to ignore it and flew into me horizontally, knocking the wind clean out of my lungs. One second I was upright, juggling the ball, the next I was staring at the sky, struggling to breathe. It was one of the biggest shots I've taken in my career and was a microcosm of the match as a whole. They were too powerful for us. We were developing a reputation for physically dominating teams, but the bullies became the bullied that day.

I was replaced by Gavin Henson after an hour. It was probably preordained, but it didn't stop the paranoia from creeping in. I'd taken Gav's 12 shirt while he'd been injured; now he was back to reclaim it. Was my tenure at an end? Had I played poorly? Had the experiment of swapping a ball player for a bulldozer run its course?

It was devastating to lose, but I loved my first experience of Paris. If the Millennium Stadium is my favourite venue, Stade de France ranks a close second. There's an irresistible romance about Paris and French sport, and I've always admired their attitude and joie de vivre. There's a certain spirit and elan about French rugby that can't be bottled. The sports fan in me loved playing in the arena in which Zinedine Zidane had inspired his team to World Cup glory a decade earlier. French victories over Wales in Paris used to be greeted with a Gallic shrug, but the extent to which they celebrated this one underlined how big a threat we'd become.

Gatland picked me *and* Gavin Henson in the next game, against Italy, among several other changes that gave the team a disjointed feel. Had it not been for an influential cameo from Tom Shanklin, we would have lost. Collectively, we were dreadful, but Andy Powell in particular had a shocker of a first half. He ran into touch from a kick-off, lost a few balls in collisions and generally played like he was wearing mittens. The cramped changing room was in a state of silent shock at half-time. I was young and reluctant to speak, but Powelly allowed his frustrations to boil over, unleashing an angry expletive-ridden tirade. 'F***ing *hell*, boys. What the f*** is going on?' He continued for a whole minute, slamming his fist into his open palm and bellowing aggressively until his voice started to crack. The veins in his forehead were throbbing as he built to a furious crescendo: 'Let's sort our s*** out, NOW!' With that, he stormed out, slamming the door theatrically behind him. Seconds later he reappeared through the same door, his dramatic departure undermined by the fact he'd walked into a wardrobe.

We were still losing with ten minutes left when Tom Shanklin came on and scored the winning try. I ran up to embrace him and, in classic Shanks style, he shrugged and said, 'Yeah, supersub, whatever.' He was humble enough, but without his contribution, we'd have suffered a humiliating defeat. It still put a serious dent in our title ambitions, because we now needed to beat Ireland by an enormous margin to retain the championship. Warren Gatland had made an error of judgement with his selection that day, and he knew it.

In the build-up to the decider against Ireland, Gatland rolled one of his grenades out during a press conference, saying the Welsh players hated the Irish more than any other nation. It was patent nonsense, and was more likely a reflection of his own fractured relationship with the IRFU. He'd lost his job as Ireland head coach amid accusations of plotting and backstabbing, and had borne a sizeable grudge ever since. He was only too happy to throw a lit stick of dynamite into proceedings. His comments caused quite a stir, but it all faded into the background for me, because I'd been dropped.

Earlier in the week, Rob Howley had pulled me aside for a chat and explained they were picking Henson and Shanklin in the midfield. It was a huge game, the title was on the line and those two were the midfield combination that had brought home the Grand Slam the previous year, as well as in 2005. I could understand the reasoning, but I was absolutely gutted. I'd been led to believe I was the future at 12, and that my assets were essential to the new game plan, so this felt like a rejection. I felt a bit like I'd been used to make an ex jealous. When it came to the crunch, when a trophy was on the line, they still considered Gav the best option. It was a big dent to my ego.

It was different from getting dropped the previous year. Then, I was an impressionable rookie who'd been delighted to get his first cap. A year on, I felt like a first-choice player who'd lost the trust of the coaches. It was natural to feel aggrieved, but I couldn't let my disappointment curdle into bitterness. I needed to be a team man, to help Gav and Shanks prepare as best they could, and that's what I did. It was a valuable lesson in learning how to cope with disappointment, and one every professional sportsman has to go through.

Gav and I didn't speak too much off the pitch, and he wasn't the sort of bloke I'd go for a beer with, but he was the ultimate professional. What we did have in common was recent experience. He'd lost his place to me after playing a starring role in the Grand Slam, and now he'd won it back. The shoe was on the other foot, so it was impossible for us not to feel a shared empathy. Throughout the campaign, he'd been patient and respectful towards me, helping to guide me through, and I wanted to reciprocate that.

Back in 2005, Ireland had come to Wales for the last game of the championship needing to win by 13 points to take the title. Two hundred thousand fans had poured into a Cardiff city centre bathed in warm spring sunshine and humming with anticipation. Mike Ruddock's Welsh team had ignited the tournament with a style of running rugby that had set pulses racing and resurrected memories of the sepia-tinged seventies. If the Irish had travelled with confidence, Wales felt as though destiny was on their side. They were on course for a first Grand Slam in twenty-seven years. Mike Ruddock was so relaxed, he spent the morning gently strumming his guitar in the hotel while the crowd outside swelled and grew increasingly raucous. I was among them, swigging from a can of cheap lager and wearing a replica Wales shirt that hung generously on my eighteen-year-old frame. Wales blew Ireland off the park, and sent the country into raptures.

Four years later, the situation was oddly similar, but with the roles reversed. Ireland were on for the Grand Slam, but a 13-point winning margin would deliver the title to Wales. The one major difference, from a personal perspective, was that I was no longer a gawky teenager. I was part of the match-day squad. It was likely to be tight, and if it was close going into the final quarter, Gatland would want to leave his experienced players on the park. It wasn't the kind of game to be giving subs a chance, so I didn't think I'd get on. As it happened, I was sprinting on after twenty-nine minutes, with the score still deadlocked at 0–0. It was as good as starting. Lee Byrne was the injured party, so Gav went to full-back and I slotted into the midfield. That was good for my confidence. We controlled the ten minutes until half-time, and went in 6–0 ahead.

We'd spent a huge amount of time analysing Ronan O'Gara's array of kicks, in particular his chip over the defence, but all the analysis in the world counts for nothing in the face of perfect execution. I was convinced he'd kicked this one too far, but it landed in-field and bounced directly into the hands of Tommy Bowe, who took it at full speed. He had the angle, and though Gav was racing across to cover, he didn't stand a chance. It was their second try in a minute, after O'Driscoll had burrowed over from close range, and with it momentum swung decisively their way.

But it's the dramatic denouement this game will always be remembered for: the elation of Steve Jones's drop goal, followed by the despair of O'Gara's. We'd been defending for our lives for two minutes when I saw Ronan dropping into the pocket, and I remember thinking, *This is the fastest ten metres you've ever had to run in your life.* I got in a three-point stance, like a sprinter, and hared towards him with as much energy as I could muster. It wasn't enough.

To this day, I don't know why Gav didn't take the last-minute penalty. Both he and Steve were world-class goal-kickers, but Gav had the bigger boot. He might have had the extra few inches to get it over the crossbar. As we know, it fell agonisingly short, meaning Ireland

were crowned Grand Slam champions. We had to watch as they
paraded the trophy around *our* stadium in *my* city. It was completely
galling. We'd gone into the game with an outside chance of winning
the title, but in the event, we finished fourth. Those are the margins
in the Six Nations. The difference between a Triple Crown and fourth
place was as little as a couple of inches, or an insufficient breeze.

A number of incentive-based clauses had been placed in our
contracts, and one was that if we finished the season in the world's
top three, our match fees would double the following season. Winning
that match would have propelled us into the top three, and someone
calculated that Steve's missed kick had cost us thirty grand a man. As
if he wasn't feeling bad enough, he now had an extra layer of guilt to
contend with. Once the raw pain of defeat had subsided, it was open
season on poor old Steve and he was buried under an avalanche of
abuse in the weeks that followed. Rugby banter can be cruel.

Returning to domestic rugby after a failed international campaign can
be a freshening tonic, and the Cardiff Blues were in the midst of their
best ever season. We'd steamrollered our way through our Heineken
Cup pool, beating Gloucester, Biarritz and Calvisano home and away.
The victory in Gloucester was particularly encouraging as we'd been a
man down for most of it, after Tom James's head butt on Olivier Azam
earned him a red card. Six wins out of six and a healthy points difference secured us number-one seeding in the quarter-final draw.

We were drawn against Toulouse in the last eight, and despite both
sides being loaded with ball players, we played out a nervy tryless
encounter, ending on the right side of a 9–6 scoreline. It was the
biggest arm-wrestle I'd played in, and a real lesson in midfield play
from the maestro, Yannick Jauzion. He was a brilliant, silky runner,
and we had to work tirelessly in defence to keep him and his fellow
three-quarters at bay. He's undoubtedly one of the greatest to have
worn the number 12 jersey.

Leicester were next, under the roof at the Millennium Stadium. It
was a far more absorbing game, but all anyone remembers about it
now is the last five minutes of the eighty, and the heart-stopping

drama that followed. With six minutes of normal time remaining, we were 26–12 down and resigned to defeat. Out of hope rather than expectation, Nicky Robinson called a line-out set play we'd practised loads in training: clean ball off the top, down to Richie Rees and out to Nicky, who had three forwards running decoy lines off him. He feigned to offload before swinging a 'tunnel ball' to me in the centre of the field. A 'tunnel ball' is one thrown in front of one player and behind another, with the two of them creating a 'tunnel' and acting as decoys to keep the defenders guessing. It was a beautiful pass, I didn't break stride and the defence parted. Once I was through the gap, I was looking for support, waiting for the moment to draw and give, but no one was trying to tackle me. I got to within 10 metres and thought, *Sod it*, putting my head down and crashing over in the corner. The celebrations were muted because we were still nine points adrift, but when Ben Blair nailed the touchline conversion, we started looking around, thinking, *Hang on, we're still in this*. Five minutes to go, seven points in it.

Leicester kicked off deep and Xavier Rush caught the ball in our 22, swivelling round and charging into contact. The ensuing ruck was messy, and the ball spilt out of the back. Richie scooped it up and two passes later it was in my hands. We were still in our 22 and I had three men outside me, but Leicester's defensive line was drifting towards the touchline. Instinctively, I ignored the overlap and cut back inside. One of England's best defenders, Lewis Moody, was directly in front of me, so I tucked the ball into my left hand and blasted through the tackle, leaving Moody on the deck and a vast expanse of green in front of me. I gobbled up the yards, crossing the 22, then the 10-metre line, with my legs pumping in an ocean of space. Once we'd advanced into their half, I passed to Tom James and he stepped on the accelerator, rounding the last tackler to score in the corner. The 40,000-strong crowd erupted. The conversion was even further out this time, just inches infield, but Benny Blair banged it straight between the posts. From 26–12 down to 26 apiece in two minutes. Unbelievable scenes.

After the electricity-jolt of the previous five minutes, extra time unfolded in a slow, turgid manner, like a record being played at half speed. Everyone was knackered, and paranoid about giving away penalties. A game of kick tennis ensued, with neither team daring to compete too hard at the breakdown. With the second half of extra time nearing its end, I heard Ceri Sweeney shouting at me from the touchline, 'Doc, you're off.' Dai Young knew this game was going to penalties, and he wanted Sweeney, a renowned goal-kicker, in the mix. He'd looked across our backline, thinking, *Which idiot here can't kick?* The final whistle blew, and rugby's first penalty shoot-out was declared. Five nominated kickers from each side, five kicks from the 22-metre line, directly in front of the posts. If it was all square after that, sudden death.

Ben Blair, Nicky Robinson, Leigh Halfpenny and Ceri Sweeney all nailed their kicks, making it 4-3, with Johne Murphy to come for Leicester. He missed. Tom James, the try-scoring hero, had the kick to win it, to send the Cardiff Blues through to the 2009 Heineken Cup final. I can only imagine how he must have felt, how those posts must have appeared to narrow as he cast his gaze beyond the uprights. He swung his left leg purposefully, and hooked the ball wide. Leicester equalised through Scott Hamilton and it was 4-4 going into sudden death. Shanks nonchalantly took it to 5-4, Aaron Mauger to 5-5. Up stepped Richie Rees. Richie's a skilful player, but as the ball left his boot it travelled on a horrible dipping trajectory before somehow clearing the crossbar. Never has an expression captured a combination of ecstasy and relief more than his at that precise moment. His smile was wide, but his jaw was clenched. Tension and release.

Then we were into the forwards. If Craig Newby missed, it would be game over, but he didn't. Martyn Williams, one of the most skilful forwards of the modern era, was next.

He's the only Welsh forward ever to have landed a drop goal in international rugby. If you could have picked any forward in Wales, let alone the Cardiff Blues, to take that kick, you'd have picked Nugget. But on that day, under that pressure, it wasn't to be. After Nugget's skewed attempt sailed wide, Jordan Crane stepped up for Leicester and booted them into the final. Game over. Nugget was inconsolable. He'd been an absolute stalwart of that side for a decade and was widely regarded as one of the best open-sides ever to have played the game. Someone had to miss, and Nugget was the man touched by the cruel finger of fate. To compound the sense of misery, it was the same set of posts at the same end of the ground that O'Gara had threaded his drop goal through two months earlier.

That was the best Cardiff Blues side there's ever been, and that was the best chance they've ever had to win Europe's premier competition. If we'd made it through to the final, we'd have met Leinster and the likes of O'Driscoll, D'Arcy, Kearney and Fitzgerald: all those Irish boys who'd won the Six Nations in front of our noses. Not revenge per se, but an opportunity to settle a score. As I watched the final a few weeks later, with the dead-eyed detachment of a neutral, I was convinced we would have won it.

9
MAN OF THE SERIES

1.30 p.m., 21 April 2009

I'm in the passenger seat of Tommy Isaacs's Ford Fiesta in the Victorian seaside resort of Penarth. The radio is tuned to BBC 5 Live, and we're gazing across the shingle beach to the lapping waters of the Bristol Channel. The warm spring sunshine is glancing off the art deco pavilion of the town's pier.

Ten miles away in the Cardiff suburb of Lisvane, my dad, three weeks into retirement, is quietly nursing a foamy pint of ale in the Black Griffin. The TV is tuned to Sky Sports News. We're waiting with a mixture of nervousness and excitement for the announcement of the Lions squad to tour South Africa.

Gerald Davies, the Wales and Lions legend, steps up to the podium and begins to read out the names of the chosen ones in his refined Carmarthenshire brogue. 'Lee Byrne, Wales. Rob Kearney, Ireland. Shane Williams, Wales. Leigh Halfpenny, Wales. Ugo Monye, England. Luke Fitzgerald, Ireland. Tommy Bowe, Ireland.' The back-three players are announced first. It's the centres next. 'Tom Shanklin, Wales. Jamie Roberts . . .'

Tommy erupts alongside me, eyes bulging, fists clenched, his animal-istic 'Woo-HOOOO!' amplified in the cramped confines of the Fiesta. I zone out for a split second, letting it sink in. Then I fling open the door and start dancing around on the pavement like a five-year-old. Joyous, uninhibited and totally unselfconscious. The pensioners enjoying their afternoon constitutional along the seafront clearly think I'm insane. Tom envelops me in a bear hug and says, 'I'm so proud of you, brother.'

Over in the Black Griffin, Norman leaps jubilantly to his feet and, experiencing a fleeting surge of generosity, offers to buy everyone in the pub a drink. The fifty or so other patrons are suddenly Norman's best friends.

*   *   *

Tommy bought me an ice cream from the doddery old Italian bloke who runs the kiosk on the pier, and my phone started burning red hot. I was deluged with texts and voicemails and became almost uncontrollably emotional. My dad called from the pub, giddy with excitement, and in that moment I felt overwhelmed with gratitude for all he and Mum had done for me over the years. The life they'd given me, the money they'd spent, the school trips they'd bankrolled, the unending encouragement and support they'd lavished on me. All that had put me on a path towards this. If being picked for Wales had been a dream come true, I'd now entered the realms of fantasy.

As a teenager, I'd worn out my dad's VHS copy of *Living with Lions*, the iconic film of the victorious 1997 South African tour. Rob Howley, Scott Gibbs, Neil Jenkins and Scott Quinnell had been my heroes. Never in my wildest dreams had I imagined I'd one day follow in their footsteps. We drove back to Cardiff via the supermarket and filled the boot with booze. As Tommy drove, I started spraying out invitations to the house party I'd just decided to throw. I invited all my schoolmates, and also my PE teachers, Keri, Dai and Huw. They had played a monumental part in my development, and it was vital they were there to help me celebrate. In among my messages was a missed call from a BBC producer who wanted me to come to their Llandaff studio for an interview. I said I was otherwise engaged, so they sent a camera crew to my house, where I was interviewed live on the Welsh news as a procession of tipsy, giggling mates were piling into my house behind me.

There were six Cardiff Blues in the squad. Gethin, Nugget, Powelly, Halfpenny, Shanks and me. The Saturday before the squad announcement, we'd stuck 50 points on Gloucester in the final of the Anglo-Welsh Cup. That performance may well have inked in a few extra names, but sadly the number was reduced to five when Shanks dislocated his shoulder the following month against the Dragons. Sport at its absolute cruellest. Had I played in that game, it could easily have been me, and my career may have followed an entirely different trajectory. It's no exaggeration to say that the tour that followed changed my life.

Mike Tindall, Josh Lewsey and Gordon D'Arcy were touted as possible replacements for Shanks, but they chose not to take anyone extra.

That left Brian O'Driscoll, Riki Flutey, Keith Earls and myself as the midfield options. Earls was the youngest, and a hybrid wing/centre, so with Shanks gone, I thought I might have a genuine shot at the Test team. O'Driscoll was a dead cert at 13, so it was likely to come down to a shoot-out between Flutey and me.

I expected the level of detail to skyrocket once I was in the Lions fold; for things to be far more intricate and complex than I'd experienced thus far. I had visions of turning up to Pennyhill Park and being handed a thick manual of plays to digest and memorise. It was the complete opposite. The drills we did under head coach Ian McGeechan during the first camp took me right back to Under-14s rugby: fixing defenders, passing, offloading. Really rudimentary stuff. I was baffled at the simplicity of it all, and broached it with my roomie, Scotland's Mike Blair, that first evening: 'Mate, did you find that really basic?' He knew McGeechan better than me, but he couldn't help but agree. Quite a few of the lads felt the same way.

It wasn't until much later in my career that I realised that that was the beauty of Ian McGeechan. A lot of coaches become swamped by complex ideas, and their messages get lost in translation. Geech understood the power of the basics: set piece, collisions, contact area, defence. If you nail those core areas, you're going to be in 99 per cent of Test matches. With rugby at that level, where differences in size and fitness are negligible, execution of the basics is critical. They'd reviewed the disastrous 2005 tour of New Zealand and concluded that a simpler, more pragmatic approach was required. That tour was a classic case of too many cooks spoiling the broth. There'd been too many players, too many coaches and way too much information. Geech understood that on a short tour, with limited preparation time, clarity and simplicity are your best friends.

What we lacked in sophistication we made up for in intensity. Our afternoon sessions were brutal, no holds-barred affairs, designed to prepare us for the biggest physical test of our careers. There was inevitable collateral damage. Hooker Jerry Flannery caught his elbow during one of the contact drills and you knew, from the tone of his agonised cry, that his tour was over.

Much is made of the makeshift nature of a Lions tour, of the clash of cultures and the supposedly immutable characteristics each country brings to the table. Clichés abound: the Welsh are shy and homesick, the English confident and brash, the Scots happy just to be there. It's all rubbish. Everyone's different, and nationality barely comes into it once you've seen your initials embroidered beneath the famous Lions badge. There were no rifts, no animosity and no bad eggs; everyone shook hands and got on with it. For the record, there were fourteen Irishmen, thirteen Welshmen, eight English and two Scots in the original selection, but the reality was, there were thirty-seven Lions. One cliché does stand up to scrutiny, though: the Welsh drink as much on tour as the other three nations combined.

Our leaving dinner was at the Natural History Museum, where all of us huddled beneath the diplodocus skeleton in the awe-inspiring Hintze Hall. Gerald Davies's emotional speech was given added weight by the setting, and everyone fell silent as his rich baritone reverberated around the chamber. Everyone apart from Tommy Bowe, that is, who was given a stern ticking-off by tour captain Paul O'Connell for tittering at the back like a naughty schoolboy.

The Lions management had organised a team-bonding exercise with the Navy down in Portsmouth the following day. We'd had a savage day's training and the lads had retired early ahead of a 5 a.m. alarm call. There had been rumblings of discontent. Team-bonding trips are often contrived and cringeworthy. No one likes being forced to have fun, and Paul O'Connell had picked up on the negative vibes. I was lying listlessly in bed, staring at the ceiling, when my phone pinged with a text from Geech: 'Tomorrow's cancelled. See you at the bar in half an hour.'

Mike Blair and I trundled down to find the entire squad assembled, pints in hand, ready for an almighty session. Andy Powell had his top off within the hour, which was early even by his standards, and by midnight we were absolutely steaming. Andrew Sheridan and I were taking turns on the guitar, Joe Worsley was tinkling the ivories and everyone else was guzzling beer and telling jokes. *That* was the bonding session we'd needed, and it brought us closer together than any sailing lesson would have done. I'm a rugby traditionalist, and there's nothing I love more than downing a skinful of beer and talking nonsense with the lads. I loved the fact that those values applied just as much to the Lions as they did to an amateur team of pot-bellied vets playing fifth-division rugby in West Wales. We had an amazing night that more than made up for the crippling hangovers that would accompany us on the plane to South Africa.

Being picked in the Lions squad had been mind-blowing, but I wanted to pull on that famous jersey and feel my studs on South African soil. My wish was granted when I was named in the starting team to play a Royal XV in Rustenburg, but it wasn't the overwhelming experience I'd envisaged. The game clashed with the Super Rugby final between the Bulls and the Chiefs in Pretoria. So while the South African rugby public's gaze was focused on their domestic showpiece, we were holed up in the back of beyond taking on an invitational side comprised mainly of brickies, plumbers and semi-pro players. We ran out to a half-empty stadium and a bunch of curious locals who could barely muster a round of applause. There were wild animals roaming around freely outside the ground and, as Lee Byrne observed with a sense of mild panic, the flies were 'the size of small birds'. This was not the Lions debut my dreams were made of.

We were terrible in the first half, and it took a couple of late tries to spare our blushes. No one covered themselves in glory, but Keith Earls had an absolute shocker outside me at 13. He couldn't catch a cold and missed a succession of easy tackles. Despite the lack of atmosphere, he got hung up on the occasion. He was gutted afterwards; you could see it in his eyes. Geech put an arm around him and told him he was getting too wound up, that it had been an off day, and hadn't been a reflection of his true talent. I was only a year older than Keith and could see how easily things could unravel. I made a silent pledge there and then to stay focused, and make sure I didn't fall victim to those sorts of mental demons.

I'll never forget the look Ronan O'Gara gave me on the final whistle. A cold-blooded death stare. He was seriously hacked off, and I couldn't work out whether I was the target of his anger or he was just furious at the world. He hadn't had a great game either and was probably worrying about his Test spot. Most of the lads were smiling guilty smiles, happy that we'd got away with it, but ROG was fuming.

I redeemed myself against the Golden Lions, pairing up with Brian O'Driscoll and running rampant at Ellis Park. I scored two of our ten tries, and was Man of the Match. It was an evening kick-off, so it was mercifully cool, but the air was thin and my lungs were working harder than they'd ever had to. Brian and I clicked, and the entire team locked into a relentless rhythm that rocked the Golden Lions from the outset. We won collisions decisively, recycled efficiently, made powerful line breaks and were razor-sharp in our execution. I caused carnage in the midfield, running purposefully and knocking defenders off their feet. Playing outside the well-oiled unit of Mike Phillips and Stephen Jones, and inside the maestro O'Driscoll, gave me freedom to roam, pick lines and whack people. The press were already beginning to salivate over my partnership with 'Drico', as Brian is known. In our first game together, we'd dovetailed naturally. I was the yin to his yang. The direct, powerful ball-carrier to his dexterous, pacy hot-stepper.

A few nights later, I returned to our Bloemfontein hotel after dark, with my face caked in blood. I tiptoed self-consciously towards the lifts, past the Lions management team who were enjoying a discreet beer in the lobby. On this tour, Warren Gatland was Ian McGeechan's forwards coach, while Rob Howley and Shaun Edwards looked after attack and defence, as they did with Wales. Rob did a double-take when he saw my ragged, bloodstained appearance. 'What the hell's happened to you?' he yelled, with a mixture of bemusement and concern.

It wasn't as sinister as it looked. A few of the Leinster boys had hooked up with their former team-mate Ollie le Roux, who now ran a farm in Free State and had invited them over for an evening's hunting. Never one to turn down a chance to try something new, I tagged along. It was one of those occasions when you step outside of yourself and realise how bizarre your life has become. A few weeks earlier I had been drinking beer in Revolution with my student mates. Now I was trundling along a dusty prairie in Africa clutching a scope rifle, shining lamps in the faces of spooked wild animals.

My hands were shaking as I took aim at a startled springbok. Dazzled by the lights, it looked at me with a pleading expression, and I almost lost my nerve. I'd never held a gun before, let alone shot an animal. On my third or fourth attempt, I heard a thud and knew I'd made contact. That was the easy part. Ollie put his foot down and sped over to the twitching carcass. Slamming on the brakes, he handed me a gleaming knife and told me to put it out of its misery. I felt sick and racked with guilt as I drew the blade across its throat. The South African farmhands were patting me enthusiastically on the back, offering their hearty congratulations.

Ollie earnestly explained that as it was my first kill, I now had to slather its warm blood over my face and eat one of its testicles. I laughed, thinking it was a ruse they tried to fool every impressionable tourist with. He was deadly serious. He sliced off a testicle and placed it in my palm. It was like a warm, slimy golf ball. Realising I had no choice, I popped it in whole, and crunched down. It tasted as rancid as it looked: veiny, sinewy, gristly and oozing liquid. I gagged several times before managing to swallow it. As unique as the experience was, I felt uncomfortable afterwards. The only thing I'd ever killed before that had been a wasp.

I sat out the game against the Cheetahs, which was closer than it should have been, before we all decamped to Durban. We were in the same hotel we'd stayed in with Wales Under-19s, right on the coast overlooking the Indian Ocean. It was a place of contrasts: beautiful, breathtaking scenery that did its best to hide a dark, seedy underbelly. When dusk fell, the sweeping golden beach became a different, more forbidding place. The tourists largely vanished and were replaced by pimps and prostitutes. It was a reminder that beyond the cosseted world we inhabited as privileged sportsmen, there lurked a darker, more shadowy realm. The previous summer, Tom James had had a gun pulled on him in a Pretoria nightclub. TJ was a handy bloke who wouldn't back down from anyone after a few beers, and had squared up to some bloke in the toilet. Within an instant he had a pistol pointed at his head. As much as we were being treated to the best of South Africa, staying in its finest hotels and eating in the best restaurants, you'd be naive to think it was a tourist's paradise. Although the apartheid era was over, its legacy remained. Taxi drivers would regularly refer to 'kaffirs' without any sense of shame or embarrassment. My mother had refused to come and support me on tour because she felt so strongly about the country's racist past.

Politics aside, I loved the place. There is an honesty and beauty about South Africa that captured my heart during my first trip there as a sixteen-year-old schoolboy. We think we love our rugby in Wales, but in South Africa it's on a different level, and their rugby philosophy resonates more closely with mine. While I admire the Welsh sides of the seventies that swerved and sidestepped their way to championships, I didn't grow up with them. I was raised in a rugby environment that was attritional and claustrophobic, where there wasn't much space on the field. I saw the same beauty in the subtleties of the set piece and the efficiency of the power game. South Africa embodies that. They prize power and brutality as highly as speed and dexterity. Combine that with the majesty of the scenery, the friendliness of the people and the amazing food and wine, and you have, in my humble opinion, the world's best touring destination.

Before facing the Sharks in Durban, Andrew Sheridan, Alun Wyn Jones and I went swimming with actual sharks, which is probably the only time Sherry's ever been frightened in his life. The freakishly strong Englishman had developed a reputation for chewing up and spitting out opposition tightheads, but he looked considerably less intimidating when a great white started prodding its nose against our flimsy cage.

Training went up a level that week. I was appraising my rivals for the shirt, keeping an eye on their GPS figures, trying simultaneously to learn from and outperform them; to pinch bits of wisdom and add extra strings to my bow. McGeechan had made it clear that every one of us had a chance of making the Test team and hammered that message home repeatedly. During a session at the magnificent

Durban High School, I noticed a significant rise in aggression levels. It was 'minute drill' time, Warren Gatland's brutal game-simulation exercise in which we recreated the physical brutality of Test match rugby, and then cranked it up a notch. It's Gats's power game distilled to its purest form: a pod of three attackers and a scrum-half going up against three defenders at full speed for a minute. Carry hard, clean the rucks, leap to your feet and go again. You get to practise your tackle technique, your close-quarter defence, your carrying and your rucking. Defenders and attackers rotate until everyone has done it. Positions don't matter: backs, forwards, whatever. You're in the attacking team once, then you do three or four sets of defending. You probably hit seven or eight rucks in a minute, which doesn't sound many but, believe me, it was intense. You can't cruise, and you can't hide. Under less exacting regimes, you'd be able to go into contact at around 80 per cent, but there was no way you'd get away with that under the piercing gaze of Gats and Shaun Edwards. I've been at clubs where it's been done with pads, but Gats wanted bone-on-bone collisions. At some point during a typical fifty-minute session, he'd call 'minute drill', and we'd have to flip the switch. Full metal jacket. It could be at the beginning, in the middle or towards the end.

Halfway through this particular session, a blood-curdling cry rang out in the humid Durban air. Stephen Ferris had caught his leg at an awkward angle, and Alun Wyn Jones, all 19 stone of him, had collapsed on top of him. Something about the timbre of the scream told you his tour was over. In a fleeting, painful moment, his dream had evaporated. He'd been a dead cert for the Test team. Quick, powerful, skilful and intelligent, 'Fez' was one of the best forwards I'd played with. His injury put a real dampener on the session, and prompted some mutterings about the wisdom of the minute drill. The Welsh boys were used to it, and saw it as a necessary evil, but the rest thought it was reckless and dangerous. I heard one Irish voice on the bus back saying we were a bigger risk to ourselves than the Springboks. It was a timely reminder of how fragile our personal ambitions were. I saw Fez sitting alone on the hotel balcony the next day, staring wistfully out at the ocean. His crutches were lying by his side, and he was lost in his thoughts. I realised then how precious this was, and how lucky I felt to still be standing.

The Sharks game was at Kings Park, the venue for the first Test in a week and a half's time. It was a chance to get a feel for the place. Mike Phillips scored a fantastic second-half try which crowned an impressive Man of the Match display and secured his place in the Test team. My partnership with Brian was continuing to evolve and the floodgates opened for us in the second half. I felt so powerful and strong, making three or four metres with every carry, and blasting holes at will. Stefan Terblanche was at full-back for the Sharks. My debut for the Cardiff Blues had almost ended in disaster when my clumsy tackle on him gave the Ospreys a last-minute penalty. Had you told me then that I'd be facing him in a Lions jersey less than two years later, I'd have thought you were high on fumes from the Brains brewery.

I felt pretty good about myself after the game, and carried that swagger with me on a big night out. I got lucky, and ended up returning to the hotel in the early hours with a South African beauty on my arm. My roomie, Keith Earls, hadn't been out as he was playing in the next match, and I was so paranoid about disturbing him that I asked my companion to remove her shoes in the lift. No matter how drunk I got, there was always something of the sensible prefect lurking beneath the surface. We padded down the corridor, and I did my best to ruin the romantic mood by giving her a further lecture about being quiet when we were outside the door. I opened it silently, ushering her towards the balcony, before tiptoeing round Keith's bed, gathering up pillows and a duvet and dragging them out to the balcony. Moonlight flooded the room when I leaned back to shut the doors, and there, bathed in its ethereal glow, was a wide-awake Keith Earls, grinning like an overgrown schoolboy and giving me the thumbs up. The two of us collapsed into a fit of giggles at the absurdity of the situation. In the cold light of day, it sounds ridiculous that I was trying to seduce a lady while sharing a room with another man, but that's life on tour.

A few weeks in, it was obvious that the tour party had split, not according to nationality, but marital status. After matches, the married family men drank together and would inevitably retire early, no doubt grateful they could enjoy a lie-in. The single lads, meanwhile, would just be warming up, getting ready to crank through the gears and hit the town. Our fitness coach, Paul Stridgeon – or Bobby as he was universally known – was very sensitive to our needs. He saw my pale complexion and hooded eyes at breakfast the next day and slid a large hydration sachet next to my drained glass of orange juice. 'Get that down your neck, kid. You're going to need it.' At times, the tour felt a glorified stag do, but there was an unwritten rule that you didn't let your after-hours antics interfere with the real business of training and playing. It was that long leash that kept morale so high. We were trusted to set our own boundaries. Being picked for the next game didn't mean living like a hermit during the build-up, but you'd be expected to take it easy and bank some early nights. Even if you had the full pass to go out and have a skinful, you were expected to turn up on time the next day. Even if there was more alcohol than blood in your veins, you were expected to front up and hold tackle bags.

Heading back from training at Cape Town's Bishops College, our unofficial tour anthem, Dario G's 'Sunchyme', came on the radio. We pulled up at a set of traffic lights near the Cullinan Hotel as the chorus kicked in, and Bobby was up and dancing in the aisle like John Travolta on steroids. All the boys were banging the seats and egging him on. A road sweeper outside started shimmying to the rhythm. Bobby slung open the door and dragged him onto the bus, before ordering the driver, who already thought he was crazy, to do another lap around the block while the whole squad, a random street cleaner and our insane fitness coach cut the rug inside the bus.

I had a day off before the Western Province game and went to meet Dad for a drink on the waterfront. As we were strolling in the midday sun, Dad noticed Gareth Edwards and Willie John McBride coming the other way, an observation that transformed him from a sixty-year-old retiree to a hyperactive child. He started tugging at my arm, and his voice seemed to go up an octave as he breathlessly pointed them out. I was placed in the surreal position of introducing these legends to Norman. They were *his* heroes, from his generation, yet I was the one who knew them. The resulting photo is the first thing anyone sees when they visit my parents' house, hanging in pride of place in the hallway.

Our winning run continued against Western Province thanks to a monster penalty from James Hook. That and Andy Powell's huge hit on Duane Vermeulen were the highlights of a forgettable game played in atrocious conditions. Shaun went ballistic in the changing room at half-time, his clipped Wigan accent lending a real edge to his anger. Our defence had been inexcusably sloppy, and he wasn't amused.

After the game, the group was split for the first time, with twelve players flying to Durban and the rest to Port Elizabeth for the Southern Kings game. Geech announced the plans with a mournful tone in his voice. Lions tours are all about brotherhood and harmony, and splitting the group can have damaging consequences. It had happened in 2005 and to a lesser extent in 2001, and Geech made it abundantly clear that this was a practical decision and nothing more.

The obvious conclusion to draw was that the 'Durban twelve' were primed for Test selection, but despite being among them, I was taking nothing for granted. The odds were in my favour, but I tried to banish any thoughts of that nature until it was made official. Riki Flutey and Gordon D'Arcy, who'd flown out as a replacement, had been picked to face the Kings, and if one of them played a blinder, there was every chance Geech's head would be turned.

The 'Durban twelve' took in the Southern Kings game in a waterfront bar, and watched with rising anger as they tried to drag the Lions into the equivalent of a barroom brawl. They weren't interested in playing rugby. There were cheap shots flying in everywhere: stray knees, high elbows, no-arm tackles, shoulder charges and swinging arms. Some of them looked possessed, and not just the impressionable youngsters excited about playing the Lions, but experienced veterans like De Wet Barry, who was marauding around like a maniac. Hooky ended up on gas and air after a really bad head knock. It was disgracefully violent, but we had precious little sympathy from the referee that night: a Welshman by the name of Nigel Owens.

We had some hard bastards of our own on the field. Simon Shaw, Nathan Hines, Andrew Sheridan and Joe Worsley were all capable of dishing it out, and God knows they must have been tempted to retaliate, but Geech's regular reminders of the importance of discipline had sunk in. Refusing to rise to the bait, they ultimately won the right way: by scrummaging and mauling them to death. It was a smart message to send and brought to mind one of Gerald's beautifully succinct motivational mantras: 'We'll have fire in our bellies, and a sliver of ice through our hearts.'

The boys flew up to Durban the following day, and we were summoned to a meeting where Geech read out the Test team. There were some big calls. Shane was the reigning World Player of the Year, and didn't make it. David Wallace edged out Nugget, and Jamie Heaslip got the nod over Powelly. I was in. A starting Test Lion at twenty-two years of age. To hear my name called out by the same guy who'd delivered all those spine-tingling speeches on the 1997 tour was an unbelievable moment. I was paired with Brian O'Driscoll, and the South African press focused on the two of us, claiming we'd be the biggest threat to the Boks' supremacy. Being the centre of attention was just what I wanted. I'd wrestled a bit with imposter syndrome at the start of the tour, but this was validation. Bring it on.

I mined Brian for so much information he was probably sick of the sight of me, but he was always so generous with his advice. I'd only played in the midfield for a year, and he was on his third Lions tour, so his supply of knowledge was virtually inexhaustible. It's difficult to describe what makes him such a phenomenal player. He wasn't the most skilful or technically the best that I've played with, but it was his ability to communicate that set him apart. Like a zen warrior, he was able to operate in the eye of the storm, to cut through all the noise and distraction of the battle, and *always* make the right call. He'd see things quicker, react quicker and get his message across with ruthless economy. You don't have time to deliver a sermon in the pressurised atmosphere of Test rugby; when he called a play it would be in language that was decisive, sharp and devoid of bullshit. That's the sign of a good leader: knowing when to talk and when to pull the trigger.

The aura that hovers around the Springboks can be intimidating. Prop Adam Jones had to have a pep talk from Mike Phillips before the first Test, to overcome an inferiority complex. Despite his elevated status, 'Bomb', as Adam is known, had to be persuaded that he belonged at the summit of world rugby. Call it arrogance or the naivety of youth, but I rarely felt that way. I was at the peak of my powers and was running into brick walls for fun. Their game was built around rugged, raw-boned physicality, but that didn't concern me one bit because I was big enough, fast enough and strong enough to deal with it. I love the visceral thrill that accompanies big hits and thunderous collisions. I thrive on operating in that space where you empty yourself and push your body to its absolute limit. There were some big names in that Springboks team: John Smit, Jean de Villers, Bakkies Botha and Victor Matfield. All World Cup winners, all players I had a huge amount of respect for, but I felt every inch their equal, and that I belonged in their company.

Willie John McBride presented us with our jerseys, the leader of the 'Invincibles' who had won every game on the South Africa tour of 1974. Ian McGeechan had played under him then and he still refers to him as 'my captain'. There was something mythical and other-worldly about McBride, a five-time Lion who'd invented the '99' call and refused to buckle in the face of South African violence and intimidation. He was an old man now, hunched in stature and hushed in tone, but his speech was dripping with emotion as he told us there would be times when we'd have to dig into the very depths of our souls.

I felt an enormous surge of pride holding that jersey in my hands. His carefully chosen words and the sight of the iconic badge connected me intimately with more than a century of history. I was ready. Mike Gibson, Dick Milliken, Jeremy Guscott, Will Greenwood: those were the names carved into the plaque above my peg. Lions legends. Seeing them there deepened the sense of significance and added an extra layer of gravitas. Talk about responsibility: I was about to represent every inside centre in Britain and Ireland. Pressure? Bring it.

*   *   *

My routine's been the same since I started for Wales. I drop my bag on arrival at the ground and head straight for the pitch to take in my surroundings. Some of the boys do their entire warm-up in the changing room, shielding themselves from the glare until necessary. I could never do that; I need to get a feel for the pitch, for the arena I'm playing in. The crowd at Kings Park was bubbling, and the atmosphere was beginning to swell, but nothing could have prepared me for what was to come.

Standing in the tunnel alongside the Springboks, you could hear an almost guttural roar emanating from the crowd. As I ran into the cacophonous din, I was struck by the overwhelming number of red jerseys in the stand. In one section, elevated above the rest, the South African green shirts appeared as tiny specks amid an undulating blanket of Lions red. It was an astonishing sight considering we were more than 8,000 miles from home.

It was probably the best run-out onto a pitch I've ever experienced, and it was the one moment I lamented the fact my mum wasn't there. Her absence was hard for me to understand. She'd supported me every step of the way, and when I'd reached the pinnacle, she wasn't there to witness it. Her negative feelings towards South Africa outweighed her pride towards me. The legendary Welsh flanker John Taylor had famously refused to tour South Africa during the apartheid regime, but I felt these were different, more progressive times. My mum, though, had grown up watching the horrors of that regime, and lived through the period when Margaret Thatcher refused to back sanctions against it, so it was recent history in her mind. I accepted her rationale, but it didn't stop me feeling a twinge of sadness when I saw the tens of thousands of Lions fans noisily cheering us out, and she wasn't among them.

The Boks started powerfully, dominating the set piece and clattering into us with a barely controlled fury. Four minutes in, they were camped in our 22, launching a series of raids off a scrum. They came around the corner several times, picking-and-going with brutal efficiency. When the time was right, John Smit chose a line inside me and I had to make a split-second decision: bite in and give him the full weight of my tackle, or keep my width in case they went an extra few phases. I chose the latter, and he bulldozed his way to the line. It was exactly what we'd prepared for all week. They hadn't been crafty or sophisticated; they just ran hard and kept coming, like a battering ram thudding into a heavy oak door. But preparing for it and dealing with it were two different things.

We could have drawn level immediately had it not been for a miracle tackle on Ugo Monye from Jean de Villiers. I was already celebrating when he crossed the line but de Villiers defied space and time to hold him up. It was an unbelievable defensive play. He was a supreme operator who delivered when it mattered most.

Twenty minutes in, and chasing down a 13–0 deficit, I got a short ball off Stephen Jones and ran determinedly between Juan Smith and Adi Jacobs. I knew if I got my hands free, Drico would be there on one of his perfect support lines. He was, and he put Tom Croft away for a try of our own. It proved a brief respite, though, as the Boks regained control through their dominant scrum, which had begun to resemble a threshing machine. Phil Vickery was getting a tuning from Tendai Mtawarira, who was more than living up to his alternative moniker, 'the Beast'. It was an emasculating experience for Vicks: so used to being the enforcer, now reduced to a bewildered victim, appealing desperately to the referee as the blood flowed freely from his battered cauliflower ears.

As a backline we felt helpless, standing with hands on hips watching our scrum being pulverised, and waiting for that depressingly shrill blast of the whistle. Steve, Drico and myself were exchanging worried sideways glances as the penalties mounted up, but there was nothing we could do. This was what the South African press had predicted would happen, and the backs became increasingly redundant as the Beast and company dragged our forwards into a street fight they didn't have the weapons to win. It didn't look great, and when an image of their enormous hooker, Bismarck du Plessis, looming over Drico with a clenched fist appeared on the big screen, it felt like a microcosm of the contest as a whole. David versus Goliath, without the slingshot. The home fans were getting noisier and more aggressive, clearly thinking their team had us on the rack. We were easy meat, like the steaks that had been thrown on the flaming braais outside the ground.

At half-time, we were 19–7 down, and in the changing room Shaun Edwards was incensed over that Smit try, enquiring none too politely how we'd 'let that fat **** through so easily'. He'd tutored us all week on how to fold defensively in order to stifle their carrying game, and he took it personally that we'd failed in our first attempt. To this day, Mike Phillips mocks my lacklustre attempt on Smit, never failing to send me the clip when it pops up on Twitter or Instagram.

Early in the second half, Adam Jones and Matthew Rees came on for Vicks and hooker Lee Mears and immediately fortified our scrum. The penalties that had been flowing the Boks' way dried up completely as Bomb set about taming the Beast with his destructive hit-and-chase approach. All of a sudden, we had a platform and were able to enjoy some sustained possession rather than living off scraps. Tom Croft scored another try, and Mike Phillips went over a few minutes from time to bring us within a score. If you take into account the chances we spurned – Ugo blew another gilt-edged opportunity when Morne Steyn appeared from nowhere and knocked the ball from his grasp – we could have won. We may not have deserved to, but it said something about our fighting spirit that we had clawed our way back after such a dispiriting opening half.

Bomb was the first to comfort a glassy-eyed Vicks in the changing room. As much as he and Paul O'Connell tried to pass off the Beast's mauling as an anomaly, Vicks knew his manhood had been compromised, and no amount of soothing pats on the back were going to heal that. Ugo was no less devastated. If a prop's primary function is to hold up the scrum, a winger's is to finish off chances. He didn't need sympathy or attention; just time to come to terms with it. Such are the fine margins on which reputations are made. If he'd scored those tries – and he so easily could have – he'd have been hailed a hero. Instead he botched both, and was dropped.

The second Test was up on the highveld in Pretoria, at Loftus Versfeld, where I'd played my first senior game as an inside centre. Now I was back for the biggest challenge of my life. The South African press had ramped up the rhetoric, and most previews were dripping with a sense of smug superiority. The bus ride to Loftus was memorable. This was Afrikaaner country, a markedly different vibe from the more urbane, English-speaking environment of Durban. As the bus rolled towards the ground, the crowd became increasingly hostile. Enveloped by the smoke of their braais, the rugged Afrikaners loomed into the road, greeting us with a mixture of mimed throat-slits and other less subtle gestures. It was pretty distasteful, more akin to a braying football mob than a rugby crowd, and it was a million miles from the faux aggression of a Twickenham car park. These guys meant it, and we couldn't have walked among them as we could among the Barbour-jacketed, prawn-munching 'Twickers' hordes. Bottles were being thrown at the bus as we sat in contemplative silence, staring straight ahead, not wanting to look any of these crazy, intoxicated country boys in the eye.

The hostility infiltrated our changing room, with even the softly spoken Ian McGeechan allowing his emotions to boil over. 'I don't want us pushed around,' he said, his jaw clenched in defiance. 'Gerald talked about a sliver of ice. I want a big f***ing icicle with a point on it going right through their f***ing hearts.' Shaun added further fuel, resurrecting his grievance from the previous week: 'First set of the Test match, and Smit walks through us, puts the ball over the try line and says thank you. Big fat **** like him. Well, you'd better set the tone tonight with our first set, and it better be more *violent* than that one.' During his playing days, Shaun was often the smallest bloke on the field, but his attitude and his aura made him seem twice as big. He once played on with a broken cheekbone and fractured eye socket, so when he spoke about playing through pain he was doing so from experience. I was willing to run through walls for him.

Once I cross the white line, I don't give an inch. I don't go out to hurt people, don't get me wrong, but if someone gets hurt as a result of me smashing into him, sorry, that's the game. There's a big difference, though, between controlled aggression and thuggery. If I was out of sight on the blind side of a ruck and had a chance to land a cheap shot, I wouldn't. That's not in my make-up. But if that person is between me and the try line, I will throw every ounce of my weight into the collision. You don't stand a chance in South Africa unless you meet their aggression head on.

Loftus is a lot noisier than Kings Park. The Boks supporters there are borderline maniacal, and there was no way they were going to be drowned out by the travelling red army. It was a sensory overload, a swirling cacophony of noise, and a riot of movement and colour. Red, green and gold blending into a seething, sweating mass of humanity. The South African anthem was raucous and passionate, and the volume swelled to deafening levels when they reached the Afrikaans section. They were up for this.

Schalk Burger had been picked for his fiftieth cap, and we suspected his brief was to man-mark me, à la Joe Worsley. It didn't take long for him to make a statement, though it was winger Luke Fitzgerald, not me, who was his first victim. The game was barely thirty seconds old when he dug his fingers up to the knuckles in Luke's eyeball. It was a grotesque and callous act of thuggery. Despite the fact the cameras exposed it as a deliberate foul of the worst kind, the referee only drew out his yellow card. It was a gross dereliction of duty. No one's denying that rugby is a brutal, uncompromising sport, and that injuries are inevitable, but this wasn't a mistimed tackle or a twisted limb; it was a malicious assault on a helpless opponent. He could have blinded him. That's not a yellow card; it's a straight red and potentially a life ban. How can something that vile warrant a mere ten minutes in the sin bin? People talk about the fact he's a lovely guy. I couldn't give a toss how nice a bloke he is. It was sickening, and the referee as good as condoned it.

We scored 10 points in Burger's absence, including a neatly taken try from Rob Kearney and a touchline conversion from Stephen Jones. We might have scored more had Gethin Jenkins not ignored my pleas for the ball after his cheeky break through the middle. I'd still have had to run 30 metres to go under the sticks, and I'm not sure I'd have made it, but I'd never admit that to Melon. He'd dished out enough rollockings to me in my short career, so it was nice for the shoe to be on the other foot for once.

It was as feisty as we'd expected it to be. The atmosphere was febrile and tempers were frayed. Mike Phillips was in full street-fighter mode, and never far away from a dust-up. A weird dynamic was unfolding between him and the Boks' enforcer-in-chief, Bakkies

Botha. Botha was on a mission, marauding around and clattering into rucks with a kamikaze disregard for his or anyone else's welfare. At one point, Mike eyeballed him and shouted, 'Are you guys on f***ing steroids or what?' Bakkies, in an unusual and disarming comeback, told Mike how 'beautiful' his blue eyes were. Mike was well used to receiving compliments on his appearance, not least from himself when looking in the mirror, but to receive one from a hulking brute like Bakkies was unsettling, to say the least.

Once Burger was back on the field, South Africa came back into it. They won a slick line-out, Fourie du Preez put JP Pietersen into a hole and he took off on an arcing run to the try line. It exposed our Achilles heel, as Luke Fitzgerald found himself in no man's land in the defensive line. Trying to get four separate nations to buy into a single defensive philosophy in a matter of weeks isn't easy. As an Irishman, he wasn't used to that 'up and in' blitz defence. South Africa knew that, exploited it and scored. If Shane Williams had been on that wing, it probably wouldn't have happened.

Just before half-time we had a midfield scrum on the halfway line. We had a play which involved me running a decoy line off Brian, before he passed out the back to Steve, who could hopefully hit Tommy Bowe on the far touchline in space. It worked like a dream, but the referee inexplicably blew for obstruction. A line break and potential try-scoring opportunity had turned into three points for them. I was quietly fuming when Rob Howley admonished us at the interval for attempting a risky attacking manoeuvre in our own half. He wouldn't have said that if we'd scored, and I'm convinced we would have if the ref hadn't made such a poor call. That said, we were 16–8 ahead, and good for our lead.

The Boks weren't enjoying the procession they'd expected, and were rattled. One of the main reasons for our superiority was the set piece. Adam Jones and Matthew Rees had banished memories of the previous week and transformed our scrum into a powerful offensive weapon. After fifty minutes spent feasting on Lion meat in Durban, the Beast had been neutered. This time it was him and Bismarck du Plessis who were popping up, the front-row equivalent of throwing in the towel, and Bomb, Smiler and Melon who were motoring forward.

It was a genuine coming-of-age for Bomb. His Test career had begun in ignominious fashion when he was considered too unfit to last more than thirty minutes and was regularly hauled off before half-time. Now, in the rarefied air of Pretoria, against one of the most feared packs in world rugby, he'd become genuinely world-class. The Beast had been well and truly tamed.

Sadly for Bomb, his dream was nearly over. Five minutes into the second half, both he and Melon were lying in agony in the medical room with tour-ending injuries. I'll leave it to the conspiracy theorists to determine whether or not they'd been deliberately targeted, but their absence changed the entire dynamic of the forward battle. There was a sense of outrage among Lions fans that Bomb had been the victim of a cheap shot. He was bent over a ruck trying to seal the ball off when Bakkies Botha clattered into him with such force that he knocked his shoulder out of its joint. Bakkies had a reputation for violence and relished his enforcer role, but on this occasion his challenge was textbook. Bomb was just the unfortunate victim of a perfectly timed wipeout.

Melon had shattered his cheekbone in an accidental clash of heads with Bryan Habana, and with both props off the field, we were forced to revert to uncontested scrums, which seemed strangely quaint in a game otherwise exploding with massive hits and crunching collisions. The one everyone remembers is the clash of heads between Brian O'Driscoll and Danie Russouw. It would probably have seen Drico sent off in this day and age, but to see a monstrous back-row forward struggle to get back to his feet after colliding with a centre was hugely galvanising. As we entered the final quarter, we were 19–8 ahead.

Uncontested scrums allow the attacking scrum-half to get wider, and they ran a play in our 22 that enabled Fourie du Preez to get to our ten channel. Centre Jaque Fourie picked a short line which I had to cover, and Drico flew up, leaving a gap between us. That's all it took. Bryan Habana is like a heat-seeking missile when he sees space and he scorched through the gap to the line. Fourie had run straight into my wrist and bent it back on itself, and as I made my way behind the posts I was trying my best to hide the excruciating pain. The physio had spotted it, though, and he trotted over and asked me to squeeze his hand. I could barely wrap my fingers around it, let alone squeeze. As this was happening, I saw Drico tramping off the pitch looking dazed and disoriented. He clearly hadn't recovered from the hit with Russouw.

A few phases after the next kick-off, I couldn't feel my hand at all. I couldn't catch or pass. However desperately I wanted to play on, I'd have been a liability. I wouldn't have been able to tackle with my dominant right shoulder because I couldn't grip. I was reluctantly subbed off and had to watch the rest of the game from the sidelines. What unfolded was as grim as any horror movie I've ever seen. Morne Steyn had just casually slotted a penalty to bring the Boks to within a point, and we had to survive the last thirteen minutes without our first-choice midfield pairing.

With so many of our key players injured, and the altitude beginning to take its toll, the Boks sniffed their chance. A series of bullocking carries took them into our 22, and they worked it wide to Jaque Fourie, who stretched for the line with the athleticism of a gymnast. Mike Phillips had done his level best to drag him out of play, and there'd been enough of a suspicion of a foot in touch for the ref to consult the TMO (Television Match Official). The wait that followed was gut-wrenching; three minutes of repeated multi-angle replays felt like a lifetime. None of them were conclusive, with each seeming to contradict the last, and the nerves were jangling horribly. Brian, sitting next to me, was away with the fairies. His eyes were on the pitch, but his expression was completely vacant. The longer it went on, the more nauseous I felt. It was eventually, inevitably, given, and Morne Steyn rubbed salt into the wound by knocking over the touchline conversion as casually as if he was practising in the park.

Moments later Stephen Jones showed his Test-match class, nailing a touchline penalty to draw us level at 25–25. Two and a half minutes left; 150 seconds to hold on and force a series decider.

It's unlikely anyone reading this doesn't know what happened next, so I won't dwell too much on the details. With barely thirty seconds remaining, Ronan O'Gara fielded a kick in our 22, running back 30 metres before launching the ball high into the Pretoria night sky. It began to descend around the halfway line and Fourie du Preez leapt to pluck it from the air. As he was airborne, ROG ran straight into him, sending him tumbling awkwardly to the turf. It was a clear penalty. On another day, at another ground, 54 metres would have been too far. But for Morne Steyn, at his home ground, 5,000 feet above sea level, it was within range. Game over. Series over.

I've never experienced a changing room like that one before or since. No one wanted to break the silence that hung like a funereal pall over the entire room. There was nothing anyone could say or do to allay those feelings of utter devastation. Not even Paulie, our inspirational skipper, could summon any words of consolation. Ronan was a broken man, physically and mentally. His head was strapped with a blood-soaked bandage, and his reddened eye was tender and swollen, but it was the unseen psychological damage that would have hurt the most. No one blamed him. He's a competitive animal and hadn't wanted to settle for a draw. Incidents that are pored over for decades afterwards happen in the blink of an eye. Those at the eye of the storm don't have the luxury of pausing and considering their options.

There was a grim irony that Ronan had been at the heart of two of the three devastating defeats I'd suffered that year. His drop goal had denied Wales the Triple Crown in March, and his mistimed tackle had handed the series to South Africa. In between, I'd watched helplessly as a wayward penalty kick had denied the Cardiff Blues a place in the Heineken Cup final. Three moments when glory was tantalisingly within our grasp. Three moments when it was cruelly snatched away.

The walking wounded among us were transferred to hospital in our torn, mud-stained kit: me, Brian, Tommy Bowe and Melon. Bomb had gone on ahead. We barely said a word all the way there. The hospital was grim: bars on the windows, mould and peeling paint on the walls, dirt and grime in the corridors. No colour, no warmth, no shiny anti-septic surfaces. It felt more like a psych hospital or a prison. Not the kind of place to lift your mood after you've just lost a series. There was only one bed available, and Melon claimed it on the grounds he was suffering the most. His face had literally caved in. He'd fractured his eye socket and cheekbone in three separate places. The rest of us were perched on plastic chairs outside his ward when he summoned me over in a panic.

'You're not going to believe this,' he said, 'but the doctor's just been in, and he *reeks* of booze.'

The surgeon preparing to operate on Gethin's face had been at the game and was three sheets to the wind. Melon was scared to death, worrying that he was going to come out of theatre looking like a Picasso painting, and he's not the best-looking bloke to begin with. Our team doctor, James Robson, had to politely but firmly tell the surgeon to go home, get some sleep and come back the next day.

An X-ray on my wrist showed nothing. The official diagnosis was that I'd sprained it. That made me feel like I'd made a fuss over nothing. Melon's got a caved-in face, Adam's shoulder's on the wrong side of his body and Jamie, bless him, has a sprained wrist. That said, I could barely move it. It was really swollen and I still had no grip strength. There was no way I was going to play in the third Test.

Our last stop was the Sandton Sun Hotel in Johannesburg, and I remember it as much for its clientele as for the traditional African reception we had on arrival. It's where all the air hostesses stay, arriving en masse at seven o'clock every evening. The hotel had an enormous central atrium, and the floors rose above it in concentric circles. You could see the doors to all the rooms from the main lobby. Once the boys had cottoned on to the 7 p.m. influx of air hostesses, it was hilarious to sit in reception, watching those who'd retired early start reappearing, all at the same time, struck by a sudden urge to have a coffee at the bar. They might as well have had signs on their foreheads saying, 'I'm coming down to ogle the air hostesses.' Rugby boys on tour, eh?

I didn't play in the final Test, but when I joined the huddle after the final whistle, I had tears in my eyes. We'd lost the series, but finished on a high with a record victory over the Springboks. The 28–9 scoreline meant we'd scored more points and tries than them over the three games. A moral victory of sorts. A tour like that drains every ounce of concentration, every last reserve of emotion, and when it all comes to an end, you need to feel like it was worth it in some way. It had been a dead rubber, but winning in that manner felt like redemption. It rescued the Lions brand. They hadn't won a Test match since the first Test in Australia in 2001. An eighth defeat on the bounce could have pushed them further along the road to extinction. The victory was a jolt to the heart of an ailing beast.

On the Sunday, a case of Bollinger arrived at the hotel with a note: 'Hard luck, lads, have a drink on me, James Bond.' It was from the actor Daniel Craig, who was a huge England rugby fan. It kick-started a session that lasted well into Monday morning, when I was awoken from a deep slumber by a call from our commercial officer, Maria, who asked me to meet her in reception. I staggered, unwashed, out of my room, in that liminal zone between being blind drunk and cripplingly hungover. Maria told me, matter-of-factly, that I'd been voted Player of the Series and needed to pose for an official photo. I was taken aback, especially as I hadn't played in that third Test. The photo has never been framed because I've got greasy hair, bloodshot eyes, and look, unsurprisingly, like a man who's been up drinking all night.

It was ridiculous. I was still looking up in awe at all the senior guys in the squad, thinking I needed to play another eight years of rugby to reach the same lofty heights. When you're a kid, playing in a Lions Test is the top of the pyramid, the crowning achievement, the summit you're only supposed to reach after years of graft and toil, yet here I was at twenty-two, a Lions Player of the Series. It felt like those boys had hauled themselves painstakingly to the top of the mountain, and I'd just taken the cable car up. What happens now? Now the challenge is to sustain it, and that's arguably a bigger test than getting there in the first place.

10

ARE YOU A RUGBY PLAYER OR A CELEBRITY?

'All right, Doc? When are you going to retire, then?' The voice belonged to Xavier Rush, Cardiff Blues' resident alpha male. Before leaving South Africa, I'd done an interview with one of the London papers in which I'd jokingly suggested I could retire happy, having won the Player of the Series award. Of course, when the article was published, that was the headline: ' "I can retire now," says Jamie Roberts.' The old stagers at the Blues were not going to let that slide. Any swagger I might have had on my return had vanished after five minutes in their company. Martyn Williams, Gethin Jenkins, Paul Tito and Rushy all took great pleasure in bringing me crashing back down to earth. There was no way they were going to let me get above my station, no matter what awards I'd won.

I'd spent the weeks after the Lions tour travelling around California in a hired Mustang with my mate David Carlson. A recent divorcee, he'd jacked in his job as a homicide detective, sold his house and set off on a two-year adventure round the world. When I got back, I went to the Ashes Test at Lord's with my mate Matt. After watching Stuart Broad rip through the Aussie batting line-up during the morning session, we got up to leave for lunch and someone shouted, 'Hey, Jamie. Great Lions tour, mate.' A few others then clocked me and a gentle round of applause started rippling from that section of the stand. By the time I'd reached the top of the steps, dozens of people had risen to give me a standing ovation. It was ridiculous and humbling in equal measure.

In the wake of such events, it would be understandable for one's ego to swell a little, so it was refreshing for it to be punctured so dramatically when I returned to the Blues. After my ribbing at the hands of the senior players, Dai Young gave me the most curt 'well done, mate' imaginable. You could tell he was proud, but he was determined not to show it. The unspoken message was 'Don't get too carried away: you've got a job to do for us.'

That autumn, Dai called me into his office and told me I'd been invited to play for the Barbarians, the exclusive, invitation-only side renowned for its attacking panache and off-field ribaldry. Would I like to go? Does a bear perform his ablutions in the woods? Andy Powell and Leigh Halfpenny had also been invited. We'd all been on the Lions tour, and had played in the autumn series for Wales, so we probably hadn't done much to justify our salaries at the Blues, but Dai knew how enriching an experience the Barbarians could be, and encouraged us to go.

Arriving at the Grosvenor House, on Park Lane, I was genuinely star-struck by some of the other players milling around in the lobby. Joe Rokocoko, Drew Mitchell, George Smith, Rocky Elsom and Matt Giteau were all hanging out, chewing the fat. A large smattering of my South African opponents from the summer were also among them: Jaque Fourie, Bryan Habana, Fourie du Preez, Morne Steyn and the Beast were about to become my team-mates. It was an outrageously talented squad, captained by Victor Matfield, and it had to be, because we were playing the All Blacks at the weekend. What followed was the most enjoyable rugby week of my life. It's so unlike any other experience because the focus is solely on getting the lads to bond. As I was introducing myself to everyone, Steve Berrick, who looks after the money side of the Barbarians, was wandering around. He thrust out a hand in greeting while simultaneously reaching into his rucksack to withdraw a bulging brown envelope. It contained five grand in cash: my 'allowance' for the week. I'm only slightly ashamed to admit that I headed straight to my room, took a photo of myself clutching the thick wad of fifty-pound notes and sent it to all my mates.

If the Lions tour sometimes felt like a stag do, the Baa-Baas pretty much *was* a stag do, but with a Test match at the end of it as opposed to a wedding. We went out four nights in a row, dining in London's best restaurants and enjoying VIP treatment at its most exclusive

nightclubs. Everything was several levels above what I was accustomed to as a simple Cardiff boy. We ate at one amazingly authentic
Italian restaurant, with pristine white tablecloths and moustachioed
chefs. After the first course, a plate was dropped, smashing into
several pieces. Everyone looked up, and one of the waiters launched
into a full-throated rendition of 'Nessun dorma'. It turned out they
were all opera singers, and the plate was just a means of capturing
our attention. It was an incredible experience.

The booze flowed relentlessly. A session at Whisky Mist off Park
Lane was particularly debauched, and while we all proved extremely
accomplished at drinking gallons of whisky and wine, we proved
rather less accomplished at rugby training. Our sessions at Richmond
RFC were, not to put too fine a point on it, embarrassing. We had a
backline littered with World Cup winners, but were incapable of
getting the ball to Bryan Habana without dropping it. It was an absolute shambles. At one point, our coach, Nick Mallett, asked us to
practise 22-metre dropouts, throwing me the ball and suggesting that
as a big lad, I should be able to get a bit of distance on it. I sliced my
first attempt directly into touch, barely a yard in front of the 22-metre
line. That was the end of dropout practice. I'd gone from the ultra-
professional environment of Wales to this: hacking about on a club
pitch with a thudding hangover. It was a throwback to the amateur
days, and I was loving it, but there was a kernel of fear at the back of
my mind: we were playing the bloody All Blacks at the weekend.

One day, on Powelly's suggestion, we took our roll of notes and
went for a 'male makeover' in Harvey Nicks. The two of us treated
ourselves to a load of new clothes, a clean shave and a haircut each. It
segued inevitably into a drinking session with the rest of the boys, and
by two the following morning, Andy was texting me with increasing
urgency to come to his room. I rushed across to find Leigh Halfpenny
lying on his bed, sweating profusely, with his breath coming in short,
shallow bursts. 'Doc, butt,' Andy wailed with his distinctive
Mid-Walian lisp, 'Leigh's in big trouble, butt. I think he's having a
heart attack.' We were still horrendously drunk, but Leigh was really
panicking and assumed, because I was studying medicine, that I'd be
able to perform some miracle and save him. Pretending to know what

I was doing, I checked his pulse while he asked me with a tremulous voice if he was going to die. My official 'diagnosis' was that he was clogged up with three days of rich food and booze and was having serious acid-reflux issues. I prescribed a good night's sleep and promptly passed out next to him.

The incident didn't stop Powelly and me going out the following night, our fifth in a row. The numbers at this points were severely depleted, and when we found ourselves at a dingy Café de Paris on Leicester Square, struggling weakly to finish a single bottle of Corona, we decided that enough was enough. We had a Test match on Saturday. It was time to hit the sack.

People think that all you learn from a Barbarians week is how to put away more alcohol than you thought humanly possible. But that Saturday I learned one of the most valuable rugby lessons of my life. At breakfast, it was obvious that all these world-class players had flicked the switch. Gone were the laughs, smiles and general merriment of the last few days. The banter had been completely dialled down and replaced by a steely-eyed resolve. Game day had dawned, we were facing the All Blacks at a sold-out Twickenham and it was time to go to work.

I'd spent the first few years of my professional career building up pressure within myself during the week. I didn't like feeling nervous, but considered it a necessary part of the process. Unless you'd trained at 100 per cent and spent every spare hour thinking about the game, you'd be going in under-prepared. I convinced myself that I had to be entirely absorbed in every aspect, even if it made me edgy or prone to broken sleep. I'd worry incessantly. Do I know my plays? Am I fit enough? Am I strong enough? Have I stretched enough? Do I know my opposite number's habits and foibles well enough? My outlook changed that Saturday morning with the Barbarians. It taught me that I didn't need to waste all that emotional energy in the week. All that matters is the eighty minutes on Saturday. No one sees what you do in training; no one cares. If you deliver during the eighty minutes, that's all that matters.

We ran out at Twickenham and blew New Zealand off the park. There aren't many living Welshmen who can claim to have done that. Habana scored a hat-trick, and I dovetailed really nicely with Matt Giteau and Jaque Fourie: the same Jaque Fourie who'd put the dagger through the Lions' hearts in that Loftus Test. Our side was littered with world-class players who'd enjoyed the equivalent of a four-day stag, but we were able to turn it on when it mattered. They had faith in their ability and enough credit in the bank to deliver. Experience buys you that.

After the Baa-Baas experience, I tried to be more like that, but it took me many years to fully absorb the lessons. I'm not suggesting that getting drunk is the best way to prepare for international rugby, just that relaxing in the week puts you in the best headspace to perform. I suppose it's like learning your lines as an actor. You can either obsess over every nuance, worry about getting it word-perfect and end up giving a wooden, stilted performance. Or you can relax, knowing you've got what it takes, and deliver.

Because I'd progressed swiftly from youth to professional rugby, I hadn't had an extended period in a 'club' environment, and the Barbarians gave me a tantalising taste of that. With rugby becoming increasingly professionalised, it's more and more difficult to capture that vibe, making experiences like the Barbarians all the more unique and precious. I'm incredibly proud of my Baa-Baas jersey. It's up on my living-room wall, unwashed and decorated with every player's autograph. It embodies everything I love about the game.

As much as I'm a dedicated professional and a product of the academy system, I'm a traditionalist to the core. Forging strong relationships is by far the most important ingredient for success in rugby, and there are few better ways of doing it than going for a beer or two with your team-mates. Knowing and respecting the bloke next to you on the field is infinitely more important than the amount of sleep you've had, the amount of time you've spent on the massage table or how hydrated you are. I'd rather play with a mild hangover, as I did with the Barbarians, knowing that I'm running out alongside a band of brothers, than be 100 per cent physically prepared in a team of virtual strangers. We proved that you can beat the best side in the world having been out on the lash all week. It wouldn't have happened if we'd spent our time staring at laptops, going hell for leather on the training paddock and retiring to bed early every night.

Hopes were high ahead of the 2010 Six Nations. Warren Gatland addressed the squad at our first get-together, telling us we should be going into it *expecting* to win. It was a defiant, tub-thumping speech, and as we stood to leave, he addressed me loudly, in front of the entire squad: 'Jamie, are you a rugby player or a celebrity now? It's probably a good time to choose.' Warren was always economical with his words, and those two sharp sentences cut to the quick. My face flushed crimson red as several of the boys shuffled out, trying to suppress their smirks.

It was true that after the Lions tour, my agent, Pete Harmsworth, had been kept busy using my growing profile to take advantage of a number of media opportunities and sponsorship offers. I'd said yes to virtually everything and at one point you could barely pick up a magazine or turn on the TV without seeing my lantern-jawed visage staring back at you. I'd been invited on multiple radio and TV shows, I'd agreed to endorse several different brands and I'd been voted Wales's sexiest man. Gats had sensed that my ego was starting to expand like an inflating balloon, and he chose that moment to pop it in front of the entire squad. I wouldn't have admitted it at the time, but it was a shrewd bit of man-management. He'd calculated that a quiet word wouldn't have the same effect. There had to be an element of humiliation for the message to sink in. He understood there was a fine line between confidence and arrogance and wanted to make sure I stayed on the right side of it. The way he dropped it in at the end of the meeting was clever, too. I couldn't argue back. He just rolled the grenade across the floor, left it fizzing and disappeared.

His expressions were often difficult to read, and unlike Dai Young, there was rarely a wry smile to soften his words. On this occasion, he'd been deadly serious, and it had the desired effect. It made me feel really small and lit a flame of anger that translated into a red-hot performance on the training paddock that afternoon. I trained harder than ever before, determined to prove that I was more committed than anyone else on the pitch. I thought about it a lot in my room that evening. Coaching isn't just about coming up with a game plan; it's about managing a disparate bunch of blokes, all of whom have different issues, motivations and insecurities. With a seemingly small gesture he'd relayed a big message. If he'd done that to someone with a more fragile ego, they might not have recovered from it. He knew I'd interpret it the right way, and as much as it appeared a tossed-off remark, it was clearly calculated.

In those first few years under Warren, I can count on one hand the number of conversations I had with him. He could be distant and detached. Later in my career, Shaun told me I was the sort of player they deliberately didn't praise in front of the boys, because they thought I played my best rugby when I felt under pressure. There would be times when I thought I'd had a really good game, but then in the debrief they'd show a video of all the errors I'd made. They knew it would make me feel my place was under threat, and lo and behold, I'd redouble my efforts and play even better the following week. They'd discussed it and decided it was the best way to push me to greater heights. Back then, I'd have preferred unfettered praise – wouldn't we all? – but with hindsight I can appreciate the subtlety of their methods. It's smart coaching.

The 2010 Six Nations turned out to be a largely forgettable affair for Wales. We lost on the opening weekend at Twickenham, conceding 17 points while Alun Wyn Jones was in the sin bin for tripping Dylan Hartley. Gatland singled him out in the post-match press conference, threatening to drop him for the next match. Alun Wyn was already feeling dreadful about his indiscretion, so being called out on television by his head coach was like pouring salt into an open wound. Again, though, it was a shrewd bit of man-management. That moment changed him as a player. Any hint of impetuosity disappeared from his game overnight, and he became the ultimate model of self-control, without ever losing any of his trademark aggression. It changed his career, and he hasn't done too badly since.

We went on to lose to both France and Ireland in rounds three and four, and had it not been for a miracle in round two against Scotland, we'd have gone into the final weekend against Italy winless and contesting the wooden spoon. That Scotland game delivered one of the most outrageous climaxes in the tournament's history. Fly-half Dan Parks had one of his finest games in Scotland colours, knocking over long-range penalties and drop goals almost at will. We were 24–14 down with five minutes to go, and a Scottish win was all but guaranteed. I'd barely touched the ball all day, but just as all hope was ebbing away, Leigh Halfpenny escaped down the right-hand touchline and scampered over for a try.

Moments later, after a relentless barrage of phases, I got the ball in a bit of space and had a crack at the line, offloading to Lee Byrne as I hit the deck. He went through, chipping over their defence, and their replacement wing Phil Godman tripped him. They were already down to fourteen men and now Godman was also in the bin. With a minute left on the clock, a heated discussion ensued between captain Ryan Jones and Stephen Jones about whether to go for the sticks and secure the draw, or roll the dice. We opted for the former and took the points, watching the clock go red as we jogged back to receive the kick-off. There was time for one more play.

Gatland's mantra about exhausting the width of the pitch was on our minds. We'd done it a million times in training, working all the way to one touchline, then back to the other, the theory being that at some point there would be a numerical advantage and we could strike. We worked our way up the field through close-quarter forward carries, coming perilously close to drifting into touch. The ball came back to Steve, and I glanced up to see a ten-on-six overlap. As I was anticipating the pass, Steve inexplicably launched a cross-field kick. It seemed to be the absolute worst option, but the ball hit the 5-metre line and bounced obligingly back into play. Halfpenny scooped it up and we all piled forward, adrenaline surging. I hit a ruck 10 metres out and a massive overlap appeared on the left: about ten red shirts against five blue. We hit flanker Bradley Davies on a short ball and as he lowered his head to try to bulldoze through the traffic, I heard myself shouting, 'Put the ball through the f****ing *hands*, man!' Seconds later,

Shane was ghosting, wraith-like, through the defence and diving over the line. It had to be Shane. I was so tired I couldn't shout or celebrate. I barely had enough energy to put my arm round him. It was the most heart-stopping, nerve-shredding, bonkers finish to a Six Nations game you're ever likely to experience.

The following day I was enjoying Sunday lunch at the Newbridge-on-Usk country pub with my then girlfriend when my phone started trilling in my pocket. It continued to buzz and vibrate for five solid minutes. My hangover-induced paranoia set my mind racing. *What did I do last night? Who did I snog? What incriminating photos have surfaced?* Eventually, I excused myself and retreated to a toilet cubicle to examine the evidence. At least half of the Welsh squad had messaged me: 'Have you seen the news?' 'Thoughts on the news?' 'WTF?' With trembling fingers, I clicked on the BBC website and saw the headline 'Andy Powell arrested for drink-driving'. I instantly thought he must have left his car at the stadium and driven home wasted, but a few sentences in, I discovered it was an altogether more bizarre story. He'd driven a golf buggy several miles down the hard shoulder of the M4, in the wrong direction.

It's part of Welsh rugby folklore now, and the first thing many people think of when Andy Powell's name is mentioned, but it's difficult to describe just how insane it sounded at the time. He was apparently ravenous and, discovering that room service wasn't available, decided to make a quick dash to the motorway services. It sounded like a scene from a Carry On film or a Benny Hill sketch. What most people don't realise is how long the journey is from the Vale Hotel to the motorway. It's the best part of a mile just to get to the end of the snaking driveway, and that's before you hit the country lanes that eventually lead to the M4. With a top speed of 10 mph, he'd have had plenty of time to reconsider. But Powelly's brain is wired a little differently.

I'd had a sense something was going to go awry the previous night when, within minutes of arriving in the Walkabout bar after the official dinner, a few of the lads already had their tops off. There was a sense of frenzy about the celebrations. Because of the extraordinary climax to the game, it was a win we simply *had* to celebrate, and we belonged among the fans because it was one of those all-time memorable matches. So it didn't surprise me that something happened; I just never would have guessed it would be one of the boys trundling down the hard shoulder of a motorway in a stolen golf cart.

Half of me thought it was hilarious, the other half knew he'd crossed the line in a serious way. He could have killed someone, and could even have faced prison. In a team sport, you all carry the can and none of us were allowed into town for more than a year after that. We spent a whole season locked away in the 'Jail of Glamorgan'. I resented the management for that. I was in my prime, in my early twenties, and spilling out into town after the black-tie dinner is a vital part of the experience. The younger lads in the squad that year missed out on all that, and it seemed wrong. I didn't resent Andy; he's too lovable a bloke for that. It's just such a shame his actions meant they couldn't trust the rest of us.

It led to a bit of tension between the players and management for the remainder of that tournament, and poor old Simon Rimmer, the WRU press officer, bore the brunt the weekend of the Ireland game. After losing the match, we had been getting a bit of heat in the press, which the boys decided was Rimmer's fault. Rimmer was a really sweet, mild-mannered bloke doing a tough job in difficult circumstances, but the boys had expected him to spin our way out of negative coverage as if he was sport's answer to Alastair Campbell. It was decided that Rimmer's punishment for *our* bad press was to 'run the gauntlet' on the team bus – just as I'd done as an initiation at Rumney Youth – and, as any sensible non-rugby-playing man would, he politely declined.

That didn't go down well with the boys, who decided he'd have to do it before we left Ireland. As he boarded the bus at Portrush Golf Club, someone declared menacingly, 'Time to run the gauntlet, Rimmer boy.' He looked pleadingly at the coaches, his only potential allies, and was dismayed to see them shrug indifferently. The poor guy got battered. Punches, slaps, digs to the ribs, pokes with coat hangers, swipes from a studded sole – they rained down on him from both sides. Everyone had their pound of flesh. He was a broken man by the time we reached the airport, with his WRU tie still askew and a haunted look in his eyes. I felt sorry for him. For the boys, it was all part of the rough and tumble of professional rugby, but we'd signed up to it, and he hadn't. If you're reading this, Simon, sorry, pal.

After the disappointment of the Six Nations, we returned to our clubs. The Cardiff Blues hadn't qualified for the last eight of the Heineken Cup, but our second-place pool finish meant we'd dropped into the quarter-finals of the Challenge Cup. It was the second-tier European competition, but there were some former European champions in it, and it was a trophy worth winning. We stuck 50 points on Newcastle in the quarter-final, before facing Wasps in the semi at Adams Park. Xavier Rush was phenomenal that day in the driving wind and rain. They had the upper hand in the scrums, but Rushy was irrepressible in the loose, and they had no answer for his surging, bullocking runs.

The odds were monumentally stacked against us in the final. It was in Marseille, and the opposition was a star-studded Toulon. Their eccentric owner, Mourad Boudjellal, had been playing his own, real-life version of fantasy rugby and had assembled a side brimming with world-class talent. Jonny Wilkinson, Sonny Bill Williams, Juan Martín Fernández Lobbe and Tana Umaga were just a few of the superstars on their roster. They'd hammered Scarlets en route to the final and were in intimidating form.

Marseille is a grimy old port city, lacking the glamour of a lot of those places on the Côte d'Azur, but I still revelled in that feeling of being in a foreign city, stepping out of the hotel after training and sipping a coffee on the waterfront. We'd been in the EDF final the year before but this was a level up. It was away from home at a hostile ground, against a team that would come to dominate Europe like no other. We were looking to clip their wings before they really started to soar. Dai Young and Rhodri Manning, the Blues' analyst, had put together a motivational video. Instead of the usual clips of us performing at our best set to a rousing orchestral soundtrack, it was the exact opposite: a bloopers reel of all our worst, most embarrassing moments. Lads dropping balls, missing tackles, messing around in training and tucking each other up, me doing my hair when I thought no one was looking. It was a masterstroke, because it calmed the nerves that had been steadily building. We left the team room laughing and feeling completely chilled.

We'd lost our playmaker, Nicky Robinson, to Gloucester but had signed Casey Laulala, who'd brought some real guile and creativity to our midfield. Whenever I took the ball to the line, he'd be on my shoulder and vice versa. He had a low centre of gravity which allowed him to stay on his feet in contact and get the ball out of the tackle. In an echo of my partnership with Drico, I was the bludgeon and he was the rapier. If I was forced to choose an all-time favourite midfield partner, it would be Casey. He was a rare talent.

Marseille was only 30 miles from Toulon, and they often played there when the big guns in the Top 14 came to town, so it was as good as a home game for them. They'd already knocked over Toulouse and Perpignan there that season. There was a small, loyal and very vocal band of Cardiff Blues supporters in Marseille, but they were swamped by the hordes of Toulon supporters, aggressively chanting their 'Pilou-Pilou' anthem. The scale of the task seemed ever more daunting as we trooped silently off the bus, surrounded on all sides by these fired-up home fans.

The first twenty minutes were awful. We were all suffering from classic big-game nerves, but we hung on in there. Our granite-hard flanker, Maama Molitika, took a hell of a shot from Sonny Bill, who virtually snapped him in half. Rushy got rocked backwards too, in a double tackle from Joe van Nierkerk and Jonny Wilkinson; you didn't see that too often. They were ahead 13–6 at half-time after a typically brilliant Sonny Bill solo try, and things were looking glum.

Seven minutes into the second half, seconds after he had narrowly missed a penalty, Jonny Wilkinson collapsed to the turf in agony. It would prove a massive turning point, as centre Tom May was forced into emergency fly-half duty, and they weren't the same team after that. Before long, the tables were turned. After a sustained period of attack, Richie Rees scooped up a bobbling ball, delivering it straight into my breadbasket as I hurtled at top speed towards the line. No one was stopping me from that distance. Twenty minutes later, we'd sealed victory after crafting further tries for Leigh Halfpenny and

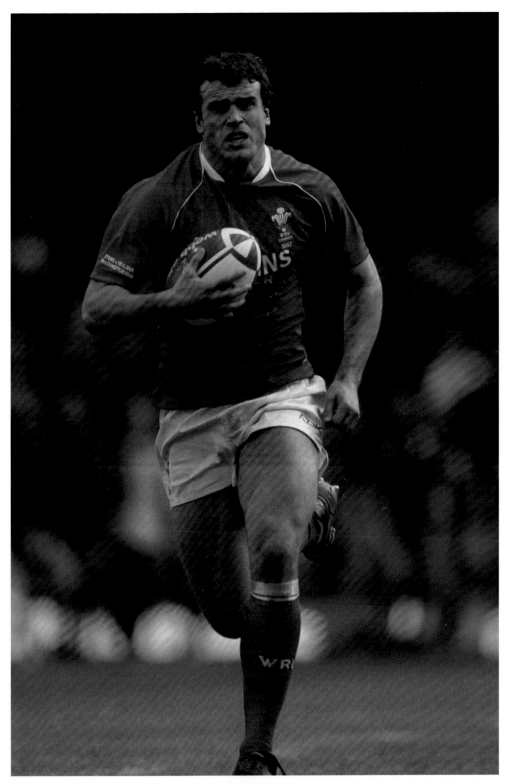

Making my Wales debut as a fresh-faced 21-year-old. I was constantly catching my breath and my adrenaline levels were off the charts, but I loved every minute.

After Dad had wooed Mum with his chat-up line about Ordnance Survey maps, they jetted off to the United States for their honeymoon. Their last taste of freedom before David and I arrived.

Enjoying a higher vantage point atop Dad's shoulders. It wouldn't be too long until I outgrew both Dad and my brother, David.

Returning to Jersey for a family holiday – where I could easily have been born had it not been for a mad dash for the boat to avoid a ferry workers' strike.

'Great try, young man.' Still smiling after having my hair ruffled by one of Wales's greatest ever fly-halves during a mini-rugby tournament at Old Deer Park, the home of London Welsh.

If the cap fits. Celebrating the end of a season in which I captained the Cardiff Schools Under-15s side. Behind me is the sacred turf of Cardiff Arms Park.

Making my professional debut for the Cardiff Blues in 2007. I nearly handed victory to the Ospreys by giving away a last-minute penalty.

The brains trust of Gatland, Howley and Edwards plotting victory against France ahead of the final leg of our 2008 Grand Slam.

A royal seal of approval. Sharing a moment with HRH Prince William after winning the Grand Slam in 2008. While I had a winner's medal, I felt more like a passenger during my first international campaign.

I played in three different positions in my first three Tests, but it was the 12 jersey that would come to define me. Here I am locking horns with the South African midfield on the highveld.

'Lad, you became a Test player today.' On the charge against Dan Carter and Richie McCaw, two of the game's most iconic players.

The aftermath of a sickening collision with Stirling Mortlock that left me hospitalised with a fractured skull at the end of 2008.

My burgeoning reputation made me a marked man. I couldn't escape the clutches of England's Joe Worsley in the 2009 Six Nations, but his man-marking mission was ultimately in vain.

Launching the unlikeliest of comebacks against Leicester in the 2009 European semi-finals.

Utter devastation for Martyn Williams and the Cardiff Blues, as Nugget's missed penalty denies us a place in the Heineken Cup final.

Being selected for the Lions in 2009 was a dream come true, but defeat in the second Test at Loftus Versfeld was one of the most heartbreaking I've ever experienced.

The photo that adorns the hallway wall in my parents' house, taking pride of place above all others. Gareth Edwards and Willie John McBride were Dad's Lions heroes, and he was beside himself with excitement to have met them on the 2009 Lions tour.

Braving the ice baths with my centre partner, Brian O'Driscoll, and fellow Welshman Stephen Jones.

Despite the series defeat, the 2009 Lions trip was an undoubted career highlight. I was privileged to be named Lions Player of the Series.

Enjoying a rare victory against the New Zealand All Blacks; a win made all the more remarkable by our 'less than professional' preparation.

Bradley Davies. It was the first time a Welsh side had won a European trophy, and to do so in that fashion, in that stadium and in those circumstances made it all the more special.

Looking back, we had the perfect blend of hard-nosed experience, selfless club servants and exciting young talent. Sam Warburton came off the bench and made a critical turnover in our 22 at a time when another score could have taken them away from us. The three try-scorers were all products of the Blues academy, which was immensely satisfying. We had some great foreign players, who formed the spine of our side, but it was a lovely touch that the guys who crossed the line had all come through the system.

It remains the only time in my career that Dad gave me a rollocking. After I had scored, wrapped up in the emotion, I cupped my hand to my ear to taunt the Toulon supporters. Richie Rees was distinctly unimpressed and nearly ripped my jersey in the act of dragging me away. After the game, when I turned my phone on, I was deluged by a flood of congratulatory messages, but the one that resonated the most was from Dad. 'Jamie, congratulations,' it said, 'that was massive, but I never want to see you celebrate like that again. That sort of thing belongs on the football field.' Like Gatland's admonishment at the start of the year, it cut to the bone.

11

PERFORMANCE, COCKTAILS, INJURIES AND LAYOFFS

It was one of the very few times I'd seen Adam Jones get angry. He'd just torn up a newspaper article and thrown it on the floor in disgust. We were on the bus to the airport in June 2010 after a humbling tour of New Zealand during which we'd been outmuscled and exposed. It had been apparent to anyone watching that they were markedly superior athletes. A journalist in the *New Zealand Herald* had written a damning article drawing attention to our lack of fitness, and Bomb and his front-row colleagues had been singled out for ridicule. There'd been a really condescending line about Bomb lumbering round the pitch chasing pies and sweets. Our conditioning coach, Craig White, had brought the article on the bus and handed it to the nearest player, telling him to read it and pass it on.

Adam, as a senior player, was at the back of the bus and had little inclination to read it once it reached him. The whole squad was spoken of in unflattering terms, but the abuse towards Bomb had been personal. Craig's decision to share the article was a little insensitive, but it was a rocket up all of our backsides. If we wanted to win the World Cup the following year, if we wanted to even compete, we had a lot of work to do. We'd been badly shown up by the best side in the world, and sometimes harsh truths are necessary.

We'd been blown away in the first Test, the last ever to be played at Carisbrook. They stuck 40 points on us and Dan Carter delivered one of his masterclasses. We'd shown a bit more grit in the second but were still way off the pace. Not many would have expected us to win, but we'd have been expected to put up a fight. Craig White may have been the messenger, but there's no doubt Gatland was the orchestrator. As a native New Zealander returning home, that article would have embarrassed him, but he knew it would embarrass us more.

Rather than spare us that, he wanted us to feel it like a shock of cold water to the face. It was a catalyst for what was to follow, as next season marked a drastic shift in our approach to conditioning, leading to the most brutal physical examination any of us had faced.

Before all of that, though, I had to get my wrist looked at. It had been bothering me since the Lions tour and had never fully recovered. I'd played the entire 2009–10 season hoping it would right itself, but it had felt as if I was playing with an arm tied behind my back for the best part of a year. I wasn't able to fend with my right hand, and at least once a game I'd clip my wrist, sending a searing pain up my arm. A scan revealed that I'd ruptured my scapholunate ligament, which is what holds your carpal bones and wrist together. It's one of the main stabilising ligaments, and I'd played a whole season without it. No wonder I'd been in agony. I was livid that the original scan in South Africa had missed it, but apparently these ruptures can be difficult to detect.

Surgery was the advised course of action, but I was conscious there was a World Cup the following summer and I worried that a six-month break would leave me out of sight, out of mind. I sent Gats a text asking for his thoughts and his response was reassuring. He said I was his first-choice midfielder, and told me to get it sorted and come back fit and firing.

You can look at an injury lay-off in two ways. You can feel sorry for yourself, wallow in misery and think about what you're missing. Or you can embrace the time off and say yes to everything that you'd otherwise have to turn down. If an opportunity falls in my lap and I think there's even a tiny chance I'll regret turning it down, I make sure I take it. I've always had that mindset. 'FOMO', I think the youngsters call it – 'fear of missing out'.

Some players would be so worried about losing their fitness, they'd base their whole life around retaining it. I took the opposite approach, pulling the proverbial rip cord, knowing I'd have ample time to get back in shape as my wrist healed. For the first three months of my recovery, I launched myself into the playboy lifestyle.

I travelled to the Grand Prix in Monza and ended up drinking into the small hours with the Stereophonics after seeing them belt out their hits in Milan. Eddie Jordan had spotted me on the balcony and dragged me into the green room. We ended up at the Cavalli club in the middle of a forest on the outskirts of Milan, absolutely legless. The 'phonics' second album, *Performance and Cocktails*, had been my bible growing up. I knew every word of every song, so to be drinking and hanging out with the guys that wrote them was special. I felt like a right charlatan.

I enjoyed another debauched weekend at the 2010 Ryder Cup, which that year was held at Celtic Manor, not far from Newport, in the company of Gethin Jones, Nugget and Ioan Gruffudd. Ioan, who'd starred in the film *Titanic* when I was growing up, was Hollywood royalty in my eyes. He may have been a humble Glantaf boy like myself, but he occupied a different universe from me now. The original invitation, from my friend Andy Allen, had been to have a few drinks on the Friday and watch some golf. I ended up leaving Celtic Manor on the Sunday, having seen virtually no play. Friday was a washout, so we spent all day on the sauce. The rain continued for most of Saturday apart from the final hour, by which time virtually all the spectators had left. It meant we had the course to ourselves and were in the surreal situation of standing next to the tee on the tenth hole, giggling tipsily, while the likes of Tiger Woods and Phil Mickelson were teeing off. A few hours and several glasses of wine later, I was spinning opera singer Katherine Jenkins around the dance floor at the official Ryder Cup ball. I finished the weekend swilling pints in Merlin's Bar with Jason Leonard and Mike Tindall, while a comatose Ian Botham snored aggressively in a nearby leather armchair.

Later that autumn, I worked on the BBC's coverage of the Wales v New Zealand match and was having a beer with Jonathan 'Jiffy' Davies outside Cardiff's Mokka Lounge when three black SUVs screeched around the corner like something out of a film. A bunch of men in pin-sharp suits got out, including a stern, intimidating-looking bloke with black curly hair. They strode towards the club, with people parting like a wave in front of them. A few of them had guns. What the hell was going on? The intimidating guy walked past me, before doing a double-take and breaking into a smile.

He beckoned over a bald, unassuming-looking man and said, 'Albert, this is Jamie Roberts. He's a famous rugby player. Jamie, this is Prince Albert of Monaco.'

I wouldn't have known him from Adam. The guy who had recognised me was Mark Thomas, son of the Wales and Lions legend Clem Thomas, who'd been in the Welsh side the day they'd last beaten the All Blacks in 1953. Mark was working with the prince, essentially acting as his right-hand man, and he invited me to join him and his entourage, so I abandoned Jiffy and my schoolmates to sink a few ales with the prince.

A few weeks earlier I'd gone to the Abu Dhabi Grand Prix and stayed in the hotel overlooking the final stretch of the circuit. Team Red Bull won and I found myself spraying champagne over Sebastian Vettel as he lifted the trophy. It was a full weekend bender with Freddie Flintoff, who proved to be a top bloke, and great company. It was one of several times that summer I caught myself thinking, *What have I done to deserve this?* I may have been a Test Lion and at the top of my profession, but at times I felt like a lucky competition-winner hanging out with global superstars. A part of me will always remain a wide-eyed Cardiff schoolboy who's gatecrashed the party hoping no one will notice.

Most of these trips were off the back of a fortuitous Red Bull sponsorship. My agent was good mates with the athlete manager there and had persuaded them to take a punt on me as a nineteen-year-old. It was the start of an eleven-year association. In those early years at the Blues, I'd get a little cash bonus for getting Red Bull on TV. I'd regularly jog out of the tunnel during televised games and 'accidentally' wander into the path of a camera while swigging from a can. It was so utterly transparent, and the boys ribbed me mercilessly for being a walking advert, but it was worth it for the £500 that dropped into my account every time I pulled it off. It didn't come without risk, though. England captain Lewis Moody was under the same management, and he once started swigging a can during a post-match interview, but what he hadn't considered was that rivals Powerade were a big RFU sponsor – and in any case, no one would drink Red Bull *after* a game. It's a stimulant, not a recovery drink. He copped a pretty significant fine, which Red Bull had to step in to pay.

It wasn't all fun and games during those six months off. Adam Beard had come in that December to shadow Craig White on the strength-and-conditioning side for Wales, and I did a lot of work with him and Frans Bosch as I was recovering from my wrist injury. Frans is a world-renowned biomechanics expert and he set about fundamentally changing my running style, using some pretty unorthodox methods. Some days I'd be in at 7 a.m., running lengths of the pitch in bare feet holding a stick above my head. Other sessions involved sprinting flat out, so Frans could analyse my stride and running mechanics. The aim was to make you as efficient and economical as possible in your movements, and to eliminate any bad habits. It was weird to begin with, and some of the exercises were bizarre, but over time it started to make sense. Rugby is about running at high intensity for short bursts during an eighty-minute match, and the exercises were designed to replicate that. The old-fashioned notion of plodding away endlessly on a treadmill was no longer in vogue.

Without getting too technical, it was about changing my 'backside' mechanics into 'frontside' mechanics. I'd always assumed that running was a purely instinctive thing, until I met those guys and had to relearn how to do it. As a tall, heavy bloke, I was never going to be the greatest runner, and certainly not the fastest, but by changing your style, you can learn to expend less energy. If you have more power in your hamstrings and hip flexors, you can get your knee through quicker, making your running more economical. You waste less energy pushing through the floor. If you can bring your hip flexor through quickly and be more reactive on your calves when your foot hits the floor, you can propel yourself forwards more efficiently. It sounds overly scientific and a bit nerdy, but after that 2010 New Zealand tour, we felt we needed to focus on the minutiae if we were to take those next few steps. The 2011–12 period would see me the fittest I'd ever been in my career, purely because of the work I had done on biomechanics. Once I'd made the necessary changes, I felt like I could cruise for 80 metres at 80 per cent of my top speed without even breaking sweat.

My return came in January 2011, in the decidedly unglamorous setting of the Galway Sports Ground, with the temperature hovering close to zero. I ended up with a nice Frankenstein-style zip scar on my forehead after splitting my head open on the frozen turf. I'd only played a handful of games for the Blues before I returned to Wales for that year's Six Nations, which was awkward. You're well aware when you're injured that your club is still paying you. The money lands in your account every month, but you're doing nothing to earn it. The lads rip into you, big time, especially if you're a Test player: 'Oh, here he is, back from gallivanting round the world. There must be a Test series round the corner. You only see him when he wants to play for Wales.' I couldn't help but feel guilty, especially as my salary had gone up considerably. Cardiff University was allowing me to spread the last two years of my medical degree over four, and I'd signed a new four-year deal with the Blues to tie in with my studies. My value had soared after the Lions tour, and my annual salary doubled overnight to £160k. By the end of the four-year period, it would rise to £190k.

I was really fortunate that this all fell into place, and I remain forever grateful to Cardiff University for their flexibility. It eased the pressure enormously. My mate Tom Smith, who was playing for the Ospreys, had made a similar request the previous year which had been denied. He quit medicine as a result, because he couldn't give his all to both. I was far from the model student, and got on the wrong side of several of the hospital consultants with my less than exemplary attendance record. Some days, I'd be absolutely exhausted from training and couldn't bear the thought of standing up in hospital for hours on end. Other days, I'd be exposed for my lack of knowledge because I'd fallen so far behind with my studies. At the same time, I was asking my rugby coaches if I could miss sessions, or was begging the conditioners to arrive early just to cater to my individual needs. I didn't want to admit that my dogged pursuance of rugby and medicine was compromising my efforts in both, and I couldn't escape the feeling that I was being judged for a lack of commitment on both sides.

The 2011 Six Nations was another forgettable tournament. We lost narrowly to England at home before labouring to away wins over Italy and Scotland. We beat Ireland in Cardiff, thanks to an 'illegal' try from Mike Phillips from a quickly taken line-out with the wrong ball. Paul O'Connell was incandescent, but his angry appeals to the referee fell on deaf ears. We finished with a heavy defeat to France which saw us drop to fourth place overall. We had the same number of wins as Ireland and France, but were undone by an inferior points difference. After the euphoria of the Grand Slam in 2008, we'd come fourth three times in a row. You'd have got pretty long odds if you'd put a bet on Wales for the World Cup that was taking place in New Zealand later that year.

The defeat to England was compounded by an unsavoury incident that night, after a few of us ventured into Cardiff for drinks. We were minding our own business outside Oceana nightclub when a total stranger took a swing at my centre partner Jonathan 'Foxy' Davies. There was no warning or preamble; he just approached from behind and punched Foxy in the jaw, knocking him clean out. I instinctively grabbed the back of Foxy's coat as he fell and hauled him back to his feet. I shudder to think what might have happened if he'd hit the deck, because he was unconscious going down; just a bag of bones. He could easily have cracked his head open on the kerb. I held him up for around ten seconds until he came round, dazed and confused, and enquiring, not unreasonably, 'What the f*** just happened?'

The red mist descended and I chased this guy down the street. I went into full Rocky Balboa mode, jaw-clenched, fists balled up, looking for retribution. Catching up with him outside Tiger Tiger, I got right up in his face, demanding to know what the hell he thought he was doing. He wasn't particularly big, so I was staring down at him, waiting for an answer, when he punched me in the mouth. The claret immediately started to flow, but as incensed as I was, Sensible Jamie told me retaliation was a bad idea. Scrapping in the street wasn't something I wanted on my rap sheet. He turned and ran, and I ducked into a nearby alleyway, hoping I hadn't been recognised. Within moments I was approached by a copper who had witnessed what had happened and thankfully accepted my version of events. The next day, I got a call from the cops telling me the CPS were deciding whether or not to prosecute. I gave my statement and headed off to training on the Monday with a few stitches in my lip, trying to pretend that nothing had happened. Unbeknownst to me, it had already made the press. Some journalism student had clocked me speaking to the copper and the story had leaked out. Nice little scoop for him.

The lads laid into me, but I honestly struggled to see the funny side. As someone who'd always had a relatively untarnished public image, I was essentially getting bad press for sticking up for my mate, and getting one in the chops for my troubles. To this day, I don't know what the guy's beef was. It had been totally unprovoked. He no doubt knew who we were, and probably thought it would be fun to have a swing at a couple of international rugby players.

A few months later, I was cruising over the Severn Bridge with the top down after another long weekend at the Monaco Grand Prix when Wales manager Alan Phillips's number flashed up on my phone. Thumper's distinctive Kenfig Hill accent came crackling through the speaker, and he wasn't happy. 'Jamie, boy. Where are you? You're meant to be in court.' Foxy's assailant was in the dock, and the court had called the WRU to enquire as to my whereabouts. I was apparently meant to be appearing as a witness. Both Foxy and I had received letters stating in block capitals that our presence would not be required. Not so, according to Thumper, and the damning headline in the following day's *Western Mail* was 'Judge blasts rugby internationals for court no-show'. I was walking through town with a few of my mates and saw it emblazoned across one of the old-fashioned newsstands on the High Street. My mum was mortified. The perception seemed to be that I was a scroat who'd been caught scrapping and hadn't bothered to turn up to court. My carefully cultivated public image had taken a major hit, and I'd done absolutely nothing wrong.

12

THE BIGGEST REGRET
OF MY CAREER

Alun Wyn Jones and Ryan Jones grunting, panting and grappling with each other in a sandpit isn't Joshua versus Fury at Wembley, but when you're marooned in a Polish forest miles from civilisation, you take your entertainment where you find it. The two alphas had been ordered to sort out their differences after an 'altercation' in line-out practice. No one knew exactly where the blame lay, but tempers had frayed and fists had flown. Warren Gatland had stressed the importance of discipline ahead of the 2011 World Cup. A loss of control in training was one thing, he'd said, but if it happened on the pitch, with the world watching, it could lead to a red card and, ultimately, an early exit. He wanted us to be on the edge, but not over it.

Discipline was at the heart of everything during that training camp, and the sandpit was the punishment for breaches. Conditioning coach Dan Baugh was torturer-in-chief. Late for a meeting? Get in the pit. Failure to 'self-monitor'? Get in the pit. Wore the wrong kit? Pit. While in there, you were made to crawl lengths without using your legs until your elbows bled. Then you'd have to do any number of exercises Dan conjured from his twisted mind. The time in the pit went up five minutes every time there was a breach, so the first person to screw up would suffer five minutes of torture, the second ten minutes, and so on. Some lads would congregate to watch, if they were feeling particularly sadistic; but the worst feeling was when they all trooped back to their rooms. You'd watch balefully as they disappeared from view, knowing Dan was about to do everything in his power to break your spirit.

This was Spala, our pre-World Cup training camp in central Poland, designed to push us to the very limits of our physical and mental capabilities. To keep going until our chests were heaving, our lungs burning, our limbs wasted and our spirits broken. It was absolutely savage and, by some distance, the most extreme training regime I'd ever endured. Gatland was a constant presence, skulking on the fringes, watching like a hawk, sniffing out weakness. He didn't mind people struggling or falling short of targets, but he did mind people just giving up. It was all about mental fortitude. The squad was going to be trimmed at the end of the week, and if you were the type of player looking to cut corners or slack off, you'd be gone by the time we arrived back in Cardiff. He knew we were skilful and talented, but he didn't think we were fit enough to win the World Cup. This was a test to see who had the minerals to survive.

Not that he practised what he preached. One evening in the gym, as I was labouring through my eighth session of the day, I looked across to see him fast asleep on a bench, slumped over with his head lolling forwards like a drunk uncle at Christmas. Never one to miss an opportunity, I sneaked my phone out to steal a photo. It was only when I looked back at it that I noticed Rob Howley scowling at me for the impertinence.

It was a far from luxurious camp. The beds, the food and the weather were awful, and there was nothing to do but train and sleep. The journey there was like something from *The Blair Witch Project*, as we drove deeper and deeper into the gloom of an impenetrable forest. When the training base eventually appeared through the trees, it felt like a mirage. It was more like an army barracks than a hotel, and the catering was similarly uninspiring. Deep-fried chicken, eggy chicken, limp salad leaves and a number of unidentified Polish 'delicacies'. Every day. We all had our supplements and were trying to eat the right amount of calories, but it was hard when the menu was so unappealing. The schedule was relentless, and often soundtracked by fitness coach Adam Beard bellowing 'Be the best at everything that doesn't require talent!' through the stadium PA system. On a typical day, we'd be up at seven for a running session, into the cryotherapy chamber, then breakfast. Full training session, more cryotherapy, lunch. Big rugby session, cryotherapy, snack. Then after dinner, we'd be in the gym for weights until eight, before a final cryotherapy session, and bed. Sleep came easily.

Everything revolved around the cryotherapy. It's what Spala is famous for. Exposing your body to sub-zero temperatures is supposed to accelerate recovery and enable you to train harder and longer. Aching muscles, ligaments and tendons are magically restored within a few minutes. It seems bearable in the initial antechamber, but then they open the door to the main chamber, where the temperature is *minus* 150 degrees Celsius. It's like walking into an arctic abyss. There are no words in my vocabulary to describe how cold it feels. To say it's *bloody freezing* would be a comical understatement. All you're wearing is a pair of shorts, knee-length socks, gloves and a headband. Your nipples are the first thing to react – they start stinging like hell – before your whole body starts to tingle and your muscles begin to throb. You have to do everything in your power to say focused. Word-association games offered the best distraction, with the loser having to get down and do five press-ups. Someone suggested licking the wall as an alternative punishment, until it was pointed out that that was a sure-fire way to lose your tongue. We were left under no illusions about the potential dangers after Stephen Jones emerged with horrible angry blisters on his Achilles tendons. He'd made the mistake of going in in ankle socks, exposing the parts of his legs where the skin is at its thinnest, and suffered third-degree ice burns. He could barely put his boots on for days afterwards, let alone train.

There were two mindsets you could adopt out there. You could buy into it and dedicate yourself 100 per cent, or you could moan, whinge and long for the day you left. I made the conscious choice to adopt the former approach and reap the rewards. It was the only way to survive.

We had to weigh in and 'self-monitor' every morning, which involved rating how well you'd slept and how alert you were feeling. It was considered an important part of the process. I forgot to do it on the very first morning. Big mistake. While we were readying ourselves for the first session Adam Beard said, 'Jamie, you're with Killer in the pool.' 'Why?' I replied, confused. 'Because you didn't weigh in this morning.' I was the first to break protocol, and he was forced to make an example of me.

My punishment was to swim continuously for an hour without stopping or touching the bottom. It was one of the most difficult things I've done in my life. Gavin Henson was there too, having broken some other random rule, and after barely ten minutes, he hauled himself out and sloped towards the changing rooms, shaking his head. Killer, one of Beardy's interns, told him, in the brusque manner of a drill sergeant, to 'get the f*** back in', but Gav continued to shake his head in defiance, claiming he was too hungry, and had had enough. I was astonished. There I was, digging in, and Gav decided he simply couldn't be bothered. He ended up leaving the camp early to go and film some reality TV series, so it was obvious his heart wasn't entirely in it. He didn't make it to the World Cup after breaking his wrist in one of the warm-up games, but there's a good chance his card had already been marked before then.

Gats was keen to foster competition within the squad, pairing us off against players in similar positions for 'king of the ring' wrestling bouts and tug-of-war contests. Under previous regimes, there'd be clandestine gentlemen's agreements between players: you win this one, and I'll win the next. Gats saw through that and wanted nothing less than absolute no-holds-barred commitment. He and Rob Howley would lurk nearby pretending to lay bets on certain players. 'A fiver says Warby takes JT here', or 'a tenner says Lydiate gets Powelly to deck in thirty seconds'. That sort of mental manipulation worked a treat on the likes of Sam Warburton, who always wanted to set the absolute gold standard.

The focus on discipline extended to the field. The ball was to be treated as a prized possession. If you dropped it before you'd completed a certain number of phases, the whole squad would have to do one of a number of fitness drills, such as 'runways', 'Hennie Mullers', or 'watt tests' – drills that fill your heart with dread and invariably end with you tasting blood at the back of your throat. It was horrible, but it helped condition the lads into respecting possession and not trying anything risky when we were in our shape. Every now and then, images of my trips to Monaco and California would flash through my mind, and I'd use them as motivation. Rather than wishing I was back there, I told myself I'd earned those trips *because* I put myself through things like this. The pleasure was in the bank; now it was time for the pain.

During a particularly savage session, Huw Bennett started spewing his guts up and Gatland pointed him out to the rest of us. I'm not sure he enjoyed the spotlight being shone on him at that precise moment, but Gats was saying, 'Look at this guy, look how hard he's working, look how much he's willing to give.' Like a teacher's pet, Josh Turnbull put his hand up, and said, 'Gats, I've been sick as well.' You can imagine the ribbing he got from the boys.

If there was any danger we were starting to feel sorry for ourselves, perspective was fully restored after a day trip to Auschwitz. On our one day off, the lads had wanted to head to the bar, but management vetoed it, proposing the road trip as an alternative. It was a genuinely moving experience, and a chance to learn about one of the darkest chapters in human history. The banter and ribaldry normally present around a bunch of rugby players was entirely absent that afternoon as we wandered the grounds in silent contemplation. It was truly sobering, and the images of the victims' personal effects remain indelibly imprinted on my mind. The pile of broken and mangled spectacles was particularly chilling. Against this backdrop, describing our training camp as 'torturous' seemed wholly inappropriate. The moaning stopped after that.

The evenings when we didn't crash out early would revolve around quiz nights, prepared and hosted, incongruously, by renowned fun sponge Gethin Jenkins. Melon was a strict, authoritarian quizmaster with no tolerance for cheating. Things would often descend into farce when someone would pipe up that several of his 'answers' were actually wrong. Mobiles would be whipped out to check fallacious facts, accusations of fixing would start to fly and Melon would threaten to abandon the whole enterprise. Much as we pretended to play it down, a competitive spirit emerged, and being on the winning team became a point of pride. Bomb was a walking encyclopaedia on sport, Alun Wyn proved himself quite the bookish intellectual and Foxy was your classic all-rounder. Nobody wanted the virtually mute Justin Tipuric, Taulupe Faletau or Leigh Halfpenny on their team; top blokes all, but with little to offer in the quiz stakes. They wouldn't even volunteer an answer, let alone get one right.

The only other thing that passed for entertainment in that godforsaken outpost was a 'play' we put on called *Shagger White and the*

Seven Dwarves. We were forced to do it by management as punishment for an unsanctioned night out in Bridgend back at the end of the Six Nations. Gatland had cancelled that year's Super Sunday – the traditional end-of-campaign knees-up – on the grounds we'd come fourth for the third year running and didn't deserve it. Our small band of rebels had naively thought that Bridgend would afford us a degree of anonymity. It didn't and the 'punishment' was to stage this play for the rest of the lads. The characters included Mike Phillips in the lead role as 'Shagger White', Jonathan Thomas as 'Jon the Bastard', Foxy as 'Quads', Lee Byrne as 'Horny' and Shane Williams as 'Stumpy'. Sadly, the script I wrote for this masterpiece hasn't been preserved for posterity, but I can safely say it wouldn't have been challenging for any BAFTAs.

We were aware the squad was going to be trimmed down before we left and when Gats summoned us all to the team room on the final evening we knew our fate had been decided. He called out the names of eight lads and asked them to go to the sports hall, telling the rest of us to return to our rooms. It was pretty obvious what was happening. Most of the eight were big characters; Andy Powell, Lou Reed and Jonathan Thomas were among them. Powelly later told me that they'd hung around in the sports hall for quarter of an hour with Rob Howley, making awkward small talk, until Warren came in and delivered the bad news. I'm not sure what the right way of doing it was, but this seemed particularly ruthless. Warren's been called out by a few players for his insensitivity around such matters. It's not a criticism of him as a coach, rather of his man-management, but at the end of the day, there's no easy way to tell eight ambitious, competitive blokes who've just given everything for eleven long and testing days that their World Cup dream is over.

The camp may have been a serious ordeal, but by the end I felt supremely fit, powerful and strong. The lads were in serious nick. We had a topless team photo in the gym before we left, and everyone looked like a professional bodybuilder. There's no doubt Spala laid the foundation for what followed. As much as there are times when you hate it, when you feel you are pushing your mind and body to their absolute limit, going through those experiences with your peers brings you closer. You struggle collectively, and when you experience adversity on the pitch, when your chest is heaving and your lungs are burning, you cast your mind back to those Spala sessions and you know you can endure it and get beyond it. You know you've been there before and found a way out.

During the build-up to the World Cup, I was drafted in alongside Melon, Nugget and some of the old stagers to represent the players in a pay dispute with the Union. At a meeting with the CEO, Roger Lewis, things got a bit tense when he started pleading poverty and Melon refused to back down, claiming he was trying to pull the wool over our eyes. It reached a bit of a stalemate when Roger stood up and theatrically emptied his pockets, declaring, 'Boys, I've got nothing!' Unimpressed, and not one to stand on ceremony, Melon told him to 'stop talking s***'. He had enough credit in the bank to take Roger on, whereas I still felt a bit callow and inexperienced. I feared that being too outspoken might negatively mark my card. It was an amusing duel between two starkly contrasting personalities: Roger, the slick, verbose businessman, and Melon, the gruff, monosyllabic prop. Gethin isn't a particularly charming negotiator, but he's very determined and wasn't about to roll over and have his belly tickled.

The crux of the debate was payment ratios: guaranteed earnings versus bonus payments. Obviously the players wanted them to be weighted in favour of the former, whereas Roger wanted the opposite. In a performance-driven environment, it makes sense for the Union to stack the heavier percentage on the latter. Our argument was that England were getting £15–20,000 a game, win, lose or draw, but Roger wasn't interested in blanket payments. A compromise was eventually reached after a good deal of needless emotional energy had been spent.

At the end of the financial year, the WRU boasted of record profits in a bumper year, a headline that, unsurprisingly, incensed the lads, none more so than Melon. So much for Roger's empty pockets!

*   *   *

We played England home and away in the first two World Cup warm-up games, and fly-half Stephen Jones went down injured just before the first. Rhys Priestland was thrust into the starting line-up and absolutely bossed it. For a quiet young bloke, he was extremely calm and assured, and had the skillset to get the backline moving. He played flat to the line rather than deep in the pocket, which is gold for someone like me. It means I'm running at shoulders more often than whole bodies – space rather than contact. England edged that game, but we beat them well the following week in Cardiff. A final warm-up win over the Pumas meant we travelled to New Zealand with a sense of quiet confidence.

The previous World Cup had ended in humiliation for Wales, but this was the new generation, a new breed of confident, gym-honed physical specimens ready for battle. Guys like Jonathan Davies, Taulupe Faletau, Sam Warburton, Dan Lydiate and George North had all emerged in the previous year. They were powerful, physically imposing athletes who'd stepped up to Test rugby with consummate ease. I'm not sure George had even started shaving, but at eighteen years of age he was already an absolute monster. Warby was a Test rookie, but he had been terrorising rucks with the authority and nous of a grizzled veteran. These guys were wiser and more experienced than their baby faces let on.

There's no doubt Gatland was fortunate that those players came through at the same time, but he was also canny enough to understand how their attributes would fit into a game plan capable of destroying physically inferior teams. He's always been a pragmatist. Whether with Connacht, Ireland, Wasps or Wales, he's always favoured an attritional, risk-averse approach. He recognised that most Welsh boys had innate rugby talent – the ability to offload in the tackle, to pass off both hands, to sidestep while running at top speed – but may have lacked an overall sense of game-management and tactical precision. An ability to see the bigger picture rather than the individual moment; the macro rather than the micro. Warren Gatland imposed that tactical framework and turned a skilful bunch of individuals into a finely tuned winning machine. Confidence was high. We were going to New Zealand to win the World Cup.

Being selected in the squad was a formality for me this time, so there wasn't the same wide-eyed wonderment I'd experienced after my Lions summons. There were a few raised eyebrows, though, at the appointment of twenty-two-year-old Sam Warburton as skipper. It was a massive call. There was a vacancy, as the incumbent, Matthew Rees, had been ruled out with a neck injury, but the smart money had been on Gethin Jenkins. Melon had reams of experience and a natural authority, whereas Warby was a shy kid, seventeen matches into his Test career. What he had that others lacked was a pure, undistilled, laser-sharp focus on rugby. He didn't drink, party or stay up late, and was out on his own in terms of professionalism. That's not to say the rest of us weren't diligent and assiduous in our preparation, but a good few of us enjoyed a pint and the opportunity to let our hair down. With a soothsayer's power of foresight, Warren realised any off-field slip-ups could derail our campaign, especially in a country as rugby mad as New Zealand. He couldn't risk another Powelly golf cart incident, or a Mike Phillips barroom brawl. There was zero chance of something like that happening to Warby. As a front-of-house poster boy, he was pure as the driven snow. He was also untouchable in that seven jersey: the only specialist open-side flanker in the squad. No one objected to the appointment publicly, but there was a good deal of cynicism among some of the senior players. I've no doubt some of them must have been wondering what they'd done wrong to have been overlooked, and I think Warby himself felt a bit unworthy, but you don't choose the captaincy, do you? The captaincy is bestowed upon you, and in the fullness of time, it proved a masterstroke.

We had the traditional haka welcome at the airport, and we then launched into a full-throated rendition of the Welsh song 'Ar Lan y Môr'. Singing is the only real thing the Welsh have in our locker, and we felt it was the most respectful way to respond to their cultural welcome. As Welsh-speaking veterans of countless eisteddfodau, Ken Owens and I led the charge, with Craig Mitchell adding harmonies more befitting of a fresh-faced choirboy than a lumpy, grizzled prop. He was a man of few words, but could certainly belt out a song. Halfers's enthusiasm for the singing was entirely dependent on how much he'd drunk. Give him a few beers and he'd soar towards the upper registers like a prepubescent Aled Jones. Ask him to do it sober, and you'd be lucky to hear him above the hum of the air conditioning. Mike Phillips alone can explode the myth that all Welshmen are good singers. The Bancyfelin-raised farmer's son sounds more like a braying cow than a human being, and is completely tone-deaf. It's reassuring to know there's *something* he isn't good at.

Warby's image as the ultimate clean-living teetotaller seemed to rub off on the rest of the squad. Our public image, as depicted in the New Zealand press, was that of a loveable band of impeccably behaved tourists, who charmed the locals with our impromptu choir sessions. It was in stark contrast to their portrayal of the English squad as a loutish, disorderly rabble. Neither was particularly accurate, but as stories of England's late nights and excessive drinking began to fill up the back pages, the myth of Wales as irreproachable paragons of virtue grew. It was nonsense. I'm not saying we were knocking it back 24/7, but we had our share of boozy nights. During the first week in Wellington, a group of us had enjoyed a particularly heavy session in Mermaids, a glorified strip club with girls swimming around naked in an enormous tank. Had photos of the lads there leaked out, the carefully crafted PR tapestry would have unravelled dramatically. The difference was that the media's lens was focused far more sharply on England, and their catalogue of indiscretions piled up into a pretty damning rap sheet by the end of their campaign.

Professionalism isn't just about doing your recovery, eating the right food or getting the right amount of sleep; it's about making the effort to form relationships with your fellow players. Rugby has to be in the business of creating good people, not just good rugby players, and I sometimes feel the scales are tilted too far towards the latter. As I've said, members of a team who laugh, drink and hang out together are more likely to have each other's backs when the chips are down and the flak is flying. That's why I was a little scornful of Adam Beard's 'wet and dry' chart. Everyone put a tenner in the kitty and those who hadn't touched a drop of alcohol by the end of the tour could split the winnings. It was all about willpower and resisting temptation, and it was the safest investment Warby will ever have made, because he wasn't even going to look at a pint of beer, let alone drink one. I could see where they were coming from because we were training hard and they didn't want us to jeopardise our recovery, but if having a few beers brought us closer together, then it was worth it as far as I was concerned. Aside from being unnecessary, it was inherently flawed because of its reliance on honesty. Melon's name was still in the dry section weeks into the tournament, which was as laughable as it was untrue.

We were in Taupo when the New Zealand press started really laying into England, and we walked into our team room one morning to find it covered with damning newspaper articles. No one mentioned it, but the message from management was clear: don't fall into the same trap. I have no doubt there was a greater appetite among the New Zealand press to try to ensnare the England boys over and above anyone else. I had it on good authority that a senior member of the Ireland squad had been in the same 'dwarf-throwing' bar, and had to be dragged from a hedge, where he'd been found paralytically drunk and unconscious. There wasn't even a whiff of that in the press. It was England's heads they wanted, and while they were being mercilessly hunted down, I had little sympathy for them. If you go out and behave as they did, it will eventually come back to haunt you.

I'd never beaten the Springboks and we had them up first in the tournament, in front of a sell-out crowd in Wellington. In keeping with its reputation as the windy city, the conditions in New Zealand's capital were damp and blustery. South Africa were the defending champions, and strong favourites, considering Wales had only beaten them once in more than a century of trying. We were expecting a no-frills forward-oriented onslaught, and that's exactly what we got. Two big, powerful teams slugging it out in an attritional, heavyweight battle. Schalk Burger was a gnarly totem of their physical, in-your-face approach, so it filled me with satisfaction to bury him early on with a dominant, bone-shuddering tackle. In a tight, tense game, our forwards more than matched them up front. Bomb defanged the Beast once again, and our back-row trio thundered repeatedly into contact, rocking their much-vaunted opponents back on their heels.

We thought we were heading for victory when Toby Faletau scored, but they came back triumphantly in the last quarter. I was partly at fault for their winning try, and was furious with myself. I was too narrow defending a ruck and allowed Francois Hougaard too much space outside me. As he crossed, I swore inwardly to myself. As defensive captain, I felt embarrassed and was dreading the Shaun Edwards backlash. It was one of the first things you thought of when you missed a tackle, and I knew I wouldn't be spared, especially as it proved the decisive score. A bit of fuss was made retrospectively over James Hook's fourteenth-minute penalty that everyone bar the referee thought had gone over. Warby was kicking himself in the changing room for not having contested it, but it was pointless crying over spilt milk.

As it transpired, losing by a point turned out to be a blessing. The day before our second game, against Samoa, we gathered in a bar to watch Ireland upset the odds by beating Australia. The result flipped the draw, meaning we'd most probably face Ireland rather than the Wallabies if we made it through the pool stages. My heart beat a little faster: our route to the final was now that much easier. Our record against the Six Nations sides was far better than our record against the southern-hemisphere big three.

It would all count for nothing, though, if we didn't beat Samoa, a team which understandably sends a chill down the spine of any Welsh rugby supporter. Twice before, Wales had met them in World Cups, and twice had suffered inconceivable defeats. The losses in 1991 and 1999 still rank among the biggest upsets in the tournament's history. The scheduling meant we'd have a full week to prepare for this one, which enraged Samoa's outspoken centre Eliota Fuimaono-Sapolu, causing him to let rip with a furious tirade about inequality between the tier-one nations and the rest. Samoa had been left with a mere four days to prepare following their opening victory over Namibia, which allowed them precious little time to recover. Given that it's often difficult to walk the day after a bruising Test match, an extra few days' recovery can make a world of difference. I understood his frustration, but his cause was somewhat undermined by some pretty unsavoury comparisons to slavery and the Holocaust.

We knew what to expect from Samoa: brutal, uncompromising physicality and a predilection for juddering, bone-crunching tackles. Our forwards coach Robin McBryde was once crowned Wales's strongest man, and had never been one to shy away from a physical confrontation. He insisted we should fight fire with fire, instructing us to 'T-bone' our opponents. That essentially means running hard and straight *at* someone, rather than *round* them. It might be considered imprudent to deliberately run headlong into some of the hardest tacklers in world rugby, but we were determined to show no deference in the physicality stakes. Early in the first half, I found myself in possession and on a collision course with Seilala Mapusua, the defensive rock in the heart of their midfield. He lined me up and threw his full weight into the tackle, but my momentum sent him crashing to the deck. It remains one of the best carries of my career, and it sent a defiant message: we're going *through* you lads; just try and stop us.

As much as we matched them physically, we were a shadow of the organised, disciplined side that had faced South Africa. Balls were being dropped, passes were being knocked on and we were incapable of stringing more than a few phases together. Jogging in at the interval, we found ourselves 10–6 behind and staring down the barrel of another seismic upset.

Hooker Huw Bennett delivered a tub-thumping half-time speech, reminding us of all the hard work we'd put in to reach this point, and finishing with what amounted to an order: 'We are *not* going home now.' I had a massive amount of respect for 'Benny'. More than anyone else, he'd put his body on the line. He would empty himself physically every time he took to the field, and those words couldn't have come from a more committed bloke. My mind drifted back to the time he was retching and spewing at the side of the pitch in Spala, and I thought, *We've been to hell and back. It* has *to have been for something.*

It remained tight and niggly in the second half, but we eventually took the lead through a Shane Williams try. The remaining ten minutes were unbearably tense as the mental demons began to rise up and whisper in our ears. It took a bit of old-fashioned skulduggery from Bomb to secure the victory. I won't pretend for a second to understand what goes on in the front row, but he explained afterwards that he'd hoodwinked the referee with one of his Jedi mind tricks. He'd basically scrummaged illegally downwards, forcing a collapse that appeared to anyone but a scrum nause to have been their loosehead's fault. I dread to think what would have happened if they'd won the ball back and launched one final, desperate attack.

We had a massive night out, making our way up Hamilton's main drag on a marathon pub crawl, finishing up in a bar rammed with supporters. A Welsh girl latched on to Mike Phillips, pestering him relentlessly about why he took so long to get the ball away from the base of rucks. He showed remarkable patience for at least half an hour before inevitably metamorphosing into 'Spike' and calmly but deliberately pouring a full pint over her head. Her hair, all done up for the night out, was now plastered across her face in dripping wet tendrils, and beer was trickling steadily from the ends onto her outfit. Had it happened in Cardiff, things may have escalated, but no bouncers leapt to her defence, nothing kicked off and no one was escorted out. Once she'd recovered from the shock, she took it surprisingly well, considering. Everyone has a breaking point; Phillsy's threshold is just a little lower than others.

I sat out the third game, against Namibia, and had the pleasure of watching from the stands, with the majestic Mount Taranaki soaring skywards in the background. Benny and I roomed together that week and we hired bikes to explore the coastline around New Plymouth. We were very different people, from different backgrounds, and wouldn't normally have gravitated towards one another, but we really bonded that week. People like him and Luke Charteris were very much under the radar, but absolutely vital to the morale of the group. As positive, upbeat blokes they acted as the glue in a squad full of big characters, and they were two of the very best Test players I've played alongside. That's the beauty of a team dynamic: everyone contributes *something*. Whether you bring the energy, the positivity, the humour or the perspective, everyone has a role to play.

We stayed in Taupo in between the Namibia and Fiji games, and I was denied the chance of doing a sky dive by the schoolmasterly Alan Phillips. If Wales's starting centre turned an ankle coming into land, he explained, Warren Gatland would have been none too pleased. I was hugely disappointed as, having done a bungee jump over the lake the previous summer, I'd been keen to 'complete the set'. Instead, we spent our time relaxing by the lake and taking in the sights. Adam Beard was beginning to get paranoid about our diets and started strictly policing our meals. One evening, I ordered a delicious-looking seafood platter which was promptly intercepted and sent back to the kitchen. Beardy knew that if anyone was struck down with food poisoning, he'd be held responsible. The following night, we were invited to a spectacular Maori banquet and treated to the local delicacy of suckling pig slow-cooked in an underground oven. He was happy enough for us to gorge on platefuls of greasy roast pork, but we weren't to go within sniffing distance of a prawn.

The media did its best to create a dramatic narrative around the Fiji game, drawing parallels with 2007, when the Pacific Islanders had dumped Wales out of the tournament. In truth, this Fiji side was a pale imitation of its predecessors and we blew them off the park, romping to a 66–0 victory. As I strolled under the posts for the first of my two tries, a bloke behind the dead-ball line spread his arms wide, waiting to envelop me in a hug. I didn't notice and completely blanked him. I later discovered it was Michael Press, a good mate of mine who was out there doing all the advertising signage at the venues. While I maintain that I never saw him, he's never quite forgiven me for the public snub.

As much as I preferred the prospect of Ireland to Australia in the quarter-finals, I was consumed by nerves ahead of the match. We hadn't played brilliantly in the pool stages and had yet to deliver a complete performance. Ireland were a well-oiled machine, with a generation of world-class players approaching their peak: Paul O'Connell, Brian O'Driscoll, Ronan O'Gara, Jamie Heaslip, to name just a few. They were on the crest of a wave and felt it was their time.

The nerves became further frayed when a mix-up at the hotel caused us to arrive at the ground late. The Ireland bus had travelled to the stadium first under a police escort, and we were made to wait until the motorcade returned to escort us in. It was taking an age, and after we'd been sitting on the drive with the engine idling for half an hour, Alan Phillips pulled rank and ordered the driver to set off without the escort. He was fuming and spent the entire journey staring nervously out of the window as a single bead of sweat glistened on his temple. It led to an almighty row between him and the police liaison officer at the ground which very nearly came to blows. The feisty hooker of yesteryear momentarily returned, and he got right up in this guy's face. By this point, there was less than an hour until kick-off, and everything was feeling increasingly rushed. I wasn't able to enjoy my usual routine of wandering onto the pitch to absorb my surroundings. I had to get straight to the changing room and prepare for the warm-up. It was business time.

Despite the imperfect build-up, the first two minutes of the game were among the best of my career. Rhys Priestland put up a huge bomb and I chased for all I was worth, out-jumping Rob Kearney to claim it in the air. Shane Williams made ground down the right before play came back my way. I called for the ball out the back, and Brian O'Driscoll came flying out of the line, enabling me to put Foxy away into their 22. As Phillsy was digging the ball out of the next ruck, I shouted to him, 'Mike! I'm coming.' He'd have been expecting to offload to a big lumbering forward folding round the corner, but in a moment of clarity, a sequence unfolded in my brain before it did on the pitch. Like a chess player anticipating a few moves into the future, I knew that I *had* to take that line.

When Phillsy picked up the ball, he could feel me thundering towards him. It's hard for the opposition in such a scenario, because they're looking at a pod of forwards, anticipating the close-quarter carry, while also trying to guard against strike runners, like me, coming from deep. Timing is everything. The later I came, the greater the chance of breaking down the door. An early, mistimed run could easily see me clatter into one of my own forwards. Phillsy popped the ball up delicately enough that I didn't have to break stride and then, *bang*, I smashed into Donncha O'Callaghan at full tilt, sending him flying into next week. One of their biggest, meanest forwards reduced to rubble. It was one of the sweetest carries of my career. Two phases later, Shane was over in the corner for the opening try. Those first few minutes had set the tone, and we never looked back.

What followed was one of the most complete Welsh performances of the professional era. We were too physical, too powerful and too aggressive, and Ireland simply couldn't handle it. Our backline, in particular, was irresistible. It was there that our best ball-carriers could be found. When we gathered a head of steam, the likes of George North, Jonathan Davies and myself offered more thrust and propulsion than the piano-pushers up front. Taulupe Faletau was strong but more of a rapier than a sledgehammer. Warby's strengths were centred on the close-quarter niggly stuff, and Dan Lydiate was an amazing defender, but carrying wasn't his forte. So while we did much of the heavy lifting in that regard, the back row as a trio were free to concentrate on their strengths and they absolutely dominated their opposite numbers.

Stephen Ferris, Jamie Heaslip and Sean O'Brien were a much-vaunted trio, but Shaun Edwards had declared pre-match that he wouldn't swap any one of them for Lyds, Warby or Toby. It wasn't empty rhetoric; he really meant it, and they proved him right. Shaun and Lyds had been working behind the scenes on the 'chop tackle', a pioneering technique that involved tackling around the ankles. It's horribly disorienting for the victim, who often finds himself flat on his back and facing the wrong way in a nanosecond. Sean O'Brien was the reigning European Player of the Year and had been terrorising defences with rampaging, bullocking runs that often sucked in two or three defenders. He'd been gobbling up the yards all season, but in that game he made a total of two metres with ball in hand. The reason was simple: Dan Lydiate. The farmer's son from mid-Wales was built like a combine harvester and spent the evening mowing him down before he was able to get into his stride. For a guy of Lyds's height to get that low and dive horizontally at people's shins is as unique as it is risky. It's easy to get stepped if your timing's off, but his rarely ever was. He was the ultimate predator: lying in wait, ready to nail you to the deck. I witnessed several of those collisions at close range, and you almost experienced the pain by proxy; you could feel the breath being knocked out of his helpless victims.

During the week, Howlers had repeatedly said that he wanted to frustrate Ronan O'Gara so much that he'd be substituted after sixty minutes. ROG was one of the best in the business at the spiral touch-finder; if you gave him time and space, he'd drill you into the corners all night long. He had an infuriating ability to identify space in the backfield and put the ball exactly where he wanted it. Over the years, whether for club or country, I'd lost count of the number of times he'd threaded the ball through the gap between our winger and full-back, watching smugly as it bobbled into touch. Gats and Howley were all too aware of this and had devised a 'two full-back' strategy to counter it. Two of our back-three players were to position themselves permanently in the 15-metre channels, so that whenever O'Gara shaped to kick, he'd see a body instead of space. It worked a treat, narrowing his options and knocking him out of his rhythm. He's a feisty, emotional bloke, and as his frustrations began to bubble to the surface, he was given the old shepherd's crook. Glancing at the stadium clock when his number came up, I noticed it was just ticking onto sixty minutes. Nostradamus Howley had called it.

While we dominated every facet, we never built a commanding lead, and as the game entered its final quarter, we were only a score ahead, courtesy of a classy show-and-go from Phillsy. A few minutes after O'Gara's departure, we were patiently working through the phases outside Ireland's 22 when the ball came to me. The midfield looked a little congested, so I ran diagonally infield, into the maw of their back row. If our secret defensive weapon was the chop tackle, theirs was 'the choke'. I was enveloped by three Irishmen determined to keep me upright and turn over possession. I pumped my legs like mad, trying to keep moving so the ref couldn't call a maul. A few of our players bound on and we started crabbing forwards for what seemed like an eternity. I was really worried the ref was going to award a scrum to Ireland, and that I'd be held accountable for failing to get to the floor. A turnover at that point could have been critical. Somehow, in the midst of it all, I managed to wriggle free and present the ball. In the blink of an eye it was shifted right to Jonathan Davies, who looked up to see a panicking Cian Healy in front of him. A nimble centre against a leaden-footed prop in open field is a non-contest. Foxy exploited the advantage, racing around Healy to touch down. It proved the decisive score.

I was absolutely battered after that game; I had a nasty, swollen black eye, and a badly broken nose, but I'd never been happier. It was such a special day and without doubt one of my best memories in a Welsh jersey. Ireland had really fancied themselves and were visibly shellshocked by the outcome. We'd been tactically smart and our execution had been slick, but it was our sheer power that had blown them away. We felt indestructible, and they had no answers. Lyds and Johnny Sexton became quite friendly when they both moved to Paris a few years later, and Johnny confessed to him that they'd been complacent heading into the match. As for us, we'd banked all the hard work from Poland and chose that day to cash the cheque. During our lap of honour, an obvious thought revealed itself: we were in a World Cup semi-final. All the euphoria to that point had centred on the fact we'd beaten Ireland in such scintillating style. It hadn't really occurred to me that we were in the semis. There were four teams left standing. Three weeks earlier we'd been staring down the barrel against Samoa; now we were 160 minutes away from ultimate glory. Up next: France.

Strolling around Auckland a few days later, I happened upon a newsagent with the papers displayed outside. A headline singled me out as Wales's danger man. France's big, barnstorming centre, Aurélien Rougerie, had declared that stopping me was the key to stopping Wales. I was well aware of my reputation as one of our principal carriers, but that brought home to me what I meant to this team. Not only was my country in a World Cup semi-final, but the spotlight was being shone directly on yours truly. It was a timely ego boost, but it also nudged open the box in my mind where I stored all my doubts and fears. There was no hiding place now: the world was watching.

In the French camp, meanwhile, it seemed there was a mutiny underway, with rumours suggesting that the head coach, Marc Lièvremont, was a lame duck whose influence had entirely drained away. Mutinies and internal coups are far from unusual in French sport, however, and there's something in the Gallic temperament that reacts positively to chaos and disorder, so we were careful not to read too much into it. They'd scraped through the pool stages, losing heavily to New Zealand and, against all odds, to Tonga, but when it had mattered, they'd knocked England over in the quarters. So, to quote that hackneyed old cliché about French rugby, we had no idea which team would turn up in the semi-final.

In a change that upset both parties, the French team were moved out of the Auckland Skytower hotel, so that we could move in. They were angry at the unnecessary disruption, and Warren resented being forced to move to a conspicuous city-centre base ahead of the biggest game of our lives. He'd have preferred an out-of-town location where we could have kept a lower profile. Personally, I enjoyed being close to the fans, and under the microscope. It's a classic Welsh trait to shy away from the limelight, but I loved it. We felt like a rock band as we battled our way through the legions of fans lining the hotel concourse, all of whom were giddy with excitement. Wales had never reached the final of the World Cup, and the belief that we might just make history was growing with every passing hour.

Nothing summed up the surreal nature of the week better than Boris Johnson calling Adam Jones to wish him good luck. An Eton-educated future prime minister ringing up a working-class boy from the Swansea Valley to chew the fat. Johnson had referred to Bomb as 'Cro-Magnon Man' in his *Daily Telegraph* column and had clearly developed something of a man-crush on him. I'm not sure what they spoke about – as far as I'm aware, Bomb comes from a family of dyed-in-the-wool Labour voters – but I remember the moment he casually announced to the boys in the team room that he'd been on the phone to Boris Johnson. 'Who the f***'s that, butt?' came the reply from an unimpressed Paul James.

There wasn't an ounce of fear or trepidation on game day. We knew if we put our best game on the park, we'd win. Their side was good on paper, but if we were firing on all cylinders, we couldn't lose. The enormity of the occasion was reinforced when Thumper told us 60,000 people had piled into the Millennium Stadium back home to watch the game on the big screen. That was more than the capacity of Eden Park where the *actual* game was being played. I'm not sure there's another country on earth that could count on that level of support.

Within seven minutes, we'd lost our Cro-Magnon Man. His calf gave way during a scrum and at a stroke we were denuded of our most destructive scrummager. With Paul James on the bench, it was a loss we could reasonably absorb, but in less than ten minutes our world was turned upside down and inside out.

France had been awarded an attacking line-out just inside our half, and I was standing 15 metres back in the defensive line. It was won cleanly off the top and their diminutive winger, Vincent Clerc, ran a line off Dimitri Yachvili's hip, hoping to thread through a gap at the tail of the line-out. Sam Warburton had anticipated it brilliantly and, planting his feet, launched himself into a powerful, offensive tackle. Eighteen stone of prime Welsh beef against a gossamer slice of French carpaccio. The physical mismatch was so stark that Clerc flipped over in mid-air and clattered to the deck in a jumble of flailing limbs. It triggered a furious reaction from the French pack, several of whom started swinging, before a shrill blast of the whistle restored temporary order. In the chaotic aftermath of clenched fists, flexed muscles and tugged jerseys, few of us noticed Alain Rolland calmly but deliberately raising his red card. The TV cameras missed it, as did the majority of the crowd.

I struggled to process what had happened. Red cards were a rarity back then, the ultimate sanction reserved for the very worst incidents of foul play. Repeated replays had shown Warburton's tackle to have been dangerous, but the outcome was accidental rather than deliberate. Warby was a fearless warrior who took pride in his physical presence, but he wasn't dirty or malicious. It was not as if he'd lost his head and thrown a punch. Had it been someone his own size coming through that channel, it would have been a textbook tackle.

Whatever the rights and wrongs of the decision, we had to deal with the reality of being a man down. We'd practised training with twelve or thirteen defenders, preparing for a worst-case scenario, but we never thought we'd have to deal with it in a game of this magnitude. Those of a negative disposition may have rolled over, but the spirit in this group was strong. Once the shock had subsided, we gathered in a huddle and told ourselves that nothing should change. We were still in the fight; we just needed to defend a bit more softly, to keep playing when we had the ball, to ensure our kick-chase game was precise and, most importantly, we needed to keep our discipline. We'd obviously miss Warby's ferocity, leadership and breakdown expertise, but we had enough nous to navigate our way through this. As sorry as I felt for him, especially when I saw his blank, forlorn expression on the big screen moments later, I knew we had to park the sympathy and get on with it. The best way for us to salve his conscience was to win.

Not long after, as we were lining up in midfield, Foxy turned to me, looking confused, and asked, with a note of incredulity in his voice, 'Was Warby sent off?' I followed his gaze up to the big screen where a red card had appeared beneath 'Wales' on the onscreen graphic. I laughed and replied, 'Are you f***ing serious?' In all the confusion, Foxy was still under the impression it had merely been a sin-binning.

The rest of the match unfolded in an almost dreamlike haze and I felt, at times, like a spectator outside of my own body. Time passed incredibly quickly, and clarity gave way to a more blurry, illusory reality. I'd occasionally look at the clock to discover fifteen minutes had passed, but I'd struggle to remember what I'd done, whether I'd hit any rucks or made any tackles. My usual sense of photographic recall abandoned me, and the game became a succession of small, atomised incidents as opposed to a cohesive whole.

Bizarrely, the red card seemed to inhibit France more than it did us. Rather than cut loose and exploit the one-man advantage, they tightened up and got more nervy as the match wore on. As the last quarter approached, Mike Phillips pulled out his ace card, finding a gap where there appeared to be none to waltz through the French defence for a brilliant solo try. It was classic Mike, a mixture of opportunism and audacity, and I was convinced that that was it: that we'd turned the tables and conjured a spectacular rearguard win against all the odds. But the conversion bounced off the posts, leaving us a point adrift.

With six minutes left, Leigh Halfpenny's 50-metre penalty attempt fell agonisingly short, but still we came, refusing to buckle or throw in the towel. We laid siege to the French line, hurling our bodies into theirs, probing for a crack, a gap or a weakness, summoning every last ounce of energy in an attempt to breach the wall. We were making a dent here, a chink there, but their ramparts were holding firm. Like a prizefighter with an iron jaw, they were soaking up everything we threw at them. Eventually, overcome with fatigue, we started going backwards, the life draining from our legs and the hope fading from our hearts.

Warby's red card remains the defining image from the game, but for me it was the final pass. Deep into injury time, Stephen Jones delivered a short ball to me on an angle, and as I thundered into contact, I spilled it. Although we'd failed to breach the impregnable French defence for thirty lung-busting phases before that, I suddenly felt the weight of the world on my shoulders. I can't imagine anyone remembers who dropped the last pass, but it haunted me for some time afterwards. What might have happened if I'd held on to it and we'd worked another five or six phases? The truth is, we were out on our feet. There was no thrust, no momentum, no dynamism; we were all running on empty.

When the final whistle blew, I collapsed onto my back and shut my eyes. My brain was whirring, conjuring fractured memories of the journey we'd been on over the past eighteen months. It felt like watching a videotape on fast-forward, spooling through all the significant way markers along the route: Spala, South Africa, Samoa, Ireland. Each episode felt like a flashbulb going off in my mind, and the overwhelming question that accompanied it all was, *What was it all worth?*

The sorrow and emptiness of the changing room was something I'll never forget. It was almost haunting. The coaches were hovering around, quietly consoling the players, but no one knew quite what to say or do. 'Shit happens, mate' was the least imaginative thing to say to Warby, but it's all I could muster when our glazed eyes met. He was smiling superficially, but he was dead behind the eyes. He gave a brief speech, praising the lads and apologising for his misdemeanour, but nobody bore him any ill will. It certainly hadn't cost us the match. To this day, people continue to debate whether or not we failed to strike the killer blow in those last five minutes. Gatland maintains there was a moment when the drop goal was on and we didn't take it.

I'm not a kicker, so I'm not going to profess to know when that moment actually occurs, nor am I going to point the finger at anyone. Those people whose job it is to drop goals will make their own judgements about whether they seized the moment or froze. Nobody is going to burn more energy thinking about it than they will themselves. If anyone has any individual regrets, they'll have to live with them. I carry plenty with me. I made a half-break outside Imanol Harinordoquy in the first half and my offload hit Foxy in the face. He'd have been under the sticks if he'd caught the ball, but my pass wasn't delicate enough. You fixate on these things and they remain with you, lurking at the back of your mind.

When we eventually returned to the hotel and shut out the outside world, my roomie, Luke Charteris, and I looked at one another with tears in our eyes and hugged it out. The emotions we'd held in check at the ground came to the fore. It was a necessary moment of catharsis. Across the corridor, Leigh Halfpenny was inconsolable, replaying the missed kick over and over in his mind. It had always been a long shot at half the length of the pitch, but his standards were so high that he regarded any miss, regardless of the difficulty or conditions, as a failure. Foxy had to virtually drag him to the bar to get a few beers inside him. He'd just wanted to curl up and wallow in his misery.

The day after, Gats thanked us for our efforts, told us he was proud and said, 'Lads, I don't want to see you for three days. Go and do whatever the hell you want.' A few boys went to the races, but myself, Charts, Alun Wyn and Benny, seeking a bit of solitude, jumped on the boat to Waiheke Island. We had a long lunch at Mudbrick Vineyard overlooking the sun-dappled Hauraki Gulf, before embarking on a haphazard pub crawl around the island. After the disappointment we'd suffered, it was the perfect tonic. Sitting with the lads, reminiscing, talking nonsense and taking in the spectacular views made the world seem a lot less bleak.

A question I've fielded perhaps more than any other in my career is whether I think we would have won the World Cup had we made it through to the final. France came within a whisker of beating New Zealand, and Welsh fans have long theorised that we'd have seen them off given the opportunity. It's a question I'm not equipped to answer, because I've never watched the final and probably never will. It's pointless to speculate and doing so only adds to the hurt. I'm extremely proud of the Herculean effort the lads put in to try to pull a victory out of the fire, but I'll go to my grave regretting the outcome.

13

GRAND SLAM

There was an air of hushed anticipation as we waited for the identity of our mystery speaker to be revealed. Team manager Alan Phillips bounded in looking very pleased with himself, and said, 'Right, boys, I told you I'd deliver the goods. Can you put your hands together and give a nice warm welcome to . . . Howard Marks.'

England had been inviting motivational speakers to their training camps. Footballer Gary Neville had delivered a talk on the culture of success, and rugby league legend Kevin Sinfield had offered his unique insights on creating a winning dynasty. They'd also lined up a former army corporal who'd been shot in the face during active service in Iraq. By all accounts the talks had been inspirational and very well received. Some of our senior players had piped up that maybe we'd benefit from something similar, and names of prominent Welsh figures like Joe Calzaghe and Ryan Giggs had been bandied around as potential options.

Leave it to me, Thumper had said, and a few weeks later, to minimal fanfare, the world's most notorious drug dealer shuffled into our team room, looking like a cross between Keith Richards and an undernourished tramp. Mr Nice himself. Thumper, rather than casting the net far and wide, had simply picked up the phone to someone from his home town of Kenfig Hill. It was so gloriously Welsh, and could easily have been a deleted scene from the cult film *Twin Town*.

We didn't learn much about how to beat Ireland that coming weekend, but we did learn which country harvested the purest strain of marijuana, and where the world's most beautiful women could be found. (Afghanistan and Argentina, if you're interested.) We trooped out of the hotel after the talk to see Howard standing there, leaning against the wall like Wooderson from *Dazed and Confused*, shrouded in a cloud of ganja smoke and holding a massive doobie. This was the start of our preparation for the 2012 Six Nations.

Rewind a couple of weeks, and Foxy and I had been wrestling on a barren, windswept beach in sub-zero temperatures. The word 'baltic' has entered the lexicon as a catch-all description for 'bloody freezing'. We were *literally* on the Baltic coast, with stinging offshore winds turning our skin to sandpaper, icy blasts numbing our extremities and sand grazing every exposed surface as we grappled unenthusiastically in the bleak winter gloom. All the while a smirking Rob Howley stood watch, protected from the elements by a thick winter coat, padded gloves and a woollen hat pulled down over his ears. Every now and then he'd blow his whistle and bark an order. 'Commando crawls.' 'Burpees.' 'Down-ups.' 'Press-ups.' 'Sit-ups.' It was hell.

Rob was normally something of a good cop to Warren's bad. We'd all take a punishing from Warren or Shaun without question: their very aura demanded obsequious obedience. Rob was different. He was more of a mate, and didn't inhabit the enforcer role nearly as convincingly. While I wanted to give it 100 per cent commitment, there was a part of me thinking, *Come on, Rob. F*** off.*

Jonathan Davies and I were both carrying niggles, so in lieu of a full squad training session, Warren had ordered Rob to take us to the beach and beast us. The session lasted an hour, and by the end I couldn't feel my hands, catch a ball or walk any faster than a snail's pace. The saving grace was that there was no one around to witness it. Nobody would willingly go to the beach in those conditions. We got on with it, but there was an element of artifice attached to the whole enterprise: Rob playing the role of psychotic sergeant major, with us as the powerless supplicants. Foxy and I spent a lot of our career training together, and while we were never in direct competition, we always wanted to do our best in each other's company. At the end of the hour, Rob asked if we'd like to walk into the Baltic Sea, in our pants, to kick-start our muscle recovery. A kind of organic cryotherapy session. Thanks, Rob, but no thanks.

This was Gdansk. Bleaker and more remote than Spala, and arguably more punishing. After our World Cup heartache, we desperately wanted to win the 2012 Six Nations, and this was a necessary step along the way. Spala had set the bar in terms of intensity, and Warren was adamant we weren't to dip beneath it. To stand still, he'd say, was to regress, so we immersed ourselves in the seventh circle of hell once more. The dark places we travelled to would serve us well during the Six Nations campaign.

We had Ireland first, in Dublin: a re-run of the World Cup quarter-final. They were gunning for revenge, and sniffed a chance against our injury-ravaged squad. Our forward pack had been decimated, with Dan Lydiate, Gethin Jenkins, 'Smiler' Rees, Alun Wyn Jones and Luke Charteris all sidelined. Shane Williams had also bowed out the previous autumn, having scored a try in the last minute of his last Test match. I was the first player he saw when he leapt up to celebrate, and I hugged him so hard I struggled to let go, because I knew it would be the last time he'd wear that red shirt. He remains the best pound-for-pound player I've shared a field with, and I knew his absence was going to leave an enormous hole.

Shane's replacement couldn't have been cast from a more different mould. A couple of years earlier, I'd gone to watch UWIC play a midweek university match in Cyncoed, sipping a few pints from the sidelines with some of my uni buddies. My attention had been drawn to a gangly winger in UWIC colours with a foppish mop of curly hair. He was tall and athletic-looking, but moved in an awkward and ungainly manner, not entirely sure where he was supposed to stand or what he was meant to do. Several minutes in, the opposition fly-half launched a cross-field kick that landed directly in his arms, and he took off on a lightning-fast arc, weaving past the flailing arms of at least ten defenders before dotting down, unruffled and untouched, in the in-goal area. I wouldn't have been surprised if he'd left cartoon-style scorch marks in his wake.

A year later, the same guy rocked up to Cardiff Blues training, introducing himself as Alex Cuthbert. He was a bit of a space cadet and every inch the student, and we got on immediately. He was raw and underdeveloped at that stage but, jeez, was he quick. After a year or two spent honing his physique in the gym, adding some muscle to his gangly frame, he was primed for Test rugby, and by the time the 2012 Six Nations rolled around he was ready to step into the shoes of Wales's greatest winger of all time.

*   *   *

There was tension in the Dublin tunnel. We'd shattered Ireland's dreams a few months earlier and they hadn't forgotten it. Both sides were lined up facing ahead, and although there were existing friendships and several of us had toured together as Lions, this was not the time for conviviality. A few fierce glances were exchanged as some of our more volatile forwards did their best to out-psych their opposite numbers. I've always been more inclined to tip my opposite number the wink in these situations. To me, that's more psychologically advantageous than staring them out or, in the manner of the French sides of the eighties, head-butting a wall. At this point, I'm focused; I know my plays and I back my skills and fitness. For me, this was the moment for retrenchment, the quiet collection of one's thoughts and banishment of extraneous noise. The calm before the storm.

We started superbly, working an overlap on the blind side, and Priest delivered a sumptuous offload to put Foxy in at the corner, only for Ireland to strike back, building a 10–5 lead by half-time. It was Cuthy's first Six Nations start and they'd clearly planned to target him in the air. He was devastatingly quick but, by his own admission, not the most accomplished footballer. I'd seen him kick the ball many times in Blues training and it was rarely a pretty sight. Early on, Johnny Sexton angled a long diagonal kick into his corner. I panicked as Cuthy picked up the ball and shaped to kick, throwing it up in the air rather than dropping it on his foot like a natural kicker. I winced as he swung his leg clumsily towards it, but miraculously his foot connected with the sweet spot, sending a majestic spiral bomb soaring into the sky. The ball travelled effortlessly from our 22 to theirs, then bounced daintily into touch. Rhys Priestland, Jonathan Davies and myself looked at each other in disbelief before collapsing into laughter. When Cuthy had stopped admiring the arc of his perfect kick, he did the same. Ireland were understandably less keen to kick to him after that.

Our second try was born of pace and power. Our back division was continuing where it had left off at the World Cup, taking it to the line at every opportunity. I'd run a decoy angle into the heart of the defence, and Priest would hit Cuthy or George North out the back. It was pure physics: when you're sending 100 kg players to the line at that pace, you're *going* to cross the advantage line. Once you've splintered that wall, the path to the try line becomes much clearer. We did exactly that off a line-out fifteen minutes into the second half. I ran the decoy and George thundered into the line like a rampaging bull, trampling through the tackle of centre Fergus McFadden before delivering the most delicate of offloads to Foxy. It was the ultimate combination of brute force and elegance. Jon did the rest, galloping all the way to the line. Tommy Bowe sneaked past George for Ireland's second, but momentum swung back our way when George bulldozed his way through heavy traffic for one of his own.

As is often the way with Ireland–Wales encounters, a controversial incident decided the outcome. We'd survived a ten-minute period earlier in the half when Bradley Davies had been sin-binned for a reckless tip-tackle on fellow second row Donnacha Ryan. He'd leapt to Adam Jones's defence at a ruck, dumping Ryan unceremoniously on his head in a move more redolent of the wrestling ring than the rugby field. Given what had happened to Sam at the World Cup, he was lucky not to have seen red.

Two minutes from time, as they were defending their slender one-point lead, Stephen Ferris was penalised for a tip-tackle on Ian Evans. It was nowhere near as bad as Bradley's and I wouldn't have protested in the slightest had referee Wayne Barnes waved play on, but he brandished his yellow card for a second time, despatching a furious Ferris to the bin. Ian Evans, never one to miss an opportunity, gave Fez a patronising tap on the head as he trudged to the sideline.

Step up, Leigh Halfpenny. His second opportunity in four months to snatch victory from the jaws of defeat. This time, with the ghosts of Eden Park no doubt haunting his thoughts, he stroked it coolly between the uprights. Leigh's an undemonstrative bloke at the best of times, but the way he gritted his teeth and clenched his fist as the ball sailed over the crossbar spoke volumes. It was the fifth and final time the lead had changed hands, and he'd delivered the killer blow. No one had blamed him for missing the kick against France, but he'd blamed himself. This was redemption. The ghosts had been silenced.

In the bar that night, Powelly, Foxy, Bradley and myself were watching the replay of the game on the hotel's big screen. Just as the ruck that led to Bradley's horrendous tackle had formed, he interrupted the conversation to point at the screen and said, 'Boys, have a look at this. I honestly don't think it was that bad.' We watched in silence as multiple replays showed him pile-driving Ryan into the Aviva Stadium turf, using his head like a pneumatic drill. Then, with impeccable comic timing, Brad drained his glass, placed it on the bar and said, 'See you in five weeks then, boys.'

He was actually banned for seven weeks, much to the chagrin of Warren Gatland, who'd publicly lambasted him for such a needless act of indiscipline. His name was added to the growing absentee list ahead of the Scotland game, along with Sam Warburton, who'd picked up a dead leg. Ryan Jones was moved into the second row and Aaron Shingler was handed his debut at open-side flanker, a position he'd never played in before. Disruption aside, there was a sense of invincibility whenever we played Scotland. We didn't feel remotely vulnerable. Dan Lydiate was back and doing what he did best, marauding around rearranging people's ribcages, and others stepped out of the shadows. If George had basked in the Dublin limelight, Cuthy did so in Cardiff, announcing himself as a genuine international class talent. He scored a beauty of a try in the second half, before creating another for Leigh Halfpenny with one of his trademark arcing runs. Halfers converted both, as well as scoring a second of his own, to round off a devastating fifteen-minute spell which saw us open up an unassailable 27–6 lead.

The only other thing from the game that sticks in my memory is the appearance off the bench of a pale angry Scotsman who'd barely been on the pitch a few minutes when he made Foxy and me look like a pair of total amateurs. We were both chasing a kick when he gathered the ball, did a cheeky little hitch-kick and burnt us both off. I remember thinking, *This guy's all right.* Stuart Hogg was his name.

Something had to give when we faced England at Twickenham. We were both unbeaten and the Triple Crown was on the line. For nigh on two decades, Welsh sides had travelled to south-west London more in hope than expectation, but this generation was different. The win back in 2008 had laid a twenty-year hoodoo to rest and dispelled any lingering inferiority complex.

Warby was significantly more fired up than usual after an incident on the way in. He was walking through the Twickenham car park, weaving his way through the crowds of Hooray Henrys in mustard cords swigging Pimm's from the boots of their Bentleys, when he heard someone intone, in clipped Home Counties vowels, 'You're s***, Warburton. It was a red card all day long.' Unbeknown to this Twickenham twerp, Warby's headphones were just a prop. He'd been keen to soak up the atmosphere and had no music coming through them, meaning he'd heard the plummy-voiced slur loud and clear. Resisting the urge to respond, he had channelled his rage into a particularly aggressive team talk. The away dressing room at Twickenham is surprisingly small, and it got pretty heated in there as Warby made some uncharacteristically malicious pronouncements about 'the English'. It was manna from heaven for some of the more bellicose boys in the squad. Ian Evans was positively salivating.

Both teams came out of the blocks firing, and aggression levels were typically high. There was plenty of niggle among the forwards and some incendiary language emerging from the claustrophobic confines of the rucks. Their centre Manu Tuilagi was living up to his hype as a one-man wrecking ball, and with the scores locked at 3–3 after half an hour, he was unleashed down the left-hand side. I'd been defending too tightly and was surprised at how quickly they managed to spread the ball wide. Despite my desperate efforts to scramble back, it was looking like a lost cause. I'd made a poor read and was about to pay the price. Then out of nowhere, from beyond my field of vision, came the rampaging figure of Sam Warburton, who mowed Manu down like some kind of cartoon superhero. It was a phenomenal piece of defending and it saved my blushes. Not that I totally got away with it; my mistake was shown on the big screen the following Monday, and once Warby had been showered with fulsome praise, I was roundly pilloried.

It wasn't long before another incident with Manu ended my match. I was in possession near the halfway line when he launched himself horizontally at me, knocking me to the ground. I felt an immediate, searing pain shoot through my knee. Not wanting to betray any weakness, I leapt to my feet and hobbled back into the line, but I knew something wasn't right. I played on, willing the pain to subside, but a few rucks later I got another massive whack on it and the pain intensified.

By half-time, I was in agony. The knee was swollen and tender and barely functioning. Foxy saw me grimacing and told me to dig in, but as much as I wanted to soldier on, I knew I couldn't run properly. I told Gats I was struggling and he made the call without hesitation. It was a tight, one-score game and he knew one mistake could decide the outcome. Scott Williams was given the nod to strip off and warm up. I felt like a right softie in front of the lads, because it was the kind of injury you could often strap up, like a popped rib or a dislocated finger, but this time my knee felt wobbly and weak. It was a horrible, empty feeling. Here I was at the home of English rugby, looking to storm their fortress with my brothers-in-arms, and it felt like I'd meekly surrendered before the battle had really begun.

I then watched helplessly from the sidelines as my replacement scored one of the most spectacular tries in the history of the tournament. Courtney Lawes had the ball and, as one of England's enforcers, thought he could just drop his shoulder and blast a hole through the Welsh midfield. He hadn't accounted for Scotty, though; he's from farming stock in Newcastle Emlyn and has never backed down from anyone. Stopping Lawes firmly in his tracks, he ripped the ball from his grasp, kicked it downfield and set off in hot pursuit. As he accelerated through the gears, leaving the English defence trailing in his wake, all he needed was a kind bounce. And he got it. The rugby ball can be a fiendishly awkward thing to control, but on this occasion it sat up perfectly for him, dropping into his hands, and he cruised over the line. It was an astonishing piece of play, incorporating virtually every skill required from a world-class centre. Strength, power, vision, awareness, composure and speed – all wrapped up in one fluid movement. It was an incredible moment, and worthy of a film script.

Never have I experienced such a kaleidoscope of emotions in such a short space of time. Delight, envy, anger, bitterness, doubt, frustration. I was swollen with pride for Scott, who'd been through a tough couple of years as third choice behind Jon and me, but envious it hadn't been me scoring that wonder try. I was euphoric for Wales, but consumed with doubt about my decision to come off. Ecstatic at the point of victory, embarrassed at my early withdrawal. Pride was the overwhelming emotion, but it was heavily diluted by all the other conflicting ones bouncing around inside my head.

Up to the point Scotty scored, the game had been horribly nerve-racking. Rhys Priestland had been sin-binned early in the second half, and the ensuing penalty had given England a 12–6 lead. It could have been the point of no return, but we kept our heads and held on to possession for eight of those ten minutes. We were patient and precise, picking-and-going and running down the clock while England hurled themselves into the contact area, trying their damnedest to turn over the ball.

Owen Farrell was standing tight to the rucks, acting as one of England's primary defenders. That's normally the domain of the back-rowers, but he wanted to be in the thick of it, putting in big hits on our heavy forwards. He was goading the likes of Alun Wyn Jones to run straight at him, which was either incredibly brave or incredibly stupid. I couldn't help but feel a grudging respect for this fearless, no-nonsense northerner who was refusing to back down. Here was a Lions colossus, nearly twice his size, and he was *inviting* him to run down his channel. Most fly-halves would happily hide behind their forwards in such circumstances.

Despite Farrell and company's best efforts, we maintained control of the ball and actually 'won' the sin-bin period 3–0. It was a valuable lesson learned from two years earlier, when we'd lost Alun Wyn to the bin and conceded 17 points.

Scotty's try came five minutes from time, but the drama was far from over. Gats had spoken a lot about 'critical moments', and the importance of maintaining pressure after going ahead. So often on the rugby field, a moment of brilliance is followed by an error as concentration levels dip. We kept our line intact for those final five minutes, but with the clock in the red, a Hail Mary of a miss-pass from Mike Brown found David Strettle on the wide right-hand side and the winger bustled his way over the line. The Twickenham crowd erupted in delight, but with Halfers, Foxy and George all scrambling brilliantly in defence, I had a good feeling he'd been held up.

As I stood there watching endless replays, my mind wandered back to Loftus Versfeld. In many ways, this was a carbon copy of that second Lions Test against South Africa the year before. Swap Jaque Fourie for the flaxen-haired Strettle, and it was an almost identical scenario. The one crucial difference was that victory was beyond England's grasp. If the try was awarded, the conversion would force a draw, but that would have felt like a defeat for us given the circumstances. The more I watched, the more I was convinced he hadn't scored. Foxy and Halfpenny's last-ditch scramble defence in the eightieth minute of a lung-busting Test match proved absolutely critical. They had combined heroically to deny him, and after five minutes of careful deliberation, the referee arrived at the same conclusion. No try. We'd won the Triple Crown for the first time ever on English soil.

I say 'we', but the truth was I felt a little detached from the celebrations. It wasn't like 2008 when I was on the periphery of the squad. I'd graduated to the ranks of first choice and had started all three games, but that defining half had unfolded without me, and to make matters worse, it had been my replacement who'd sealed the victory. It was the first time in my career that my position had been genuinely under threat.

In the introduction to the BBC's *Scrum V* programme the following day, the AC/DC song 'Thunderstruck' was used to soundtrack Leigh Halfpenny's defensive read. Via the overhead angle, we saw just how much ground he'd covered scrambling from one touchline to the other. He was flashing with a sort of radioactive glow, like a character from a computer game. 'Thunderstruck' has a jittery, syncopated intro which was playing as he sensed the danger and set off to cover the full width of the pitch. As he reached Strettle and launched himself sideways, the main riff kicked in. If there's ever any moment that encapsulates Leigh Halfpenny's will to win, it's that. He's not a flashy full-back who scores length-of-the-field tries, stepping six or seven defenders like Christian Cullen used to, but that moment showed his value to our team. It was brave, selfless and born of sheer determination. He was actually being treated for concussion during the TMO deliberations, and didn't realise we'd won the Triple Crown until he staggered back onto the pitch sporting a black eye and a swollen lip.

I self-consciously hobbled on to celebrate with the boys, and Foxy maintains that he's never seen anyone on crutches move so fast. He insists that my sole motivation was to get next to Sam in the team photo and claims I was elbowing people out of the way to get there! It's categorically not true; I was genuinely that excited, and just wanted to be among the lads. I knew I'd be confined to barracks with my injury that night, so this was my one chance to bathe in the glory of a rare Twickenham win. Sure enough, while the boys stayed in London to celebrate, I headed back down the M4 with physio Mark Davies, known as 'Carcass', listening to Bob Seger's entire back catalogue at ear-splitting volume. His choice. I finished the evening eating crisps on the sofa with a bag of frozen peas on my knee.

I'm not usually a jealous person, but in the wake of that match I experienced a good degree of envy and was determined not to let it curdle into bitterness. It's only human to feel that way, but it's unhealthy to allow those emotions to blot out the positive ones, especially in a team environment. I was on the physio bed, having my knee looked at before the team to face Italy was named, when Gats appeared by my side. In his usual brusque manner he looked me in the eye and said, 'You owe me a big performance this week.' Holding up his thumb and forefinger so they were millimetres apart, he added, 'We were this close to starting Scotty.' He'd made his point, and turned on his heel before I had a chance to respond. It was a fairly typical exchange, if you can even call it that. In the ten years I worked under him, I never had a genuinely in-depth conversation with Warren, and I wasn't alone in that regard. He maintained an almost permanent distance from his players, preferring to keep them constantly on their toes.

As I walked out of the room, I spied Howlers and Scotty deep in discussion over in the corner. It was clear what was being said, and Scott's expression betrayed his obvious disappointment. I'd had the lifeline and Scotty, despite his heroics, was being given the bad news. I put my head down and got the hell out of there, ducking through the laundry corridor to avoid bumping into anyone. I was shaking and felt inexplicably nervous. For several minutes, I sat alone among the laundered sheets and whirring tumble dryers, allowing what had just happened to sink in. It was the news I'd wanted to hear but it came with a caveat: *You'd better raise your game, because someone's breathing down your neck.*

As I jogged out for that afternoon's training session, I heard Ryan Jones's foghorn of a voice from within the huddle of lads pitchside: 'Here he is, boys: Lazarus. Back from the dead.' A peal of laughter rang out as several of his acolytes picked up on the new nickname. 'All right, Lazarus?' 'What's happening, Lazarus?' 'Got a sniff of glory, did you, Lazarus?' As someone who's never been shy about dishing out the banter, you could say, excusing the pun, that I didn't have a leg to stand on.

As amusing as it was, I'd be lying if I said it didn't touch a nerve, especially in an environment in which bravery and durability were so prized. I still vividly remembered Shaun Edwards calling out Mark Jones in 2008 for not getting up against England because he hadn't 'been knocked out or broken a leg'. I didn't regret coming off, because I genuinely didn't have an option, but I couldn't escape the feeling that some of the lads thought I was a bit soft, or even worse, a glory hunter.

Shaun had a massive go at us on the day of the Italy game, for not being sufficiently pumped up. Not everyone needs to be stomping around head-butting the walls, but he'd sensed an air of complacency that didn't sit well with him. Gethin Jenkins was about the only player old and experienced enough to answer back, and he did so in his own inimitable style. 'Pipe down, Shaun. There's four hours till kick-off.' He had a point.

It wasn't as convincing a win as we were hoping for against Italy, but on a personal level, I scored one of my most satisfying tries for Wales. From a turnover, Priest squared up nicely to put me into space, and I ran 50 metres unopposed. The work I'd done on my running technique with Adam Beard and Frans Bosch had paid off handsomely. My stride length had improved, I'd addressed an issue with my trailing leg and I felt like I was gliding over the pitch. I'd transformed myself from a chunky station wagon straining in fifth gear, to a sports car purring at top speed. It was the classic adage of minimum effort, maximum output – proof that good running is a combination of instinct *and* technique. You never stop learning.

That try settled the nerves somewhat after what had been a niggly first half. The Italians may be renowned for their sense of style and sartorial elegance, but their rugby is the very essence of no-frills. Hard-nosed, uncompromising and almost wholly lacking in flair, they've become experts at dragging their opponents into a dogfight. It took until the last quarter for our superior fitness to tell. There's always a moment against Italy when they run out of steam. The urgency goes, they're slower to get to their feet after tackles and they start giving away needless penalties. The 24–3 final scoreline was comfortable enough, but the dressing room felt strangely subdued. It may have been an underwhelming performance, but it was good to have got it out of our system ahead of what would be the Grand Slam decider against France the following weekend.

The week's build-up was disastrous. The weather was wet and dreary, the ball was constantly greasy, we couldn't hit a line-out and couldn't go more than three phases without messing up. There were knock-ons and fluffed moves galore. It was like watching a hungover pub team train, or a slapstick film without the jaunty soundtrack. Mistakes like that become self-perpetuating and what usually comes naturally becomes forced. Some of the younger players were getting twitchy, and the mounting mistakes led to further frustration and a swelling sense of panic and confusion. We were fortunate that there were enough old heads who'd won Grand Slams and knew how to cool the temperature. Ryan Jones, Gethin Jenkins and Adam Jones were on a quest for a third, and it fell to the usually taciturn Bomb to deliver a motivational speech. As someone who'd spent the best part of a decade in the Welsh shirt, his words, though few in number, carried weight. He gathered the team into a huddle and told us, in no uncertain terms, to calm down. The only pressure we were feeling, he insisted, was the pressure we were putting on ourselves. Our pattern hadn't changed and our tactics were ingrained; we just needed to relax and trust the system.

It's impossible to overstate how significant the Six Nations is to the people of Wales. Its climax coincides with the turning of the seasons, as the bleak frosty winter gives way to blue skies and warmer temperatures, and success can alter the mood of the nation more dramatically than the coming of spring. We were standing on the brink of history and helping to forge a new, modern Welsh identity. So much of our national pride was centred on the misty-eyed romanticism of the seventies. The success-starved eighties and nineties had forced us all to look backwards for inspiration. This was an opportunity to write a new chapter, and to usher in a new golden era.

I'd developed a well-worn routine for home games which unfolded to a familiar, faithful music playlist. I'd board the bus at the front entrance of the Vale, making my way towards the back. As it began to roll up the drive that day, there were hundreds of supporters lined up on the pavement to wave us off. It was at this point that I pressed play on Bruce Springsteen's 'Thunder Road', the plaintive harmonica ringing in my ears as we wound our way up the drive and past the golf course. By the time we reached the motorway, it had segued into Swedish House Mafia, the more urgent tempo matching the heightening sense of drama. As the suburb of Canton hove into view, it was time for the Verve's 'Lucky Man', a reminder of the good fortune that had got me to this point. The coach slowed right down by Westgate Street, and that's when 'This Is the One' by the Stone Roses came on. That day, the corner of Castle Street and Westgate Street was different. It's always thronged with fans, but this time there were twice as many, and they were ten times as loud. Brandishing giant leeks and daffodils, they were all clustered together, swaying, singing and holding their sloshing pints aloft. It felt like the entire population of Wales, all three million of them, had poured into Cardiff.

It dawned on me at that point that while the whole nation was behind us, there were only twenty-three people who got to pull on that red jersey and run onto the fabled Millennium Stadium turf. As Owen Sheers had put it in a specially commissioned poem, it was a moment 'when the many, through the few, become one.' It was a privilege. As we edged down Westgate Street, I was roused from my reverie by the sight of a massive banner of yours truly adorning the side of the stadium. It was a photo from an Under Armour shoot I'd done months earlier, but I had no idea it would be given such a commanding position. As we passed through the gates and into the stadium, the hypnotic breakbeat of Mobb Deep's 'Shook Ones (Part II)' started playing through my headphones. To the uninitiated, it's the song from *8 Mile* where Eminem is rapping in the mirror. It's always the last thing I hear before entering the sanctity of the home dressing room. The atmosphere inside was serene and focused. We'd built an almost irresistible sense of momentum and felt it was our destiny to win the Grand Slam.

As defensive skipper, I'd deliver a few key messages before Warby's rallying cry. Against France it was pretty obvious. First, man up, because they're big boys and they'll be coming for you. They're very good at exploiting momentum, so those first-up hits have to knock them back and suck the juice out of them. We decided that we'd have to gang-tackle a few of their big carriers like Louis Picamoles to stop them building up a head of steam. Second, avoid turnovers, because they're deadly on the counter-attack. And third, guard the blind side, because their nines are very good at playing off the touchline; they'll always look to have a dart and can create carnage in tight spaces. Shaun had taught us not to cram our brains with too much information, but to distil the strategy down to a few key points we could easily recall in the heat of the battle. It's important to enter the fray with complete clarity of thought: no distraction, no confusion, no room for error.

Dan Lydiate took care of number one all by himself. He was an absolute bulldozer of a player, with a raw natural strength derived from hours spent hauling bales on his remote family farm. We'd marvel at his effortless power in the gym, as he continued to add weights on top of weights long after the others had given up and tapped out. Combine that freakish power with his never-say-die attitude and you have a defensive weapon par excellence. His ability to get low and parallel to the floor has become a priceless attribute in today's climate of low-tolerance for high tackling. In 2012, he was essentially tripping players up with his shoulder. I'd been on the receiving end of a few Lydiate specials at club level, and it's a uniquely unpleasant experience. Unlike a regular tackle, you don't see it coming, and are unable to brace for impact. It's the unexpectedness that's so disorienting. One minute you're gliding smoothly across the turf, assessing your options, the next you're splayed out facing the wrong way and wondering what on earth has happened. It's like being taken out by an unseen sniper. The nickname 'Silent Ninja' was well earned.

The French knew we were on a roll, and had vetoed our decision to shut the roof, allowing the rain, which had fallen steadily all day, to coat the pitch in a greasy sheen. It was a cynical ploy which turned the first half into a game of chess rather than the free-flowing encounter the crowd had hoped for. Running rugby was off the menu. The continuous parping of vuvuzelas in the stands told you all you needed to know about the lack of inspiration on the pitch, as the ball was pinged tediously back and forth, with neither side willing to take a risk. The entertainment, such as there was, was provided by Dan Lydiate, who delivered his defining performance in a Wales shirt. His match-day transformation from mild-mannered country boy to testosterone-fuelled warrior was always astonishing to watch, and that day his aggression levels were off the charts. He was launching himself at the knees and ankles of French ball-carriers with abandon, sending them crashing to the ground in a thrashing jumble of limbs. Wesley Fofana, Thierry Dusautoir and Jean-Marcellin Buttin all became bewildered victims of the Mid-Walian Chopper, and all looked equally emasculated by the experience.

He made twenty tackles that day, but the most significant by far was the one on Thierry Dusautoir after twenty minutes. The ball was swiftly snaffled by a predatory Alun Wyn, and we snapped into attack mode. Lyds was back on his feet to play scrum-half and got the ball away to Rhys Priestland, who did his usual thing of finding space where there seemed to be none. He got a pass away to Alex Cuthbert, who absolutely *shredded* the French defence. I watched admiringly from the other side of the pitch as he scorched a path to the line. It was the bludgeon and the rapier working in perfect unison: Lyds with the destructive tackle, Cuthy with the silky finish. He's the quickest I've ever played with bar none, but it wasn't his sheer pace so much as his ability to change direction at top speed that impressed me the most. At that point in time, there was no better finisher in Europe.

The second half was all about concentration and composure. Full-back Jean-Marcellin Buttin found a few holes in our otherwise water-tight defence, but we always scrambled to safety. Leigh Halfpenny uncharacteristically fumbled a high ball, which led to a frantic defensive set as both Harinordoquy and Picamoles charged into us with renewed ferocity, but we held our nerve, and our line. Penalties were exchanged and we took a 13–9 lead into the final quarter. An act of French petulance allowed us to stretch the gap to seven when François Trinh-Duc threw the ball into the stands after being tackled into touch. Halfers nailed the penalty, making that cushion a little more comfortable. We weren't going to lose in those final five minutes. Our defence was too strong, and France had run out of ideas. It was an energy-sapping last stand as they hurled themselves at us with increasing desperation, but we felt equal to the task. Eventually the ball went loose and Priest banged it hard and high into the stand. We'd done it. We'd avenged the World Cup defeat and secured another Grand Slam, Wales's third in seven years.

The sense of relief was overwhelming. The crowd erupted with joy as we bounded, leapt and hugged one another with unalloyed delight. A girl in the crowd blew me a kiss and threw me her pink sparkly cowboy hat which, against my better judgement, I placed on my head. It remained there as we strode round the stadium milking the applause and adulation. It wasn't until the following day, when I saw the official photos, that I realised how monumentally camp I looked. Like a giant mud-stained fifth member of the Village People. That aside, it was an awesome experience, especially given the disappointments and near-misses I'd suffered. I was chuffed to bits for Jug, Melon and Bomb, who were celebrating their third Grand Slams and joining an elite band of Welshmen to achieve that special goal. I could now call myself a Grand Slam winner. Yes, officially I'd been one in 2008, but I'd felt more of an observer than a participant. This one was real.

It felt like redemption after the 2011 World Cup. We'd experienced hurt and anger on an enormous scale, and the heartbreak had driven us to become better people and better players. When you've experienced the pain of losing at the highest level, it lingers constantly at the back of your mind, always there, like low-level tinnitus or a scab that never heals, and every time you're under intense pressure on the pitch, the memory of those losses drives you to another level.

By the end of the 2012 Six Nations, we were powerful, so physically dominant, that we felt virtually invincible. We beat teams up, sapped their spirit and forced them into mistakes. We were bullies and we revelled in it, but despite what some of our detractors would have you believe, it wasn't all about brute force. Yes, we had a set of three-quarters who could dominate collisions, but we also had the artistry of Rhys Priestland, the athleticism of Alex Cuthbert and the accuracy of Leigh Halfpenny. It was a potent brew that had come to the boil at exactly the right time.

We had a great session on the Sunday in Cowbridge. There were some casualties from the official celebrations the night before, but the hardcore all made it out. The so-called 'Super Sunday' celebrations were always more informal and relaxed, giving us a chance to mix with the fans and luxuriate in our achievement. In the course of the afternoon, I remembered how Mike Phillips used to do this party piece where he'd pin twenty quid on the dartboard and challenge people to try to win it. You had three darts from three distances: one right in front, one from the oche, and a third from twice that distance again. It was two quid to play, and if you hit the note with all three darts you got to keep it. Mike was a canny operator and always left with a tidy profit, and now, half-cut, I decided I fancied a piece of the action. I had a fifty-pound note in my wallet, so I whipped it out, pinned it to the board and set the entry fee at three quid. Jonathan Davies placed his pint on the bar, rolled up his sleeves theatrically and dropped three pound coins into my palm. With a minimum of fanfare, he punctured the note with each dart before strolling to the board, retrieving the note and sliding it casually into his pocket. The lads erupted with almost as much enthusiasm as they had when we won the Slam. I got exactly what I deserved for waving a fifty around like I was John D. Rockefeller. I should have known better: Foxy's the son of a pub landlord.

It had been a coming-of-age tournament for that gawky student I'd seen roaming around on the UWIC pitches a few years earlier. Alex Cuthbert had started every game, terrorising defences with his lightning speed and scoring three spectacular tries, including the one that sealed the Grand Slam. He did all of that while drawing an academy salary at the Cardiff Blues, earning about the same as a shelf-stacker at Tesco. A few weeks after the tournament ended, he received a six-figure bonus. He'd earned more for five days' work than he had in his life to date. For some time after, his nickname was 'Rags to Riches'.

14

DEFYING THE CRITICS

It was five in the morning and the country lanes were shrouded in an inky darkness that matched my gloomy disposition. My headlights illuminated the road, but I knew every twist and turn intimately. I'd made this journey hundreds of times. My destination was the luxurious Vale Hotel, but I'd rather have been a thousand miles away. I was wrestling with a simple, recurring question: *What the hell am I doing?* While the rest of the Wales squad were tucked up in bed, getting the rest and recuperation they needed, I was trundling along the lanes in the middle of the night feeling weary, exhausted and racked with doubt. For the last seven years, I'd been driving two trains running on parallel lines: rugby and medicine. In less than a fortnight, there was a danger they were going to career off the tracks and crash spectacularly into one another. I was preparing to sit my final medical exams *and* face Wales's biggest rivals in a career-defining, championship-deciding game. My two worlds were about to collide.

I pulled into the car park, turned off the engine and slumped back in my seat. This had been a regular ritual for the last seven weeks: driving to the Vale in the small hours to cram in three hours of revision before the world woke up and training began. Today my tank was empty. I'd reached the end of my tether. I felt claustrophobic, as though the weight of responsibility was crowding in from all angles, pushing down on my shoulders and chest. I considered restarting the car and driving away with no purpose or destination. Just *away* from there, away from all the pressure and scrutiny. I was gambling with both my rugby and my medical careers, putting it all at risk. Was I doing everything in my power to be the best rugby player I could be? Absolutely not. I was pushing myself to the point of exhaustion. Was I giving myself the best chance of passing my finals? Definitely not. I was trying to prepare for an international Test match, relegating my studies to the hours before dawn. I felt like I was disrespecting the medical profession and betraying my country at the same time. I was spreading myself too thinly, giving too little of myself to each. I'd always taken pride in my ability to spin plates, to keep busy, to stay focused. Now there was a danger the plates were about to come crashing down.

The euphoria that accompanied our 2012 Grand Slam evaporated as quickly as the morning dew on a summer's day. Rob Howley had taken the reins while Warren was on Lions sabbatical and we'd gone into a tailspin, losing seven games on the bounce. My troublesome knee had forced me out of the summer tour to Australia, and I was recovering from anterior cruciate ligament reconstructive surgery while the boys were down under, sinking to a 3-0 series defeat. It had been billed as a north-south summit of sorts: the Six Nations champions against the Tri-Nations champions. We lost the first match fair and square, but the second and third were absolute sickeners. We had them flailing on the ropes in both, only for them to recover and land the killer blow. Two defeats by a combined margin of three points. The Aussies proved once again that they never know when they're beaten.

While the lads were having their post-mortem, I had myself another summer to remember, using my injury lay-off to step off the hamster wheel and travel. I met up with the England cricket lads at the Silverstone Grand Prix, hung out at the Henley Regatta and went on another road trip round the south of France, before bowling up at the Monaco Grand Prix. Putting my contacts to good use, I blagged a room in Monte Carlo's Casino Square. From there, we went on an amazing boat trip to Antibes on one of those wooden VanDutch boats. It was the stuff of dreams: a 'Carlsberg' weekend. By the time the 2012-13 season rolled around, I was mentally and physically refreshed.

Wales were whitewashed in the autumn for the first time in our history. Played four, lost four. I lasted quarter of an hour against Argentina before being knocked out cold by a rampaging Gonzalo Tiesi. Samoa beat us with their superior physicality, the All Blacks with their pace and dexterity, and the Wallabies - true to form - broke our hearts at the death. The narrative remained the same, but this one was personal for me as defensive captain. We were 12–9 ahead with less than a minute to play, and Australia were deep in their own half. I warned Foxy and a few of our backs that they were going to play to width, but we didn't react quickly enough. Australia shifted the ball across their backline with razor-sharp precision, finding a sliver of space on the outside. It led to a brilliant try from Kurtley Beale, but we'd essentially waved them through. As I was under the sticks trying to process yet another last-gasp defeat, I looked up to see their lumbering lock forward Nathan Sharpe lining up the conversion attempt. It felt like they were rubbing our noses in it.

The knives were out for Rob Howley. The team was largely the same and the game plan hadn't changed, yet it seemed as if we couldn't win without Warren. Without his golden touch, our sheen had seemingly rubbed off. I'd never seen Rob looking so gaunt. His default expression became one of resignation and despair, and he appeared to age visibly during the campaign. A number of mocking videos started appearing on social media, depicting him as clueless and out of his depth. I think those hurt more than the damning headlines.

The defeats tapped into a lingering insecurity we'd managed to suppress for several years. Maybe we *were* flat-track bullies: capable of dominating European sides, but simply not good enough to beat the southern-hemisphere giants. The Wallabies defeat was our eighth in a row against them, we hadn't beaten South Africa since 1999, and the games were still being shown in black and white when Wales had last beaten New Zealand.

Howley was a convenient target, but the wrong one. There were no cracks, cliques or divisions in the squad, but there was a growing realisation that the pattern we'd been playing to – this attritional, low-risk game plan – might be a busted flush. Warren could be quite thin-skinned, and repeated suggestions he was a one-dimensional, unimaginative coach didn't go down well. I'd had the same crap slung at me throughout my career, and I took it personally. I was seen by some as the personification of what became referred to, pejoratively, as 'Warrenball'. When we lost to more agile, creative sides, we were portrayed as clumsy, lumbering brutes who lacked the wit or skill of our opponents. It was a reductive criticism, but one that undoubtedly had a grain of truth. Debates raged around whether Wales should employ a southern-hemisphere-style 'second five-eighth' in the 12 jersey: a rapier rather than a bludgeon. Such a move would arguably make me redundant, especially as the skills I'd honed before moving to midfield were now like the rusty contents of a toolbox languishing at the back of the garage.

My job description since 2009 had been simple: carry hard, win collisions, smash defenders and put Wales on the front foot. If I wasn't carrying the ball, the threat that I *might* be would create space for others. I didn't resent abandoning the other aspects of the game I'd enjoyed, because I was good at what I'd been asked to do. When it worked, I was considered the chief architect of big victories, but when it didn't, I was often blamed for defeat. It was chastening to have won a tournament in the manner we did in 2012, only to watch it all unravel so dramatically. It may have been arrogance, naivety or a bit of both to think the same approach would work against southern-hemisphere sides. When you're in the thick of it as players, it doesn't always occur to you to challenge the coaches on their overall outlook. Looking back, we were naive not to air our concerns or lobby for more variety to our attack.

There was little time for navel-gazing, though. We had a title to defend and a reputation to restore. That said, rugby was far from the only thing on my mind. My medical finals were scheduled to take place during the last week of the 2013 Six Nations. As the dates drew ever closer, I'd repeat to myself what had become something of a mantra: 'Pressure is a privilege.' Not many people get the opportunity to put themselves under *real* pressure. Some people aspire to have an entirely stress-free existence, but I need pressure to feel alive, to feel that I exist and have a purpose. I know that the minute I stop playing rugby, I'm going to have to seek it elsewhere. It could be the pressure of having people's health and lives in my hands as a surgeon, but that feels like a long way off right now. I see pressure as a vital stepping stone on the path towards achievement. It's only by feeling it, confronting it and overcoming it that you appreciate the buzz of accomplishment. The deeper the pressure, the greater the buzz.

Around this time we had a psychologist attached to the squad. His name was Andy McCann and he'd become an influential figure for the likes of Sam Warburton and Leigh Halfpenny, who swore by his methods. They used him to overcome fears and insecurities ahead of big campaigns. Before this tournament, Sam had developed an irrational fear of breaking his ankle that was stopping him clatter into breakdowns with his usual ferocity. Andy helped him overcome that. Leigh would get the yips when lining up important kicks. Andy told him to imagine himself back at Gorseinon RFC, kicking goals for fun as a teenager.

It wasn't for me. I always saw value in finding solutions myself. If my form dipped or I'd had a bad game, I'd work out the reasons why, and the process of doing so would restore my confidence. I guess it's both a strength and a weakness to internalise things like that, but we're all wired differently. If I found my own way out of those troughs, I would feel stronger and more empowered. I'd see it as a challenge *not* to go and see someone. Dealing with stuff on my own, I reasoned, would make me more resilient further down the line. It's probably desperately unhealthy, and not great for my mental well-being, but I'm pretty stubborn when I want to be. My fiancée, Nicole, tells me I can be cold and emotionally distant during times of intense pressure. There were lots of times during this period when I really struggled. I was convinced that both my rugby and my education were starting to suffer, because of all the competing demands on my time. I learned to see it as riding a metaphorical wave: there'd be peaks and troughs, and ups and downs. I just had to stay on the board and avoid a wipeout.

There was no internal discord leading up to the 2013 Six Nations, no rising panic or fear of mutiny. We trusted that things would come good. Our first game was against Ireland in Cardiff. They'd suffered two painful defeats against us, and arrived with the scent of blood in their nostrils. Welsh rugby was on its knees and we weren't about to be helped to our feet by our Celtic cousins. They ripped into us from the first whistle, running rampant and carving holes in our worryingly porous defence. We were a meek, cowed version of our former selves and had no answer to their all-out aggression. The pitch was heavy, and I felt slow and sluggish. Ireland's debutant winger, Simon Zebo, had no such issues, scoring an early try and producing a sublime piece of skill. Jamie Heaslip's pass was low and marginally behind Zebo, so instead of stooping to collect it, he let it drop to his boot before casually back-heeling it into his hands. It was the sort of thing Maradona would have been proud of. It kept their attack moving and forced our defence to scramble desperately. A few phases later, Cian Healy was burrowing over in the corner.

If our confidence had been fragile coming into the game, it was now well and truly shattered. Normally strident voices within the team were muted; no one was talking, and we were staring down the barrel of an ugly defeat. World-class players were looking decidedly ordinary. Foxy, by his own admission, was having a nightmare. His radar was completely off, and on one occasion he passed the ball directly into touch. It was a nervy, jittery performance, which betrayed how much negative energy we were carrying around with us.

The half-time team talk was simple and delivered in fairly industrial language. *Just get hold of the ball and f***ing keep hold of it.* Within minutes of the restart, Brian O'Driscoll had gone over for another try, stretching their lead to a daunting 30–3. They were channelling all the fury of their recent defeats to us and exacting sweet revenge.

Then, strangely, things began to happen. The Drico try, rather than killing us off, sparked a recovery. With the game beyond reach, we relaxed and rediscovered our rhythm. My decoy lines started sucking in defenders and creating gaps, one of which was exploited by Cuthy, who ran a neat line off Dan Biggar to go under the posts. Within moments, Leigh Halfpenny had dotted down in the corner to make it 30–15. Prop Craig Mitchell's close-range score came too late to complete what would have been a miraculous comeback, but our blushes had been spared. It didn't alter the fact, though, that it was another defeat, our eighth in a row.

Only Wales seems to suffer feast and famine on this scale. Grand Slam champs to chumps in less than a year. The changing room was like a morgue. I looked at the three feathers on my chest and the usual pride turned to shame. I'd let the jersey down in a big way; we all had. Warren Gatland had been in the crowd wearing his Lions blazer, pencilling in names for his squad. It didn't take a genius to discern that not many would have been wearing red. The next game against France was going to be crucial. If we retreated any further into our shells, we could wave goodbye to the prospect of a Lions trip, no matter how much credit we had in the bank.

I was feeling the heat more than most as, once again, our failings were being blamed on our style of play. The power game that had eviscerated Ireland in our previous two encounters had been analysed, broken down and neutered. The press was calling for wholesale changes, and the axe was hovering most threateningly over my head. The hard-running crash-ball centre, so feted a few years ago, had become passé.

No one gave us a hope of winning away in Paris and so, in keeping with the backs-to-the-wall mentality, Alan Phillips took us away from our regular accommodation on the Champs-Élysées. Gone was the usual opportunity to have a mooch around Paris and enjoy a coffee with Foxy and a few of the boys. Thumper wanted zero distractions, so we holed up in a remote, soulless hotel on the outskirts of the city. It worked. We turned up at the Stade de France with our sleeves rolled up and delivered a gutsy, nuggety win.

It wasn't sexy, it wasn't glamorous and I did nothing that would make it onto a showreel, but it was one of my proudest performances in a Welsh shirt. There was a doughtiness to it, a refusal to roll over and accept the preordained narrative. We stripped our game back to its basics: watertight defence, an aggressive kick-chase and a ruthlessness when opportunities arrived. George North produced a world-class finish from a chip kick to score the only try, which was celebrated theatrically by an exuberant moustachioed pitch invader. The man's attempt to hug George wasn't reciprocated, with George brushing him away dismissively before he was bundled off by a bunch of officious stewards. It was only afterwards that he discovered it was his dad. Realisation dawned via a phone call from his mum explaining that she'd be late coming to meet him, as she was at a Paris police station trying to persuade the gendarmes that her husband was just a mad Taff, and not a terrorist.

My emotions got the better of me during the post-match interview. It was the day I'd won my fiftieth cap, and I'd exchanged glances with my brother, who was working as a pitch-side cameraman, as I'd walked off. Those two factors triggered a flood of emotions, and as I spoke on live TV, tears welled in my eyes. The pressure valve had been opened and all my pent-up frustrations came gushing out. I knew I was coming to Paris next year because I'd signed for Racing Métro 92 in November. Winning with Wales was the absolute priority, but I also wanted to prove to the French that they hadn't signed a dud.

Rob Howley boarded the bus with blessed relief etched across his features, and as he took his seat, a booming voice from the back hollered, 'Aren't you going to say thanks, Rob?' It was the unmistakable Carmarthenshire accent of Mike Phillips, already a few beers to the good. 'Thanks for what, Mike?' 'For saving your f***ing job, butt.' The whole bus erupted into laughter, and the tension of the last eight months dissolved in that moment. Timing is everything.

The coach dropped us off on Rue de Rivoli, by the side of the Louvre, and we went straight into the VIP Room club, striding down the steps and across the dance floor to the main tables, where a stash of vodka bottles was waiting for us. After months of feeling increasingly tightly wound, we suddenly felt lighter than air. It was important to celebrate that win after enduring such misery. Foxy bought me a bright yellow VIP Room beanie from the merchandise shop as a nod to my fiftieth cap, along with a couple of expensive Cuban cigars to toast the victory. Some of the French boys joined us, and the lads kept asking Richard Hibbard and a mystified Dimitri Szarzewski to pose for photos on the grounds they looked like identical twins. I'm not sure the suave, urbane Szarzewski appreciated the comparison. The French guys didn't stay long, and the image of their team bus pulling away to reveal Andrew Coombs throwing up into the bushes pretty much summed up the night. French dejection versus Welsh abandon.

The next morning felt like a throwback to the amateur era, with Alex Cuthbert sleeping in and missing the bus, and a dusty, hungover Mike Phillips continuing to taunt Rob Howley at the breakfast bar. Rob put up with it, because he knew it meant Mike had recovered his swagger. When Mike's cocky off the pitch, he's commanding on it, and Howlers wasn't about to clip his wings. The dynamic between those two was fascinating. A month later in Edinburgh, one of the lads ordered a load of beer and burgers to their room from the late-night menu and didn't settle the bill. The leftovers were abandoned in the corridor, and there was a bit of confusion about who'd ordered the greasy, calorific midnight feast. In the absence of a confession, Howlers blamed it on Mike, questioning his professionalism and needling him constantly during the week that followed: 'Where's your self-control, Mike? Would Fourie du Preez be scoffing burgers in the earlier hours? I thought you were meant to be the world's best scrum-half?' Mike hated it; it really got under his skin. He thought he was being victimised, but it was actually a clever bit of coaching. Whether Howlers believed it had been Mike or not, the constant prodding and poking kept him angry, and he was at his snarling, confrontational best when he was angry.

On the journey to the airport, all the lads, without exception, were hanging. Bloodshot eyes, hair all over the place, crumpled clothes and more alcohol than blood in our veins – it looked more like Glyncorrwg's team bus returning from a fixture in Pontrhydyfen than the Welsh national side after a landmark win in Paris. The notion that you have to be ultra-professional all the time is just nonsense. We connected as a group more than ever that night, and the entire experience – the victory against the odds *and* the celebrations that followed – proved a catalyst for a remarkable turnaround in our fortunes.

The pressure was off when we travelled to Rome, and after the captain's run, Jonathan Davies, Alex Cuthbert, Ken Owens and I enjoyed a long, relaxed afternoon ambling around the city, before making camp at a café near the Pantheon and watching the world go by. We went on to beat Italy comfortably at a rain-lashed Stadio Olimpico, and had another good night out in Rome. The referee,

Romain Poite, ended up joining us, and for reasons that have faded from memory, one of the lads ripped his shirt off. I'll forever associate that night with the surreal, slightly disturbing image of a topless Romain Poite, dancing terribly to pounding house music.

When I returned to the hotel in the small hours, I found Foxy slumped outside our room. He had lost his key and passed out. Moments later, Shaun Edwards came stomping down the corridor in his vest and pants, checking on the boys and whispering through the doors: 'You all all right, lads? Everyone OK? Did you have a good night? All right, let's get our heads down, then. Night, lads, good night.' It was incredibly sweet. He must have had a few himself, but still considered it his duty to make sure everyone was back safe and tucked up in bed, like a kindly uncle who couldn't rest until his extended family were all safe and sound.

That night, I was aroused from my slumber by a splashing sound and awoke to the image of Foxy urinating on his shoes. I peered at him through sleep-encrusted eyes, and politely enquired as to what the hell he was doing. He just grinned, nodded and climbed back into bed. He had no recollection of it the following morning.

If this campaign is beginning to sound like an extended stag do, let me put you straight. These nights out were one-off blowouts amid an unbelievably intense six-week period for me. Every day we were scheduled to be at the Vale training during that campaign, I would arrive, under cover of darkness, having driven through the wintry, frost-laden country lanes, to start revising for my medical finals. They were looming large on the horizon, and as mentioned, for the first time in my professional career, the parallel tracks I was travelling on were due to converge. My last exam was on the Thursday before the last round of the championship, when we just happened to be playing England. As the weeks progressed, and the ignominy of the Ireland game began to recede in the rear-view mirror, we started to realise that the England game may yet be a championship decider.

Before every training session, I'd sit down at a conference-room desk for a three-hour studying stint before breakfast. It's the most

pressure I have been under in my entire life, and it was the culmination of everything I'd worked for to that point. The climax of seven
long years of study, coinciding with my last tournament as a Welsh
rugby player in Wales. I had made a conscious effort on day one to
establish a rigorous, disciplined routine. The alarm would trill in my
empty house at 4.15 a.m. and, resisting any urge to hit the snooze
button, I'd crawl from beneath the covers, pull on a tracksuit and
munch my way listlessly through a bowl of cereal, before entering a
world populated only by milkmen and dog-walking insomniacs.

A lot of the boys would stay at the Vale for the duration of the tournament, but I slept better at home. Sleep was massively important,
especially when every second of my time was allocated and accounted
for. On top of those twin pressures was the prospect of the 2013 Lions
tour, which was hovering at the back of my mind in the tiny space not
occupied by seven years' worth of medical theory. It was a real test of
my resilience, and in keeping with my stubborn single-mindedness, I
was determined to do it on my own. To have had a girlfriend or a
housemate would have been a major distraction. I would finish training, gobble down some snacks and drive home to work again from
five until ten o'clock. Go to bed, wake at 4.15, go again. My colleagues
at university were doing the same amount of revision, but that was
their sole focus. To be doing all of this while also being involved in
one of the biggest sporting tournaments in the world seems, with the
benefit of hindsight, ludicrous. At the time I didn't have the luxury of
perspective.

The conference room I worked in was free of distractions. Just my
laptop, notepad, pens and a cafetière I used to pilfer from the team
room on my way up. Every day I'd focus on a different sub-specialty
– cardio, respiratory, gastro, neuro – cramming my brain with information as my team-mates slept blissfully in their beds. I wasn't
always productive. One morning, after half an hour, though my pen
had been scrawling across the page, it felt like it was being moved by
a spectral presence. I was physically holding it but my brain wasn't
remotely engaged. I had hit the equivalent of the 'wall' that long-
distance runners talk about. With a dramatic sigh, I slammed the
book shut, strode down the stairs, got changed and slid into the

jacuzzi. I had the pool to myself, and an hour and a half passed before I moved again. Like a mobile phone with a flat battery, I needed time to recharge. As I sat, glassy-eyed, staring into the rippling water, I felt myself slowly reanimate.

The Scotland game was a pretty drab affair. The fact it set a world record for the number of penalty kicks tells you all you need to know, but once again we came out on top, and we were now setting the right kind of records: it was our fifth consecutive away win in the Six Nations and, since the defeat to Ireland, our try line hadn't been breached. Our defence was back to its mean, impenetrable best. I flew home on my own straight after the game. My exams were on the Tuesday and Thursday of that week, and I couldn't afford to waste half a day bumming around Edinburgh waiting for a flight. It was a lonely end to the weekend, but it was necessary. The next day, I had the England–Italy game on mute while I was poring over the books, watching absent-mindedly as they laboured to an 18–11 win. It kept their Grand Slam hopes alive, but the modest margin meant we could win the championship if we beat them by eight points. It had been an astonishing turnaround.

My wobble was behind me. I'd had that moment in the car park at 5 a.m. when it felt like the walls were about to come tumbling down, and I'd pushed through it. You sometimes need to reach breaking point to understand what's at stake. You cannot fully appreciate the light without the shadows. It's in those moments of quiet despair that you remind yourself why you're putting yourself through it. Once the panic subsides, your mind becomes clearer and your focus sharper. I may have cracked a little, but I didn't shatter.

Rob Howley approached me the Monday before the England game and asked if I was ready. He meant well, but I was insulted. This is Wales–England. How dare you even suggest I'm not ready? I didn't reply; the look in my eye was enough. I was excused from Tuesday's training session to sit an exam, but reported for duty on the Thursday directly after finishing my final one. It was so liberating to stride out of the exam hall knowing that it was done and I could focus exclusively on beating England. Driving straight to the Vale Hotel, I pulled up to the side of the pitch just as the backs were starting their unit sessions. I changed by the side of my car and jogged towards the lads with adrenaline coursing through my veins. I was on an incredible natural high and felt like I was floating on air. Rob could see I was unusually hyperactive, and told me to calm down and warm up properly. The last thing he or I needed was a pulled hamstring on the final stretch.

I don't know what people think an elite sports team does the night before a huge match, but they probably don't imagine players lounging on bean bags watching *EastEnders* and devouring burgers, chips and double helpings of apple crumble drowned in custard. That was our typical pre-match ritual, and it was no different this time. André the chef knew we had to get the calories in, and would adjust the menu accordingly. Dan Biggar supplied extra cakes. He had a connection with Gower Cottage Brownies and would regularly turn up with armfuls of them. It was always harder to pass the time before home games. Being anonymous in Paris, Rome or London was easy. You could have a wander, sit and sip coffee on some bustling square, dip in and out of the shops, and generally melt into the background. Cardiff offered no such luxury, so that night, once I'd gorged myself on Bigs's brownies, I donned a baseball cap and drove to the cinema in Treforest to escape into the silver screen for a few precious hours.

Nothing stirs a Welshman's soul like England coming to Cardiff. Sprinkle in the fact they were unbeaten and aiming for a Grand Slam, and you have the ingredients for a box-office thriller. The English papers were billing us as potential 'party poopers', which was a little rich. This was *our* party and *our* house, and destiny was in *our* hands. We'd spoken of the points difference required, but hadn't laboured the point. The message, as boring as it sounds, was 'Let's win the game, and see where we are in the last twenty minutes.' We couldn't get ahead of ourselves.

The crowd outside the Vale was three times what it normally was. There are two routes to the bus from the team room: one under the building via the laundry corridor, and another through the main foyer and into the heaving throng of supporters. The crowd would cost you at least ten minutes of your time in photos and autographs, and that day I was craving that attention. I showered early because I wanted to see it, feel it and embrace it. I didn't know when or if I'd experience another day like this. It was almost Shakespearean in its sense of drama.

The ignition rumbled, the bus eased out of the horseshoe-shaped driveway and on went 'Thunder Road'. I don't hate the English, but I love the David and Goliath narrative. Look at the number of players in England, the resources at their disposal, the standard of their league and the calibre of players it produces. We knew we had a group that was as good as, if not better than them, but it was not much deeper than thirty players. If twenty English players vanished into thin air, the next twenty would come in and do an equally good job. You're always the underdog against England.

As we rolled into Cardiff, the monitors above our seats dropped down and a video started playing, with Eminem's 'Till I Collapse' as the soundtrack. There were clips of England players like Ben Youngs and Chris Ashton saying they were coming to Cardiff to take the Grand Slam, interspersed with moments of us at our dominant best: crunching tackles, thundering charges and dives for the try line. The juxtaposition was perfectly pitched. Welsh hwyl and passion versus English complacency. My jaw tightened, my fists clenched, my focus narrowed, and as we rounded the corner to the stadium, I had one thought: *Bring it . . . just f***ing bring it.* As we filed into the changing room, the Six Nations trophy was standing on a plinth, gleaming. It was a powerful moment, a reminder that it was *our* trophy, that *we* were the defending champions and it would be a cold day in hell before we allowed England to come and take it from us.

Out in the stadium, the lights were dimmed, the flames were erupting and the atmosphere was febrile as the band struck the opening notes of the English anthem. God Save the Queen is often dismissed as a tuneless dirge, but that day it was a rousing call to arms, sung as passionately as I'd ever heard it. I wondered whether there'd been a mix-up in the ticket allocation and too many white-shirted supporters had been allowed in. We were left in no doubt that England, and their army of travelling fans, were bang up for this.

Then our anthem began and order was restored. It was like the headliners taking to the stage and blowing away the support act. It was so loud, you felt it in your chest as much as you heard it in your ears. When the chorus arrived, the band dropped out and the rest was sung a cappella with the male voice choir harmonising behind us. I'm not sure there's a more stirring, inspirational sound than 75,000 people singing Hen Wlad Fy Nhadau in that stadium. As a Welsh speaker, the words resonated deeply, and I felt passionately at that moment that I was representing three million people: every man, woman and child that had risen to their feet in the stadium, and in the pubs, bars and living rooms the length and breadth of the country. Everyone out there living their dreams vicariously through you. *Pressure is a privilege.*

As the last note rang out, we walked away feeling invincible. I felt twice as strong, twice as fast and twice as sharp as the English boys, who suddenly appeared shrunken, cowed and fearful. I looked into the determined faces of my friends – Foxy, Bigs and Phillsy – and in that moment I knew we were going to win.

They almost cut straight through us off an early scrum, when Manu Tuilagi came on the charge. Foxy got quite narrow and only a dropped ball got us out of jail. It was a wake-up call for him and me: time to tighten up. Manu was a big unit with a low centre of gravity, a bristling ball of muscle who performed a similar battering-ram role to me. Moments later, another assault. The ball was floated off the top of a line-out and Tuilagi came barrelling towards me. Here we go. I set myself, dropped my shoulder and absolutely *buried* him. He looked confused as he returned to his feet. He was used to bulldozing through players. Not today, pal. One-nil.

As the first half progressed, my duel with Tuilagi intensified. I felt like a boxer racking up points against a heavyweight rival. For every tackle where I knocked him back, I'd have a carry where I gained yards. Not easy yards, but my momentum was getting me beyond the first hit and keeping us on the front foot. I was back in my element, coming on those lines, running as hard as I could against the grain, backing my weight and power in the tackle. In a game of that magnitude you don't feel pain. You could snap your arm in two and not realise. It gets me excited just thinking about it.

The first half flew by in a frenetic blur, and we started winning the fifty–fifty calls. Steve Walsh was the man in the middle, and he loved being the centre of attention. Every time a big decision was due, his gaze would drift to the magnified image of himself on the big screen. England had dropped an early scrum, which planted a seed in Walsh's mind. Rightly or wrongly, he decided that we had the superior scrum, and the penalty count started mounting in our favour.

We were 9–3 ahead at the break, and comfortable. As well as dominating the scrum battle, we had England in trouble at the breakdown. Dan Lydiate's injury had opened the door for Justin Tipuric, and he and Warby had formed an impressive 6–7 partnership. 'Tips' is special, and would have had countless more Test starts if he hadn't been in direct competition with Sam. He's as skilful as any back, but what sets him apart is his engine. He's the sort of bloke you can picture running five miles up a mountain every morning without ever getting out of breath. He may not be the biggest, most powerful model on the forecourt, but in terms of fuel efficiency he's in a class of his own. Unlike a regular human whose output dips as time ticks on, he has as much energy in the eightieth minute as he does in the first. He never gets tired, and never makes mistakes.

With the game entering a critical period, a fired-up Ken Owens tore into contact, ripping the ball from Tom Wood's grasp. Tips pounced, and we snapped into attack mode, a transition we'd practised many times in training. Two quick passes to get the ball into space. In the blink of an eye we'd shifted it to Cuthy on the right wing. He had 40 metres of open space still to cover, and Mike Brown had the angle on him, but he put the hammer down and flew past him on the outside, dumping him with a textbook hand-off. It was a sensational finish.

If that try sent the crowd into raptures, the next was enough to blow the roof off. It began on our own 22 when Toby Faletau's dancing feet helped him evade a number of flailing tackles. Warby, less inclined to employ the sidestep, took the Roman Road, pumping his knees and arms all the way to their 10-metre line, where Owen Farrell just about scragged him to the floor. We'd aligned perfectly behind the ruck, finding our width and depth in time for Mike to unleash our three-quarter line into the heart of the backpedalling England defence. Fix and give, fix and give. Biggar to Halfers, Halfers to me. Manu flew out of the line to shut me down, but I just about managed to get the pass away. Tips did the rest. Mike Brown was again the last line of defence, and he was trying his best to shepherd Tips towards the touchline. Any other back-row forward would have put his head down and charged into contact. Instead, like a chess grandmaster, Tips was able to run several options through his mind and choose the one most likely to unlock the defence. He sold a dummy to check Brown's momentum before changing his angle to run directly at him. Brown committed to the tackle, leaving Cuthy unmarked and in space on the outside. All he needed to do was collect Tips's pass and dive over the line.

Tips could have scored that try himself. He'd done all the hard work and bamboozled the defence, only to give the glory to someone else. Delivering that level of precision when the stakes are at their highest is mind-blowing. During that period, Warby took all the accolades and rightly so, but if pushed, I'd have to say that Tips is the best open-side Wales have ever had.

Those tries are so firmly ingrained in the minds of every Welsh fan that Dan Biggar's drop goal is often forgotten. That was arguably the decisive moment. It came between the two tries and isn't remembered with the same degree of giddy excitement, but it was the score that put the game beyond doubt. It took us from 17-3 to 20-3, extinguishing any hopes of an England comeback. Bigs had never quite won the hearts of the misty-eyed romantics who thought all Wales fly-halves should be jinkers and dancers in the mould of Phil Bennett and Barry John, but he was and remains one of the most tactically astute players in the game.

It seems arrogant to admit it, but while we were waiting to receive the kick-off after Cuthy's decisive try, he and I were already planning our celebrations. Do we go back to the Vale after the dinner, or stay in town and push on through? Where would we start? Cuthy and I were the party animals and knew Cardiff's haunts better than anyone. It was an entirely novel experience knowing that we couldn't lose. Big games like that are usually so tense that you can't even begin to relax until long after the final whistle has blown. There were still fifteen minutes left to play, but England were dead and buried, their Grand Slam dreams trampled into the Millennium Stadium turf.

The final score was 30-3. A record victory against England and a second successive championship. Although it wasn't a Grand Slam, it felt more special than 2012 because of the journey we'd been on to get there. Rob Howley had had a hell of a time of it. He'd been mocked, patronised and pilloried during the eight-game losing streak, but he'd toughed it out and finished with his hands around the trophy. Some of the other players didn't have the same level of respect towards him that I did. Each to their own, but Rob was one of my biggest influences, and I couldn't speak too highly of him.

I think some people missed the subtleties of his coaching. Sean O'Brien criticised him after the 2017 Lions tour, suggesting that Johnny Sexton and Owen Farrell were running the attack and that Rob was largely redundant. I wasn't there, but knowing Rob as I do, that would have been a deliberate play. He's always been keen on empowering players and making them feel involved in the decision-making process. If you feel ownership of an idea, you're more likely to act on it. Rob has an incredibly analytical rugby brain, and is more than capable of coming up with the plays and strategies required to unpick defences, but he wasn't dictatorial about it. He'd start a conversation, ask the players what they thought, and often, because of the environment he'd created, they'd come up with solutions that matched his own. He'd achieve his aim without having to force it down their throats. That's clever coaching.

He encouraged me to be a leader for Wales, and would always be on my shoulder asking what I thought the best plays were, when he knew the right answer. It was about encouraging me to think rather than telling me *what* to think. About being a collaborator rather than a dictator. If players got it wrong or weren't on the same page, *then* he'd assert his authority. That's where the subtlety lay. His hands-off approach was interpreted by some as a lack of insight, when actually the reverse was true. During that year, he'd stood firm as the storm raged around him, and helped deliver an emphatic victory in the most satisfying circumstances. For that he has my lasting respect.

Gethin Jenkins may have been an authoritative captain, but his post-match speech was a disaster. Bellowing orders during the white-heat intensity of a Test match comes naturally to Melon, but delivering a speech to a roomful of suits and blazers is as far from his comfort zone as he can get. He fumbled his way through a few insincere thank-yous, sensibly opted not to tell any jokes, and sat down with an enormous and audible sigh of relief. I recorded the whole thing for posterity and will always have it as a blackmail option should I need it.

A few hours after the formal dinner, my shirt was unbuttoned, my tie was round my head and I was behind the DJ decks at Revolution nightclub, drenched in sweat and imploring everyone to get up on the dance floor. I don't have a clue how to DJ, so it wouldn't have been the best half hour of people's lives, but I didn't have a care in the world. That's about the only memory that's in focus. Things got very blurry after that.

As I was checking out of the Vale the day after with a thumping headache, Shaun sidled up to me. With a minimum of fuss, he thrust a bottle of Dom Perignon champagne into my hand, along with a framed photograph of the two of us. Inscribed on it was the message 'From Shaun to Jamie. 2013 Champs. Four hours, 38 minutes. No tries. Thanks for your leadership.' It was a special moment, and a reminder that after that opening game against Ireland, no one had crossed our line. He was a man of few words, not given to overt displays of affection, so that small gesture meant the world to me.

The champagne remained in its box for the best part of a month until I received my exam results. I'd passed. As soon as I'd torn open the envelope, I sounded the Horn of Gondor and organised a spontaneous celebratory session. Ten of my closest mates were there within the hour, and we headed to the Cricketers down the road. When I popped the cork on Shaun's Dom Pom, it felt like a defining moment. The end of a chapter.

That moment had been in the making for more than a decade, ever since I'd joined the Cardiff Blues academy at sixteen. To win two trophies on the bounce with Wales and pass my medical finals was a hugely satisfying reward for all the graft and stress I'd put myself through. It would take me a few more years to realise that the eight years of work were the achievement, not the piece of paper that said 'pass'. The amount I'd grown, developed and prospered during those eight years had made me a better person. It felt like a fitting juncture to park my studies for a while and concentrate on being a rugby player. Medicine could wait.

15

HAMSTRUNG

Warren Gatland was a master of psychology. In a Lions year, every member of every home nations squad is measured up for suits. You know it has no bearing on selection, as *everyone* gets their measurements taken, but it offers a tantalising glimpse of a distant prize. After the tailors had left in 2013, Gats circulated among us, telling anyone within earshot how astonished they'd been at our vital statistics. 'Jeez, boys. They've never seen a group of lads so big and strong.' Our chests, arms, quads and shoulders were bigger, wider and more rippling than those of our counterparts in England, Scotland and Ireland. It was Trump-esque, in that it was almost definitely nonsense, but the more he said it, the more we'd start to believe it. Us Welsh are not possessed of the same self-assurance as the English, and he understood the benefits of tickling our egos.

As it turned out, the denouement of the Six Nations was all the evidence he'd needed to prove we were the superior international outfit. The final game had a huge bearing on the composition of Warren's Lions squad to tour Australia in June and July. When the stakes were at their highest and a Grand Slam was on the line, we'd put our foot on England's throats and choked the life out of them. Several of their players saw their Lions hopes wilt as dramatically as a saturated red rose.

Fifteen Welshmen were picked, the most from any nation, and it was entirely justified. If there had been a question mark next to Justin Tipuric, it had turned into a big green tick. The same was true of Ian Evans. They'd transformed themselves from 'maybes' into dead certs over the course of eighty minutes in Cardiff. Richard Hibbard was another. His explosive hit on Joe Marler arguably got him on the plane at Marler's expense. He may as well have done it on the Heathrow runway. The reverse was true for a number of England players. Chris Robshaw had been the bookies' favourite to claim the captaincy. In the end, he didn't make the squad.

Unlike 2009, I felt like I belonged this time. There were no hysteri-
cal outbursts on Penarth Pier, no expensive rounds for the old man. I
hadn't listened in nervously to the official announcement, finding out
instead from my Blues team-mate Dan Fish, who casually informed
me I'd been picked when I walked off the training pitch.

The only Welshman from the starting XV that beat England not to
make it was Dan Biggar. Gatland had only picked two specialist fly-
halves and Bigs lost out to Johnny Sexton and Owen Farrell. Bigs has
never lacked for confidence, but that must have been tough to take. It
wasn't until the tour had ended that I felt able to wind him up about
it. I had a Lions jersey for a charity event and took it to a Wales session
to get some Lions autographs on it. 'Warby, mate, put your signature
on that, would you? Here you go, Tobes, can you sign that? Tips, let's
have your autograph mate. Bigs . . . oh no, sorry . . . Foxy, scribble
your name there, please.' By then, enough water had passed under the
bridge for him to see the funny side, and God knows he's dished out
enough banter himself.

During our first week's training at Ireland's Carton House, I made
a conscious effort not to hang out with people I already knew.
Gravitating towards close colleagues is the easy option, especially for
some of the more insecure Welsh boys. The confident, privately
educated Irish lads would take great pleasure in invoking the stereotype. 'Look at the Welsh boys over there, chatting amongst themselves.' The likes of Toby Faletau and Justin Tipuric would be in the
corner, mute and disengaged, while the likes of Rob Kearney and
Jamie Heaslip would be holding court, bellowing stories in their
clipped Dublin brogue, lords of their own manor. Their rugby set-up
wasn't as advanced as ours, but the golf courses were amazing, and
Owen Farrell, Sean Maitland, Alex Cuthbert and myself spent as much
time as we could on the fairways and greens of Carton House. We had
a good night out in Dublin at the end of the week, untroubled by the
laser focus of the media that would have followed us around in Cardiff.

Things got a bit tasty the following week when we lined up against
the Wales squad preparing for their tour of Japan. We were expecting
a casual walk-through, but the Welsh boys absolutely tore into us,
and within five minutes there had been several flare-ups, a few ripped

jerseys and some comical snarling and gnashing of teeth. It was obvious they were in no mood to defer to the Lions, and the session soon
acquired the intensity of a Test match.

Days before we were due to fly, Dylan Hartley was handed a ban
that ruled him out of the tour. He'd always been something of a
pantomime villain in Wales, and I'd never been his biggest fan, but
he'd surprised me at the official squad meeting. Expecting him to be
stand-offish, I was taken aback by how different he seemed from the
aggressive caricature portrayed in the press. When it emerged that
he'd sworn at the referee during the Premiership final, I was
gobsmacked. Why? It was the ultimate act of self-sabotage, and it
denied him the tour of a lifetime. He claimed it was directed at someone else, but with a rap sheet like his, that was never going to wash.

I was positioned near the front of the photo on the plane steps, after
being hidden at the back in 2009. Within four years, I'd developed
from a callow youngster into a seasoned international. Hong Kong
was our first stop, for an exhibition game against the Barbarians.
There was only a modest welcoming committee at the airport, and we
were largely anonymous as we strolled across the concourse. All of us
apart from Richie Gray. The locals were utterly transfixed by this
shaggy-haired giant, and he was swamped by a gaggle of excitable
Chinese girls desperate for a photo and a stroke of his blond locks.

In the grand tradition of touring teams, our mission was to make
the first night one to remember. We travelled en masse to Happy
Valley for the races, and enjoyed an enormous buffet surrounded by
the neon lights and high-rise towers of urban Hong Kong. When the
sun eventually rose, we stumbled out of a Wan Chai whisky bar
having guzzled copious quantities of fiery single malts. Within a few
hours, I had to report for media duties, emerging from my air-conditioned cocoon into the blast furnace of daytime Hong Kong. I was
interviewed on the roof of the hotel, where the heat combined with
my crippling hangover to give me a disorienting case of vertigo. I
spent the entire interview feeling paranoid that I was going to fall off
the roof.

I nursed the rest of my hangover in the company of two of my best mates, Rhys and Tom, who were backpacking round the Far East and had timed their trip to coincide with the Lions. We climbed up Victoria Peak, sweating out the toxins before I had to get down to serious business. The drinking stopped there. The same can't be said for the Barbarians, who spent the entire week drinking and partying, despite a ludicrous claim to the contrary. Their coach, Dai Young, had told the press they were dispensing with a century of tradition and applying an alcohol ban. He hadn't reckoned on the advent of smartphones and social media, though, and as the week progressed several photos of the Baa-Baas luxuriating on yachts and clutching enormous cocktails found their way into the public domain. Who was Dai kidding?

As a consequence, they were done as a competitive force before half-time. The conditions were debilitating enough without the added handicap of a thudding headache and a week-long hangover. They might have got away with it in London, but playing a game in soporific heat and humidity when you're already a dehydrated husk is danger-ous, and several of their players were struggling big time. The ball was as greasy as a bar of soap, and breath came in short gasps rather than long draughts. Because of the humidity, the surface of your skin was coated in a slippery, sweaty sheen, and moisture was gushing from every pore. There were huge fans at the side of the pitch, designed to cool us down, but the ambient temperature was so high, it felt like standing in front of a hairdryer. There was no respite, and no matter how much water you drank, you felt permanently parched. I played for sixty minutes and lost a kilogram in weight for each of the three quarters I played in. Some of the big lads in the tight-five lost a lot more than that.

Brian O'Driscoll had missed a few of the training camps because he'd played in the Pro14 final, so Foxy and I were given the first shot in the midfield. Though the Barbarians were an absolute rabble, I felt quick and strong, and even out-jumped Joe Rokocoko for a high ball, which hardly ever happened. Despite the Baa-Baas' undercooked approach, the game didn't lack for a competitive edge, as shown when the normally mild-mannered hooker Schalk Brits took a swing at his Saracens clubmate Owen Farrell. Ultimately, though, their spirits wilted, and we cantered to a 59–8 win, scoring eight tries in the process. It was a very different experience from the opening match of the South African tour in 2009, when we'd been in danger of outnumbering the crowd.

There'd been a healthy degree of cynicism around the fixture, which many had dismissed as a meaningless sop to the sponsors. The Lions claimed it had been a vital part of their mission to spread the gospel, but that was undermined when a local player who'd trained with the Barbarians all week wasn't picked in their side. A raft of newspaper columns questioned the wisdom of the stop-off, claiming it was an unnecessary match played in debilitating conditions that was likely to hinder rather than help our preparations. I took a simpler view. As a rugby traditionalist, I knew that these were two of the most iconic jerseys in our sport, and to be involved in a match between the Lions and the Barbarians was to be involved in a small piece of history. That was enough for me.

The opposition wasn't much better when we arrived on Australian shores. Western Force were the weakest of Australia's Super Rugby sides and had been further denuded by the absence of their internationals. The Wallabies coach, Robbie Deans, had banned his Test stars from playing in the warm-up games, a move widely condemned as being out of keeping with the Lions spirit. It was a cynical ploy to starve us of quality opposition so we'd arrive at the Test series undercooked. It may have protected their Wallabies from getting injured ahead of a series they were desperate to win, but it denied them the chance to pull on their club jerseys against the most famous touring side of all. It was a cold, clinical decision.

Brian O'Driscoll played with Manu Tuilagi in that game and they went well, putting the pressure back on Jonathan Davies and me. Watching them dovetail together from the touchline, regardless of the opposition, made me a bit twitchy. Drico still oozed class, and Manu was a blockbuster player capable of inflicting serious damage. There was little forceful about Western Force's performance, and they were buried under an avalanche of points. It was another emphatic win, but any joy was tempered by the tour-ending injury suffered by Cian Healy. Cian is one of life's eccentrics: an old-school tourist with a sneaky cigarette habit and a caffeine addiction. It was particularly distressing to see such a vivacious character lying there, crying tears of pain and frustration so early in the tour, especially in a game of such little consequence.

My heart fluttered when the team was announced for the next game, against Queensland Reds in Brisbane, and I wasn't in it. Foxy and Manu had been picked in the midfield. I understood the rationale – they wanted to try all the different combinations – but it meant I'd now been ignored for the first two games in Australia. Were they resting me, or was this a sign? Years of being Gatland's go-to man at 12 didn't stop me getting nervous. I knew the game after that was against Combined Country, a team put together from players from Queensland Country and New South Wales Country, which didn't really whet the appetite. It would be like the Royal XV game four years earlier against a scratch side of plumbers and electricians. If Manu and Foxy dovetailed well against the Reds, I'd then have to shine in a game where we'd be expected to rack up 80-odd points. It's hard to excel in those games because they're never a true test.

I didn't get the reassurance I sought from Warren Gatland, who remained as distant as ever. I was used to his ways, but some of the other lads found him a bit aloof. There was a clear method to his approach: it kept players guessing and ensured he wasn't accused of favouritism. That was something we were all conscious of. A tour party containing fifteen Welshmen and led by Wales's national coach could easily fracture if a strict hierarchy wasn't maintained. He was professional, but never intimate. Interactions were transactional rather than emotional. He didn't do much actual coaching, and what he did do was mainly with the forwards, so as backs, our exposure to Warren was limited to opening and closing huddles on the training park. The specialist coaches led the sessions, but there was no doubt who was in charge. He'd cultivated an image as an all-seeing overlord, an enigmatic presence hovering in the background.

We were expecting more resistance in Queensland than we'd encountered in Perth. Queensland is rugby country, and the Reds were at the peak of their powers, having won the Super Rugby title in 2011. Their coach, Ewen McKenzie, was being touted for the Wallabies job, and a Lions scalp would definitely have enhanced his burgeoning reputation. They played an attractive brand of rugby, spearheaded by their maverick fly-half, Quade Cooper. Few players divided opinion like Quade. His unorthodox, singular style was as likely to lose you a game as win you one. Depending on your perspective, he was either a magician touched by genius, or a rampant narcissist with a tendency to self destruct. Robbie Deans's opinion leaned towards the latter, as he'd left him out of the Wallabies squad. His loyal fan base was outraged at the snub, and he became something of a cause célèbre ahead of the match. The Wallabies' loss, according to the local press, was very much Queensland's gain. I was delighted he wasn't in the Wallabies squad. He'd been a nemesis of ours for a number of years, and I was sick of the sight of him in a green-and-gold jersey. Wales hadn't beaten Australia for five years, and he'd been one of the key antagonists in that Australia side.

At the airport ahead of our flight to Brisbane, I bumped into my old PE teacher, Dent-head Dai. He'd taught me from year seven at school and was now here on the other side of the world to watch me on the Lions tour. It was a poignant moment, and one of several occasions on tour when I felt like I was right back in Cardiff. I'd seen Dai Young, Casey Laulala and Rhod Manning in Hong Kong, and had met my parents for coffee in Perth. I may have been 12,000 miles from home, but there was a constant stream of reminders connecting me with my rugby past.

I watched helplessly from the stands as the Reds ripped into the Lions, causing them a serious amount of trouble. Their star Wallabies may have been absent, but they proved ferociously competitive even without the likes of Will Genia, James Horwill, Rob Simmons and James Slipper. Their rampaging long-haired Beau Robinson looked more like a surfer than a back-row forward, but he covered every blade of grass as he went toe to toe with Sam Warburton in the battle of the breakdown. Elsewhere, our supposedly superior scrum was shunted back several times by a fired-up home pack desperate to land a blow before the Test series began. The lads eventually came through,

Andy Powell and I attempting to shackle Chris Paterson during the 'miracle game' in 2010. While the drama was unforgettable, the game will be forever remembered for what Powell did afterwards.

Touching down against Toulon en route to our Challenge Cup triumph in 2010. My dad would later berate me for taunting the French fans in the stand.

The opening two minutes of the 2011 World Cup quarter-final were among the best of my career, and the match remains an all-time personal highlight.

A rare hug with Gats after the victory over Ireland. It was particularly gratifying for him given the unsavoury way his time with Ireland had come to an end.

My biggest regret. There was precious little I could say to console Sam Warburton after we'd lost by a point to France in the semi-final.

Lazarus! After Scott Williams's match-winning cameo against England in the 2012 Six Nations, I had a point to prove against Italy.

Grand Slam! Revenge was sweet as we toppled France in Cardiff to claim a second Six Nations clean sweep under Gatland.

Rags to Riches. Alex Cuthbert went from earning the same wage as a supermarket shelf-stacker to a six-figure bonus as his lethal finishing proved a point of difference in our surge to Grand Slam glory.

The purest natural high I've ever experienced. Jamming with the Manic Street Preachers in Melbourne.

Hamstring hell. Meeting up with the family at Sydney's Opera Bar in 2013 was a welcome distraction from my inner demons as I wrestled with the injury that nearly denied me a place in the Lions Test team.

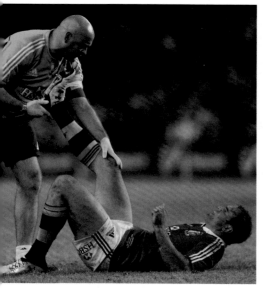

It felt like a knife had plunged into my thigh. The moment when I thought my Lions dream was over.

A win against the All Blacks in the red of Wales is one of the few things that eluded me in my career. I'd happily have swapped my Man of the Match performance in 2014 for a victory.

Heading towards the try line in the decisive Test between the Lions and the Wallabies. The series win was the Lions' first in sixteen years.

The breathtaking views from our 2015 World Cup training camp in Switzerland almost made up for the daily floggings we received.

I loved my time as part of a star-studded squad at Racing 92, though it didn't end as I'd have liked it to.

The irresistible force against the immovable object. The press hyped up my duel with England's Sam Burgess in our 'Pool of Death' match at the 2015 World Cup.

Another Twickenham triumph for Gatland's Wales; a result that would ultimately see England become the first tournament hosts to fail to reach the knockout stages.

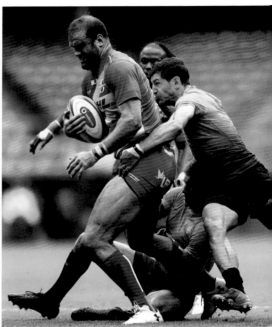

I didn't last the distance, but my appearance for Cambridge University in the 2015 Varsity Match was a proud moment, and a welcome departure from the pressure cooker of international rugby.

My South African sojourn with the Stormers was meant to be the perfect denouement to my career, but the global pandemic put paid to that.

Flying high at Quins. I enjoyed the swashbuckling approach at the Stoop, but I came crashing back down to earth when a contractual dispute led to the end of my Wales career.

Above: My omission from the 2017 Lions squad allowed me to fulfil a lifelong ambition and captain my country on a tour of the South Pacific. Here I am leading the team out in Apia, Samoa.

Left: Becoming a parent has put everything into perspective. Nicole and I with our beautiful baby boy, Tomos Rhys Roberts.

but the game wasn't without its casualties, as a forlorn-looking Tommy Bowe trooped off clutching what appeared to be a broken hand.

From Queensland, we travelled south to Newcastle, a place that holds the title (once held by Cardiff) of being the biggest coal-exporting town in the world. The rugby league side Newcastle Knights are based there, so rugby union came a distant second in the eyes of the locals, making our appearance something of a novelty. This match against Combined Country was the very definition of a missionary game: a mis-match against a ragtag brigade of semi-pro players for whom playing against the Lions would be an undisputed career highlight. One of their props was the grandson of a former Scarlet, who admitted afterwards to being a staunch Wales and Lions fan. His broad Aussie accent was a little incongruous, considering his name was Dylan Evans. He later resurfaced at the Scarlets.

It was a lose-lose game for me. However well I played, it was never going to be a yardstick for Test selection. Win by a narrow margin, and we'd have been pilloried for not putting an inferior side to the sword; win by a landslide, and the game would have been dismissed as pointless. It was the latter scenario that unfolded as we ran in ten tries and scored 64 unanswered points. I was back in the saddle with Drico in the midfield, but we were playing outside a rookie fly-half in Stuart Hogg, who'd barely ever worn the ten jersey. That didn't stop Mike Phillips naming him 'DC' after Dan Carter, because what he lacked in age and experience, he made up for in confidence. Whether it was genuine self-belief or a bit of bluster, he thought nothing of bossing his infinitely more experienced forwards around.

I hardly needed an alarm on tour, as I spent so much time rooming with Matt Stevens, and the first thing I'd hear in the morning would be his dulcet tones emanating from the shower. He had quite the repertoire, encompassing the chart hits of the day, classic rock tunes, show tunes and the occasional madrigal or sea shanty. His positivity was infectious, and I'd bound out of bed as he'd be hitting the high notes. His selection for the Lions tour had been a big surprise after a cocaine scandal and two-year ban had derailed his career. At the age of thirty, he'd thought his best years were behind him, but Gatland recognised in him someone who could lift the mood purely by the force of his personality. He was so energetic and sociable, and seemed to know someone in every town we stopped in. Our bags would barely have touched the floor before he'd whipped out his phone and started making plans to meet friends for coffees, beers and meals out. He was incapable of sitting in the room and chilling. During that Newcastle trip, he sneaked out on his own for a massive slab of cake, and was spotted by fitness coach 'Bobby' Stridgeon as the boys returned from a training session on the bus. He'd chosen a café right on the main drag, and Bobby ordered the driver to pull up outside and honk his horn continuously while Matt scoffed his cake. If he thought it was going to shame him into leaving it, he was wrong. Matt just sat there grinning and shoving forkfuls into his mouth until there was barely a crumb left.

The next game, against the New South Wales Waratahs in Sydney, was seen as a dry run for the first Test, so I was mightily relieved to get the nod. We delivered our best performance of the tour by some distance, carving the Waratahs to shreds. Our backline clicked into place, and as the game progressed we developed a near-telepathic connection. The game plan was basic enough: we played on the front foot with tempo and pace and allowed our ability to do the rest. We were smart, disciplined and physical, and they couldn't live with us. There was history in this game. Twelve years earlier, in one of the defining episodes of the 2001 Lions tour, Ronan O'Gara had been the victim of a thuggish, violent attack by Duncan McRae, who'd unleashed a furious barrage of punches during a sustained assault. O'Gara was barely recognisable afterwards, his eye forced shut and his face horribly swollen. It may have influenced forwards coach Graham Rowntree's pre-match speech when he told us that the time for being polite tourists was over. We were to go out there and 'smash up their house'.

There had been a load of negative stuff written about us in the Aussie press. We'd been labelled, derisively, as 'slabs of meat', supposedly lacking the subtlety and creativity so prized down under.

The Waratahs game exposed that nonsense for what it was. Leigh Halfpenny had one of those games where everything he touched turned to gold. He couldn't miss from the tee, knocking over everything that came his way, and bagged a couple of tries, for a 30-point haul. It was the culmination of everything that had happened on tour so far, the performance we'd been building towards. Then disaster struck.

With thirteen minutes left, and the Waratahs flailing on the ropes, I stooped to collect a low pass and sank to my knees in agony. It felt like someone had plunged a knife into the back of my thigh. A disorienting warmth flooded my leg, and my immediate thought was *Tour over*. It wasn't an innocuous click or a pop; it was a rip, and I didn't need my medical training to tell me I'd torn my hamstring. A reel of film footage whirred through my mind. Images of Jerry Flannery, Stephen Ferris and Cian Healy danced before my eyes, Lions who'd been cursed by injury's fateful hand. I was now one of them. *It's happened to me. I'm not going to be a Lions Test player again.*

Play continued around me while Eanna Falvey, our head of medical, ran on. I was so emotional I could barely speak as I shook my head despairingly and pointed to my hamstring. By then the pain had subsided, but I knew instinctively that it was a bad injury and not something I could run off. Eanna's disposition did nothing to reassure me.

I'd grown up watching the *Living With Lions* DVD of the 1997 tour, and one of the most heart-rending episodes was the injury that ruled Rob Howley out of the Tests. He was arguably the best scrum-half in the world at that time, and he was robbed of the chance to go head to head with Joost van der Westhuizen. The image of him in tears, inconsolable on the physio bed, had stayed with me. Now, in a strange circle-of-life moment, I was that inconsolable Welshman, and it was Rob, in his role as assistant coach, who was trying to comfort me. I pointed it out to him through tear-stained eyes, and we both laughed a hollow laugh. The contrast in emotions was stark as the boys trooped back in at full time, joyous and triumphant, and I sat staring into space. A few of the lads came up and put a hand on my shoulder, but no one could relate to the depth of my pain.

A scan revealed it was a grade-two tear. A grade-one tear is a mild strain, and a grade-three is a complete tear or avulsion that usually takes months to heal. Mine was somewhere in between, and it normally requires a four-to-six-week lay-off. I'd resigned myself to an early flight home, and when tour manager Andy Irvine approached me on the Monday, I assumed he was the harbinger of bad news. There was no point keeping me on tour as a dead weight. I was lying on the physio bed when he approached and I braced myself for confirmation of the worst. His opening gambit took a few seconds to compute. 'Jamie, I've spoken to Gats, and we're keeping you on tour. Let's do everything in our power to get you fit.' The medics had persuaded them that I *might* be fit for the third Test, and that was enough for them to keep the faith. It was an enormous show of loyalty, and my spirits soared immediately. I wasn't stupid, I knew the chance remained wafer-thin, but they were willing to take a punt.

As much as I'd been in championship-winning sides in 2012 and 2013, I'd had some major disappointments. The Lions series, Six Nations and Heineken Cup defeats in 2009 still rankled, and the 2011 World Cup semi-final remained an open wound. My career had been peppered with agonising defeats, and I'd persuaded myself that this tour was a shot at redemption, a chance to wipe away those festering memories and swap heartbreak for glory. There was still a chance.

All the joy was sucked out of the tour during the week that followed, as every waking hour was devoted to my recovery. And there were more waking hours than usual. If I had any hope of making that final Test, I had to ice the hamstring every two hours, day and night. We moved on to Canberra after Sydney, and I barely slept for four days. Physio Prav Mathema had given me a contraption to wrap around my hamstring every two hours, so my alarm would sound off with depressing regularity. To ensure my nocturnal icing didn't disturb anyone else, I was given my own room, which increased the feeling of isolation. Made by Game Ready, it was essentially a cryotherapy cuff: a compression sleeve that wraps tightly around your hamstring, with near-freezing water circulating within. It was a crucial part of the process, and the only way to reduce the swelling.

Canberra was like a fever dream: I existed in a zombified state, punctuated by brief periods of broken, shallow sleep. The Lions' defeat to the Brumbies almost felt like it didn't happen. Concerned that injuries were mounting up, Gats had called in Billy Twelvetrees, Brad Barritt, Christian Wade and Shane Williams and thrown them into the same backline after just one training session together. I'd lost track of how many farewell games Shane had had, but unlike his final bows with the Ospreys and Wales – when he scored in the last minute on each occasion – this was no such fairy tale. They were hostages to fortune, and the result, while depressing, wasn't a huge surprise. I watched it through a fug of sleeplessness, and was alarmed at the ease with which we surrendered possession on the deck. This was a big strength of the Wallabies, and here we were, days out from the first Test, being schooled at the breakdown by a half-strength Brumbies side.

It also ignited a furious debate about the cheapening of the Lions jersey, which ruffled feathers on both sides of the divide. The players picked in the original party may have thought their status was diluted by the presence of a bunch of hired guns, and those hired guns probably considered themselves little more than cannon fodder, collateral damage in the pursuit of a Test series victory. Shane was an exceptional case because he was a former Lion, but the other three weren't necessarily the next cabs off the rank, just the nearest back-up players to Australia. George North and Tommy Bowe were also sidelined with injury at this point, and Warren was desperate to preserve the fit first-choice backs he still had left. Part of me thinks they weren't Lions, just mercenaries who got to wear the shirt, but that wasn't my concern or theirs. From a purely selfish point of view, I was just fighting to get fit.

The euphoria of being kept on tour had waned by the time we returned to Brisbane, and the monotony of my rehab was getting me down. Brisbane, with its stunning sun-dappled coastline, is a beautiful place to pass the time, and its warm climate is reflected in the sunny disposition of the locals, but my mood was increasingly dark. I was desperate to repay the faith Gats and Andy Irvine had shown, but the prospect of playing again felt increasingly out of reach. I was barely able to walk without limping, so how on earth could I be in contention for a gladiatorial battle in a fortnight's time?

Prav told me to walk as far and for as long as I was able, but not to put any load through my leg. I couldn't stretch, couldn't bend and certainly couldn't lift weights. Ice, walk, massage. That was it. Ordinarily, it would be the dream ticket: a fortnight off to explore Brisbane, to dip in and out of its coffee shops and gaze dreamily at the yachts in the harbour, to amble without purpose around the South Bank and Epicurious Garden. But as earnest as it sounds, I was there on a mission, and right then I felt helpless and frustrated. I couldn't train, and while they meant well, the constant barbs from the lads about being a 'freeloader' were beginning to grate.

Foxy was selected at 12 for the first Test, on 22 June. I sat down with him and went through some of the intricacies of playing inside centre, and that was about the limit of my input. To the untrained eye, 12 and 13 are interchangeable, but there are big differences. As a 12, or inside centre, you get more direct traffic in your channel, and everything happens tighter to the set piece, which gives you less time to make decisions. Someone is always coming at you off a maul, line-out or scrum, so you have to commit early. When you're at 13, or outside centre, you're more worried about the space between you and your winger, whereas with 12 there's always a part of you that's looking after the fly-half on the inside. It's a channel teams target to get forward momentum, so there's a big responsibility to stop that at source. Foxy was my mate, and had been in outstanding form, so I was more than happy to pass on a couple of tips, but I was devastated to be watching from the sidelines. Clapping the lads out from the changing room was a far cry from being strapped up, pumped up and ready for battle.

Foxy set the tone early by knocking Christian Leali'ifano out with his first carry. It was unfortunate for Christian, who got himself in the wrong position, but it was a significant marker to lay down. We had some serious power players, and an early psychological blow had been landed. They'd lost only one man, but had to reconfigure their entire backline as a result. He was also, and this would prove critical, their main goal-kicker.

If we had a range of power athletes, the Wallabies had themselves an absolute freak. Controversy has followed winger Israel Folau at every turn since, but back then the world was able to revel in what he'd surely call his God-given talent. He'd starred in rugby league and Australian Rules, and had brought those skills to bear in the union code. Early in the match he went up for a high ball, planted a knee in the back of one of our players and caught the ball above his head. I'd not seen that kind of raw athleticism in union before.

He struck the first blow on the scoreboard too in what was a typically Australian try. We were in our attacking shape in their 22, patiently going through the phases, when the ball spilt loose, allowing scrum-half Will Genia to set off on a mazy, weaving run. We snapped into scramble-defence mode, but he made it to our 22 before we'd recovered our senses. The Wallabies flooded the field, giving Genia options inside and out, and it was Folau who received the kick-pass to canter over the line.

George North, clearly miffed that Folau was getting all the attention, decided to get in on the act, and single-handedly scored one of the best individual tries the Lions has ever seen. Gobbling up a loose kick, he set off on a counter-attack, bamboozling the first two defenders with a double step, before accelerating through the gears and cruising around Genia on the outside, taunting him with a raised finger before touching down. He later apologised for that, but he could be forgiven in the heat of the moment.

The gauntlet had been laid down, and Folau responded with interest. With half-time approaching, the ball was worked out to him on the wide right-hand side. He had three defenders to beat and 40 metres to cover and did so with barely a hand laid on him. He beat Sexton with a sidestep and handed off Alex Corbisiero, before rounding Halfers with a lightning injection of pace. It was a masterclass in three-quarter play. Balance, dexterity, strength and speed in one fluid movement. His ability to change direction at full throttle was astonishing. He may have been a similar sort of build to me, but he was twice the athlete I was.

Ten minutes into the second half, Cuthy scored a wonder try of his own. The Wallabies backline was in disarray by that point, with Christian Leali'ifano, Berrick Barnes and Pat McCabe all off injured. It meant Michael Hooper, a flanker, had been pressed into emergency midfield duty, and he was no match for a rampaging Alex Cuthbert. He came thundering into the line, collecting Sexton's flat pass at top speed, before galloping over to score. The travelling fans were in raptures. Not only was their team 20–12 ahead, but they were being treated to some of the most sumptuous rugby the Suncorp Stadium had witnessed.

I knew from seven years of playing against the Wallabies that they never know when they're beaten, and it was their stubborn refusal to roll over that kept them in the game, eventually narrowing our lead to 23–21. Ironically, it was one of our greatest strengths that proved our Achilles heel at the death. Our scrum hadn't dominated in the way we'd hoped, but we'd begun to get a shove on during the second half. In classic northern-hemisphere style, we saw the scrum as a potential source of penalties, as opposed to a platform to launch attacks. With that in mind, we'd often keep the ball in the scrum even when it had been successfully hooked to the No 8's feet. That way we could go for a secondary shove, hoping for a collapse and an easy penalty. That's exactly what we did in the dying moments of the Test, and it backfired on us. The penalty came, but it went the Wallabies' way. After all the hard work, and the dominance we'd enjoyed, they'd risen from the dead again.

My heart was thudding in my chest as Kurtley Beale lined up the kick. It was within his range, but the turf around him had been churned up by the scrum. It was a huge moment. If the Wallabies could pull this out of the fire, our hopes of a series victory would shrink dramatically. They're a dangerous beast at the best of times, but with the wind in their sails they're virtually invincible. The stadium fell eerily silent as Beale went through his routine. It was the same Beale who had shredded Wales's defence in the last minute of our last defeat to the Wallabies. Was he about to inflict similar misery on the Lions?

The entire stadium held its breath as he began his run-up. As he swung his leg towards the ball, he lost his footing and slipped, still making contact but without the force he'd hoped for. Sixty thousand fans gasped in unison as the ball sailed into the night sky. Despite his slip, it still appeared to be heading for the posts. I watched through my fingers as it bobbed and weaved through the air for what seemed like an age before eventually dipping beneath the crossbar and into the grateful arms of Leigh Halfpenny. Beale dropped to his knees in despair and his team-mates rushed to console him, as we leapt to our feet in delight. That's sport. One man's devastation is another man's elation.

My delight was tempered by the distance I felt. The boys who'd masterminded the win were out there in the full glare of the flood-lights, bloodied, battered and victorious. My heart was thumping like theirs, but I was just a fan in a Lions suit. I wanted to be down there amongst it, with heaving lungs and aching muscles, sharing in the camaraderie of my comrades.

No one was getting carried away, though, because we knew the outcome could easily have been so different. Brian O'Driscoll hammered that point home after the match. He'd been there in 2001 when the Lions had won the first Test, only to see it unravel in the next two. Beale's last-minute miss was one of five wayward kicks that night. Any one of them would have given the Wallabies victory. Plans for a wild celebration were dampened down by Drico's speech. He wouldn't even allow Adam Jones to buy a case of celebratory cigars in case it jinxed things the following weekend. A few of the boys ventured into Sydney for a couple of beers and a burger, but it was another night of broken sleep for me as my troublesome hamstring kept me awake and the mental demons crowded in. I was beginning to feel like the spare part the boys were labelling me as.

My mood was lifted by a text from James Dean Bradfield, frontman of the Manic Street Preachers. I'd met him a few years earlier in a greasy-spoon café behind Cardiff railway station and we'd swapped numbers, but it was still a surprise to see his name flash up on my phone. The

Manics are mad rugby fans and had organised a tour to coincide with the Lions, so I'd known he was in the country. I assumed he was getting in touch about the injury, but it was a whole lot better than that: 'How do you fancy playing a song with us on stage this Friday night?'

Not to put too fine a point on it, these guys were my heroes. Their albums had been the soundtrack to my youth. The first CD I ever owned was *This Is My Truth Tell Me Yours*. I won it in a competition on Radio Cymru. Playing alongside them was dream territory. Excitedly, I messaged back saying it would be an absolute honour, and as I was doing so, it crossed my mind that the medical team might try to veto it. All I'd be doing was standing on stage strumming an acoustic guitar – I wasn't planning on donning a spandex jumpsuit and doing Dave Lee Roth-style scissors kicks – but the medics were understandably conservative when it came to risk assessment. I knew I'd have to keep it under wraps. I wasn't training with the others, so I could easily disappear for a clandestine meeting with a rock god without any suspicions being raised.

I took a taxi to the venue at lunchtime on Friday, and wandered in during their soundcheck. For several minutes, I was treated to a private concert from my idols, James's powerful voice giving me goosebumps as it reverberated around the empty arena. When the feedback from 'A Design for Life' died down, he summoned me up to the stage and thrust a beautiful-looking acoustic guitar into my hands. He'd decided we were going to do one of their early anthems, 'You Love Us'. It was a song I'd heard a million times, but that rendition, with him sitting inches away from me, was easily the most special. Luckily, my part was pretty straightforward. I had a few chords in my locker, and he patiently taught me the changes in what amounted to my own personal guitar lesson. Even in that intimate setting, with the emotion dialled down, it was difficult not to be moved by his voice. There was familiarity in every inflection, and the singalong chorus evoked so many happy memories.

My heart quickened as I looked out at the cavernous space in front of me, picturing myself back there in six hours' time with thousands of people filling that space. I wrote the chords down on the back of my hand, went back to the hotel and dined alone, without telling a soul where I'd been. There was a guitar in the team room that Matt Stevens had been hacking around on, but two of the strings were broken, so I wasn't able to practise. Before that, I'd taught myself a bit online, but I wouldn't have had the audacity to refer to myself as a 'guitar player', certainly not in the presence of James and his bandmates. Hopefully my muscle memory would kick in when it mattered. The nerves I experienced ahead of a one-song cameo in a 3,000-capacity venue far exceeded what I was used to dealing with ahead of running out for Wales or the Lions in front of 75,000. I belonged on a rugby field, not on a sound stage. I spent a good hour in my room just deciding what to wear. As most of my clothes were Lions-branded leisurewear, I had limited options and eventually settled on skinny black jeans, black trainers and a dark shirt with the sleeves rolled up.

When the moment finally came, James introduced me to the bemused crowd as 'Jamie f***ing Roberts', and as I walked out self-consciously they burst into a chant of 'Lions, Lions, Lions'. It was utterly surreal. James struck the opening chord of 'You Love Us', the band kicked in and we were away. I couldn't hear a thing I was playing, and have no doubt my guitar was turned down to zero in the mix, but I couldn't have cared less. It was such a unique experience it's hard to put it into words. It flew by in a rush of adrenaline, but I was conscious of a voice in my head saying, *Drink it in, revel in the moment, this will never happen to you again.*

The song finished, the crowd erupted and I walked off, buzzing from the purest natural high I'd ever experienced. I've never taken drugs, but I can't imagine it would feel any better than that. I walked off the side of the stage, melted into the crowd and watched the rest of the gig as a fan. When the euphoria died down, I worried that people might judge me, might think I wasn't taking my injury seriously enough, but the truth was, if I couldn't stand and strum a guitar for three minutes, I certainly couldn't strap up and face the Wallabies in a week's time. That evening, my phone was inundated with messages, predominantly from my mates back home who'd seen the videos popping up all over YouTube. They were fuelled largely by jealousy rather than admiration. 'You lucky bastard' was the overriding sentiment.

The second Test in Melbourne was horrendously tense. It lacked the box-office moments of the first, but George North and Israel Folau continued their personal duel for world's best winger with a moment that would provide one of the defining images of the tour. George had the ball and Folau was blocking his path. If an attacker decides to hold on to the ball rather than pass, he generally has two options: run around the tackler or run through him. George came up with a third: run into him, pick him up in a fireman's lift and keep going. It was simultaneously baffling and awe-inspiring. I'd never seen that done before, and didn't think it was even possible. It defied physics. The tackler is supposed to pick the ball-carrier up, not the other way round.

Alex Corbisiero and Paul O'Connell had joined the injured list after the first Test, and the reconstituted pack struggled to assert itself, with Mako Vunipola conceding a succession of scrum penalties. When Sam Warburton hobbled off during the last quarter with what looked like a tour-ending hamstring injury, things were starting to look bleak. As in Brisbane the week before, it came down to a last-minute kick. This time, it was our chance to steal a victory we didn't deserve, but Leigh Halfpenny's kick didn't quite have the distance and the Aussies clung on for a nail-biting 16–15 win. It was a devastating outcome. We'd had a chance to put the series to bed, and we hadn't taken it. Now, the momentum was all in their favour. Our hopes, and my chances of recovery, were like the dregs of an emptying bath, circling round the plughole a few more times before disappearing altogether.

Afterwards, the Aussie press, which had been uncharacteristically subdued, dialled up the hubris. All of a sudden their boys were world-beaters and we were the charlatans they'd always assumed us to be. The Wallabies were in the ascendancy and we were falling apart at the seams. During a routine dip at St Kilda beach for some cold-water recovery the following day, a group of bikini-clad girls trotted gaily into the ocean and surrounded us. It felt like a classic bit of subter-fuge, and our suspicions were confirmed when a phalanx of photog-raphers appeared with their shutters flashing nine to the dozen. I was single, injured and quite open to a bit of female attention, but most of the married boys sheepishly retired to the beach, praying that photos of them frolicking with a bunch of tanned, athletic young ladies didn't make it to the back pages of the British and Irish papers. It turned out we were being paranoid. They were the Victoria Maidens American football team, who *played* in bikinis, and Adam Beard had invited them down as part of his endless quest to glean knowledge from other sports. Quite what he expected to learn, I'm not sure, but it certainly enlivened an otherwise unpleasant session.

To prepare for the final Test, we decamped to the coastal resort of Noosa, in a move described by the former England and Lions coach Clive Woodward as a 'massive and unnecessary distraction'. On the contrary, it was a master stroke. 'Noosa' is an old Aboriginal word meaning 'place of rest', and that was exactly what we needed, particu-larly the boys who'd slogged it out in both Tests. All rugby was cancelled, and we had three days to chill. The level of scrutiny had increased exponentially as the tour progressed, and after six weeks away from home, we'd all become a little tightly wound. We had a huge blowout on the Sunday, sinking Jägerbombs at a local bar and singing until our voices grew hoarse. The Monday and Tuesday were ours to do with as we wanted. A bunch of us went surfing, and a few of the boys hired jet skis or went hiking on the coastal path. It was blissful. The town itself was a funky, bohemian little place full of art galleries and organic cafés selling smoothies and artisan coffee. The locals wandered the streets barefoot, and the vibe was mellow and relaxed.

I could manage a paddle in the ocean, but I hadn't attempted to run since my injury. On the Wednesday, Prav took me out for a light jog to test the hamstring and see where I was at. I didn't break sweat but still felt quite ungainly and restricted in my movements, and I ended the session consumed with doubt. I'd seen Tommy Bowe and George

North make Lazarus-like recoveries during the tour, but time didn't appear to be on my side. The leap from a gentle, stiff jog to a full-blooded Test match in four days seemed enormous. I rated my chances as fifty-fifty, and that was being generous. Warren would rely on the medics' advice, but I was the one that knew deep down whether I was ready.

It was turning out to be a serious moral dilemma, and my emotions vacillated dramatically back and forth during the week. My hamstring was still tight and causing me pain, but I was desperate to play. That desperation was almost certainly clouding my judgement. Was I kidding myself? It was the biggest game of my career, and from a self-ish perspective, I couldn't bear the thought of watching it from the sidelines. But what if my hamstring blew out in the first ten minutes? I'd be letting the team down and jeopardising their chance of glory. I knew I'd heal further in the next two or three days, but it remained a guessing game. Team versus self, the biggest dilemma of my career, and it crossed my mind more than once to take the decision out of Warren's hands and pull out.

A quarter of an hour before the team was due to be announced, I was playing table tennis in the hotel courtyard. Out of the corner of my eye, I saw Warren Gatland and Rob Howley approach Brian O'Driscoll, and the three of them walked off together. It could have meant one of two things. Fifteen minutes later we were assembled in the team room and, with his usual lack of ceremony, Gats pulled the crumpled piece of paper from his pocket and dispassionately read out the team for the deciding Test. 'Fifteen, Leigh Halfpenny. Fourteen, Tommy Bowe. Thirteen, Jonathan Davies. Twelve, Jamie Roberts . . .' My heart started to pound as the rest of the team was named. I was in. I'd bloody made it.

The team room is always a whirlpool of conflicting emotions after a big announcement, but these are usually processed quietly and internally. Overt displays of emotion are considered inappropriate. The same couldn't be said for the public reaction when it filtered through that Brian O'Driscoll, the four-time Lions tourist and darling of the Irish press, had been dropped. The quiet solitude of Noosa was replaced by a rabid media frenzy as sections of the Irish press went into full-on attack mode. Gatland, they said, had displayed the latent bias they always suspected was bubbling beneath the surface. When the pressure was really on, he'd reverted to his tried-and-trusted formula. I was one of ten Welshmen in a XV containing seven changes from the week before. Mike Phillips was back after recovering from a knee injury, Taulupe Faletau replaced Jamie Heaslip, Alex Corbisiero returned to bolster the scrum, Richard Hibbard was picked ahead of Tom Youngs at hooker, and Alun Wyn was handed the captaincy in Warby's absence. All of these, though, were trivial subplots compared with the dominant narrative of Drico's omission. He hadn't even made the twenty-three.

If the teams for the first two Tests had been chosen by consensus, this one had Warren's stamp all over it. The buck stopped with him, and he had put his neck on the line. Jonathan Davies and I were a championship-winning partnership and knew each other inside out. Foxy had deputised admirably at 12 in the first two Tests, but my return meant he could shift to his natural position of outside centre, casting Drico to the margins. The Lions had failed to make a single line-break in the second Test, and Gats craved the element of power I brought to the position. My brief was to get out there and do some damage.

I sat next to Foxy on the bus to training and, with characteristic understatement, he said, 'The next few days are going to be interesting.' We were well aware of the affection Brian O'Driscoll was held in, and knew we'd be public enemy number one among the Irish supporters. Brian mounted the steps and immediately came to shake our hands. He'd publicly heaped praise on Foxy earlier in the tour, not realising that Jon's rise would accelerate his own downfall. He'd have been hurting desperately, but he did the right thing in offering his congratulations. I felt horribly torn: overjoyed to have claimed my place and delighted for my mate Jon, but at the same time gutted for Drico, who'd been my partner and mentor four years earlier.

Out on the field, with the sun blazing down, Gats ambled over with his arms casually folded and asked, 'Are you ready, Doc?' My silent nod of assent was in raging conflict with my inner monologue, which was screaming, *No, I'm not!* He replied with a nod of his own, and wandered off. That was the extent of it: no questions about the pain, the stiffness, the doubts, the fears. I'd done a job for him for the past five years, and a nod was all that was required.

The sense of serenity we'd bathed in since our arrival in Noosa evaporated during that afternoon's training session, as testosterone levels soared. Johnny Sexton is rarely ever relaxed, but his patience cracked spectacularly as the handling errors piled up, and Richard Hibbard found himself on the wrong end of a lashing from his acid tongue. In my experiences with Wales and Cardiff, I'd not witnessed any player speak to a team-mate like that. I'd experienced the death stare from Paul Tito and Gethin Jenkins plenty of times, but never verbal abuse of that kind.

For a brief moment, I thought Hibs was going to knock his head off. Johnny may have been the tactical leader, with the authority to call plays, but Hibs wasn't a bloke to be messed with. He was from the mean streets of Taibach, where they were more inclined to settle an argument with fists than with words. Had the red mist descended, we'd have been looking for a new fly-half. Instead he fixed Sexton with a murderous glare, and the Irishman sensibly rowed back. The threat of violence aside, it was an incident that sharpened all of our minds. While Johnny's conduct crossed the line, it was evidence of his ultra-competitive spirit, and a reminder of what was at stake.

After the captain's run in Sydney, Foxy and I jumped on the ferry to the beach suburb of Manly. It was the last afternoon before the defining Test of our careers, and we needed to escape the pressure bubble. Whenever we roomed together we'd try to get out for a coffee the day before the game. Whether it was on the Champs-Élysées, outside the Pantheon or on George Street in Edinburgh, we'd always try to absorb some of the energy of the place we were in. The number of Lions supporters in Australia had swelled immeasurably since the Test series had begun, and there were swathes of red jerseys everywhere. The friendly faces, pats on the back and shouts of encouragement were in stark contrast to the poison pouring through Foxy's social media accounts. He's the most laid-back bloke I know, but even he was shocked by the level of vitriol being spewed in the wake of Drico's omission.

He showed me one tweet that read, 'Just landed in Sydney. Off to track down @JonFoxDavies to break his legs.' I couldn't help but laugh. Foxy was getting all the heat for taking Drico's place, when it was actually my return that had ousted Brian. Foxy was a 13, and had only been deputising at 12. Once I was back in the midfield, he was always going to shift back to his natural position. He had been one of the outstanding players on tour and was never realistically going to lose his place. Brian would be the first to admit he hadn't played brilliantly, and as much as it would have hurt him, deep down he'd have known it was the right selection. Warren had given him his first Ireland cap back in 2000, then denied him his Lions swansong. It was conclusive evidence, as I'd later discover to my cost, that he didn't allow sentimentality to cloud his vision. His choice had essentially been to either bring me back or retain the Foxy–Drico axis. But although it was my return that had forced Drico out, the slings and arrows of the outraged Irish were hurled exclusively in Foxy's direction.

I offered him as much sympathy as I could muster, but I had issues of my own to deal with. My hamstring was killing me. I've taken more anti-inflammatory pills in my career than I'd care to remember, and before every Test match I used to have a diclofenac jab in my backside. It wasn't so much a dependency as an accepted reality. I couldn't expect to put my body through the pummelling I routinely did and not require severe pain relief. The night before the Test in Sydney, I was desperate for something extra, but reluctant to confide in anyone. I feared that if I brought my doubts into the open, they'd become real. Secrecy and denial were my preferred coping mechanisms. The last person I wanted to infect with my doubt was my centre partner, who was idly flicking through a magazine on the bed opposite me. I was still in considerable pain, and didn't want Jon to know.

Sleep was difficult to come by as I wrestled with my dilemma. Doubts and anxieties always seem magnified in the small hours. The enormity of what was ahead was difficult to comprehend, and my mind was at war with itself: This could be the highlight of my career.

My hamstring is still tight. A sell-out Test match in Sydney's Olympic Stadium. *It's actually really hurting.* A series decider for the Lions. *What if I injure myself in the warm-up?* The chance of a first series win for sixteen years. *I haven't played a Test match since the England game in March.* You may never get an opportunity like this again. And on and on, through the night.

The portion of my brain normally reserved for clear-headed focus was flooded with nervous energy and doubt. All I could think about was what might go wrong: I wouldn't be able to run, I'd miss a crucial tackle, I'd collapse with the try line at my mercy. Strip all the emotion away, and the decision was an easy one. Pull out. Stop kidding yourself. But I couldn't; this was a monumental opportunity.

The day dawned, and it began with a lengthy hot shower. In private, my doubts continued to intensify. I was testing out the hamstring, stretching, leaning into it as the steam rose, willing it to feel more supple and trying to ignore the niggling pain. *Imagine how you'll feel*, I said to myself, *watching from the sidelines for the third week running as the Lions make history.* I had to at least try.

Three hours before kick-off, while Foxy was going through his usual exhaustive stretching routine, I was watching with envy at the ease with which he was moving. That was it. I went to track down Prav and Eanna, the medics. It was confession time. I told them of the pain I was still feeling, of the doubts that had kept me awake, and looking Prav in the eye, I said, 'Mate, what is the strongest stuff I can take here?' I needed the biggest legal painkiller that was allowed. Prav delved into his medical bag and retrieved a diclofenac suppository. More concentrated than a tablet or an injection, it ensures more of the drug gets into your bloodstream. It was my only hope. I surreptitiously slipped into the bathroom while Foxy was still stretching. The relief was immediate. Prav had also given me the maximum dose of tramadol, which helped numb the pain further. It was the most powerful combination of drugs I'd ever taken, and within minutes, the laser focus returned. This was one of the biggest moments of my career and I was not going to let a bit of pain get in the way.

Warren reminded us of what Geech had said four years ago, about the privilege and responsibility that went with wearing the jersey. But the difference, he said, between four years ago and now was that we had a chance to win the series. With the timing of a Shakespearean actor, he said, 'That's a big difference,' and left a long, heavy pause for it to sink in.

The coach ride to the ground was only half a mile, but it was an assault on the senses. The number of Lions fans was overwhelming and the Wallabies supporters were virtually swamped by the swirling, heaving mass of red. It was baffling to consider the fact that 40,000 fans had spent their life savings crossing continents and time zones to come and see us play. The atmosphere grew increasingly tense as the stadium hove into view, with an almost celestial light shining from the open roof. This was crunch time. Seven weeks, nine games, and it all came down to this. A winner-takes-all grand finale was the perfect dramatic climax, and it amplified the feeling of pressure and expectation on the bus.

Silence reigned as we glided inexorably to our date with destiny. My mind drifted back to my first tentative steps in junior rugby, the timing races with Dad and David at Roath Park, the thrill of my first tackle, the joy of my first try. Everything had been building slowly to this moment. This, in the celebrated words of Lions coach Jim Telfer in 1997, was my Everest. I knew my parents were inside the stadium, feeling their own kind of pressure, their own sense of expectation. As the bus pulled into the car park and the engine died, I flicked the switch. Only the present mattered now, the eighty minutes that were about to unfold. My thoughts turned from the general to the specific. I thought about my first carry, about how hard I would run, how much mayhem I would cause. I needed to make a statement.

There was a palpable energy in the dressing room. It felt like a tinderbox ready to explode if the temperature rose above a certain level. Alun Wyn delivered a calm, assured speech, devoid of histrionics. We didn't need a Churchillian call to arms, just a cold-blooded appeal to our animal instincts. He echoed defence coach Andy Farrell's words about 'taking the Wallabies to the hurt arena', while also emphasising the need for discipline, clear-headedness and an iron will. 'Never give up' were the words that continued to resonate as we strode out in front of 83,000 expectant fans.

We had a dream start. Will Genia, their X-factor scrum-half, dropped the ball off the kick-off and we surged forward, determined to capitalise. Our forwards piled into theirs from the resultant scrum and, after a series of powerful carries into the heart of their defence, Alex Corbisiero crossed for the opening try. The changes up front had transformed our pack, and the resistance the Wallabies had shown in the first two Tests began to crumble. Their scrum was in constant retreat, and we were pulverising them with the force and ferocity of our tackles and carries. Richard Hibbard was like a human cannonball, launching himself gleefully into contact and scattering Aussie defenders at will. One sickening head clash with their veteran flanker George Smith left them both looking battered and disoriented. Astonishingly, both played on.

Every Aussie indiscretion was punished by the dead-eyed accuracy of Leigh Halfpenny, who coolly kicked us into a 19–3 lead. In true Wallabies style, though, they fought back strongly. We knew they had the ability to cut us to shreds, and just before the interval, fly-half James O'Connor took advantage of a gap in our defensive line to jink his way over. The half-time score of 19–10 felt a good deal less secure than 19–3, and to compound matters, they scored first after the break. And then again after that. Thirteen points in six minutes. If 19–3 had seemed unassailable, 19–16 was as good as a reset scoreboard.

As a Welshman, I started suffering awful flashbacks. We'd experienced enough Aussie comebacks to know how dangerous they could be. As strong and powerful as we felt, they were like an agile boxer avoiding the big swinging haymakers while prodding insistently at their opponents' weak spots. Was mental strength our weak spot? Did we really have the belief, deep down in our souls, that we could win this?

The answer arrived in the last quarter with an avalanche of points. The Wallabies had thrown all their punches and run out of steam. At the end of a long, gruelling season, we dug into our reserves and discovered a gushing well of energy and dynamism. In ten breathless minutes, we delivered a series of devastating blows that left them sprawling on the canvas. Three tries in quick succession. First Johnny Sexton, then George North and finally, in what proved to be my final act in that fabled red shirt, me.

Halfpenny was instrumental in the first two, proving that place-kicking was just one weapon in his armoury. The ball was whipped quickly away from a ruck towards the left touchline and Leigh cut the line beautifully to get behind the defence. Subtly drawing the last tackler, he then delivered a deft offload to put Sexton through the gap. Not long after, he set off on a magical solo run, incorporating two dummies and a swish of the hips before putting George away. It was the crowning moment of a magnificent tour for Leigh, putting his status as Player of the Series beyond doubt.

My try was born of years of dogged repetition. I ran a line off Conor Murray that I'd run, without exaggeration, *thousands* of times over my lifetime. Very rarely would it even lead to a line-break. I'd either get gang-tackled and stopped in my tracks, create space by attracting defenders, or find a soft shoulder to make enough of a dent to cross the gain line. When Conor Murray came off the maul, George came onto his hip to fix James O'Connor, and I completely blindsided Christian Leali'ifano. It was a lovely flat pass from Murray, and as the field opened up in front of me, my overriding thought was *Have I got the gas to make this?* I was praying my hamstring would hold on. Will Genia was the only defender close enough to tackle, but I think he'd given up by then.

What followed was almost surreal. While the crowd erupted into a joyful cacophony of noise, I felt as if I'd been plunged underwater. I can't explain why, but in the immediate aftermath, I was enveloped by a strange, calm inner silence. The noise was registering but it was muffled and distant. Then, all of a sudden, the volume surged back up to ten and the enormity of what we'd achieved struck home. Four years ago, we'd had our hearts torn from our chests. This was redemption and euphoria on an unimaginable scale.

A few plays later I was subbed off. We were 25 points ahead, and I had the luxury of watching the final few moments unencumbered by fear or anxiety. I embraced Gats at the final whistle with tears in my eyes: the only time we've enjoyed anything more intimate than a handshake. In the blink of an eye, the whole squad transformed from elite sportsmen into big kids, our childhood dreams realised in the most dramatic of circumstances. Alun Wyn and I started doing snow angels on the pitch among the tumbling confetti, while the red-shirted fans threw their beers gleefully in the air.

A besuited Sam Warburton raised the trophy with Alun Wyn Jones, and Brian O'Driscoll was at the heart of the celebrations. As a four-time Lion, he could finally sign off with a series victory. Yes, he'd prefer to have been lifting the trophy in a torn, mud-stained jersey, having spilt blood for the cause, but he was now a winning Lion, and no one could take that away from him. Leigh and I were collared for a TV interview and asked if we were proud Welshmen. I replied that we were proud Lions. There were no schisms, no cliques and no national boundaries. We'd arrived as Lions, and we'd won as Lions.

I had been spellbound by the history of this mystical, travelling band of warriors since I'd first picked up a rugby ball in North Cardiff, and now here I was, standing on the shoulders of giants, carving my own name into Lions history. If the very concept had seemed imperilled after three consecutive losing tours, our exploits out here and the presence of tens of thousands of jubilant fans had surely guaranteed its survival for decades to come.

I wanted the lap of honour to last forever. When you've taken on as much as I had, and had pressure coming in from all sides, the feeling you get when you eventually reach your goal is indescribable. The exams, the injury, the scrutiny, the Drico situation, the weight of history, the public expectation: all those things combined felt like a balloon that was ready to burst. Now I experienced the blissful feeling of release as all the air rushed harmlessly out.

Daniel Craig appeared from nowhere and I started loudly humming the James Bond theme like any drunk Welsh bloke spotting James Bond would. Within seconds, the whole squad had joined in and he was surrounded by thirty-seven hairy blokes bellowing in his face. A bottle of champagne exploded, spraying its contents all over his expensive suit, but he didn't care.

I went into the Wallabies changing room, where I swapped shirts with Christian Leali'ifano and cracked a beer with Adam Ashley

Cooper. The morgue-like silence was in stark contrast to the chaos unfolding within our room. Both teams were physically and mentally drained, but while the Wallabies were slumped in their seats, licking their wounds, we were gearing up for the party to end all parties.

After that, everything unfolded in a drunken haze, and it wasn't until a few days later that individual scenes began to return to me in flashback: Simon Zebo tumbling fully-clothed into a rooftop swimming pool, Richard Hibbard puffing nonchalantly on a huge Cuban cigar, Stuart Hogg striding through the hotel lobby in a pair of nylon budgie-smugglers, Leigh Halfpenny missing the bus to Bondi and trying to hail a taxi in his pants. If there was ever a time to go absolutely nuts, this was surely it. I'd graduated from medical school, Wales had won the Six Nations and now I'd scored the decisive try in a career-defining Lions victory.

After two days of unrelenting celebrations, I woke on the Tuesday with a pounding head, a parched throat, a throbbing hamstring and what felt like a broken wrist. The combination of the suppository and the anaesthetising effects of the booze had kept my injuries at bay. I hadn't even realised that I'd damaged my wrist, which gives you some indication of the strength of the painkillers. As I prepared to board the plane home, the mother of all celebrations was about to be succeeded by the mother of all hangovers.

And it was worth every painful minute.

16

PARISIAN SKIES

I woke up bleary-eyed and disoriented to find a gaggle of angry-looking children staring at me. Rolling gingerly into a seated position, I looked around to discover I was inside a soft-play centre next to my friends Mike and Andrew, both of whom were blissfully snoring away. The low moan of a ship's horn woke them with a start, reminding me where we were. We were on the Dover to Calais ferry, and it appeared we'd spent the entire journey comatose in the boat's only play area. If the kids were angry, you should have seen their parents.

I was moving to Paris for the 2013–14 season to start my next chapter, and Mike and Andrew had offered to help. The problem was, we'd gone a little over the top during my last night in Cardiff and had boarded the ferry after very little sleep. After muttering a few embarrassed apologies, we wandered down to the vehicle deck, located our van and hit the road to Paris.

My initial destination was a hotel, after a falling-out over living quarters had nearly led to the tearing-up of my Racing Métro 92 contract. I'd been over to Paris flat-hunting earlier in the summer and had been shown around the facilities by Simon Raiwalui, the former Fiji and Newport lock forward, who was now team manager at Racing. It felt surreal being welcomed to my new club by a guy I'd hero-worshipped from the terraces at Rodney Parade back in the day. I found a lovely two-bedroom flat, in Boulogne-Billancourt, the sporting hub just to the west of Paris. Longchamps race course, Roland Garros, the Parc des Princes, Paris Saint-Germain and Stade Français's ground were all a stone's throw away. It was perfect.

The summer had passed in a breezy haze of trips and holidays without the burden of study weighing me down. Two days before I was due to move to Paris, I was sitting by the harbour on the Croatian island of Hvar when my agent called, sounding nervous. Jacky Lorenzetti, the billionaire president of Racing, had found out where I was planning to live and wasn't happy. My agent spelled it out for me: 'You'll have to tell the landlord to rip up the contract.' I nearly spat out my coffee and immediately went on the defensive, arguing that I could live wherever I damn well pleased. I could live in Germany and commute every day if I wanted to. As long as I'm in work on time, what does it matter?

I heard my agent take a deep breath before he began to lecture me on the tribalism of French rugby. As a Racing Métro 92 player, he explained, I'd be representing the people of the 92nd district, which is in the southern suburbs of Paris. It followed that I had to live there, socialise there and generally be seen to ingratiate myself into the local community. Furthermore, Racing's rivals, Stade Français, were based in Boulogne-Billancourt, and he didn't want me potentially socialising with their players. I'd always thought that Welsh rugby was parochial, but this was on a whole different level.

In my arrogance, coming off the back of the success I'd recently enjoyed, I threw a massive wobbly, telling my agent that Jacky could get stuffed if he thought he could dictate where I lived. I called his bluff, saying that if that was a deal-breaker, I wouldn't come. I was moving to Paris as a single bloke in search of adventure. I wanted to absorb the magic of one of the world's most alluring cities and place myself right in its bustling heart. It was a cultural experience as much as a rugby one, and I wasn't going to go and live in the faceless suburbs on my own. I might as well be anywhere in the world. For a club whose image was based on raffish eccentricity, whose players used to wear pink bow ties and quaff champagne at half-time, this seemed a bafflingly draconian rule.

A tense stand-off ensued, before my agent called back the next day to announce, with some relief, that Jacky had acquiesced. Not only that, he'd sourced me a bigger, grander fifth-floor apartment right in the heart of Saint-Germain that he was willing to subsidise, because the rent was an eye-watering 4,000 euros a month. It was incredible. A cavernous place, 100 metres squared, with two king-size beds, huge high ceilings, an ornate wooden door, extravagant lighting, embroidered rugs, polished parquet flooring and toile fabrics, all augmented by various ornaments and antiques. It was genuinely, authentically

French, and the location was even better than the one I'd found, strad-
dling the border of the sixth and seventh arrondissements off Boulevard
Saint-Germain, behind the Musée d'Orsay. Within seconds of leaving
the flat, I'd be on the banks of the Seine, opposite the Louvre.

I'd landed on my feet. For the following two years, I commuted to
work on my Vespa. Whether it was crisp and sunny or hammering
down with snow, I'd stick a new album on and weave in and out of the
traffic, past the Eiffel Tower and down the Left Bank before veering off
into the southern suburbs. It was a dreamy existence. I started to
develop an appreciation for the finer things, shopping in fashion
boutiques, refining my palate in small Parisian cafés and drinking in
wood-panelled bars, where I developed a taste for expensive red wine.
Out went the boot-cut jeans and check shirts; in came tailored slim-fit
trousers and plain T-shirts. The Cardiff boy was doing his best to melt
seamlessly into the Parisian hipster scene.

Jacky Lorenzetti owned a chateau in Margaux, near Bordeaux, and
loved his wine, so the post-match functions were a far more sophisticated affair than I'd been used to. Instead of necking eight pints of
gassy lager, we'd congregate around tables with perfectly laundered
white tablecloths and sup expensive wines. Then I would take my
leave and head down the Champs-Élysées to my city-centre sanctu-
ary. There were times when I had to pinch myself.

When I first arrived, the club had just appointed new coaches who'd
come from Castres as a pair. Laurent Labit, who's currently attack
coach with France, and Laurent Travers. It was a new start for them as
well as me. The set-up was light years away from what I'd experienced with Cardiff. Our training venue felt like it belonged in the
Premier League. Its sumptuous reception area gave way to a full
restaurant, where you could cook your own food. Once a week we'd be
given steaks to cook to our liking on the hot plates, and there'd be an
overwhelming selection of beautiful gourmet side dishes. The gym
was ultra-modern, the pitch was like a bowling green and the changing rooms were sleek and luxurious. It was all in stark contrast to the
pitch we played on, which was absolutely shocking. Stade Colombes

had been built as an Olympic venue in 1924, but was now crumbling into the ground. The pitch was a proper ankle-turner, festooned with divots and bare patches where the grass no longer grew. Their new home, La Défense Arena, was still in the advanced stages of planning. It has since become one of rugby's iconic venues, but sadly I never got to play there.

The coaching in France was far less sophisticated than I was used to. Passion and spirit seemed to be more prized than technical expertise, and there was a much stricter hierarchy. I was naive enough to think I'd been hired for my international pedigree and trophy-winning nous, but any attempts to help shape our game plan fell on deaf ears. Myself, Johnny Sexton, Dan Lydiate and, later, Mike Phillips and Luke Charteris were mere foot soldiers hired to follow orders. It was their way or the highway. Johnny felt as frustrated as I did. He'd won the Heineken Cup twice before arriving in Paris, but couldn't exert any kind of influence over what was, at times, a stifling and dictatorial environment. He'd try to bring ideas to the backs: kicking tactics, certain attacking and defensive structures, but they were always waved away with a dismissive Gallic shrug.

I fought it initially, before learning to accept it as a fundamental cultural difference. I was the outsider and it was up to me to adapt and be the right guy for the team. The language was an obvious additional barrier. The meetings were all in French, and I'd sit there with a furrowed brow, wondering what the hell was going on. Other cultural differences I had to accept were a laissez-faire attitude to time-keeping and a take-it-or-leave-it approach to fitness. Nine o'clock in France could mean ten past, twenty past, or whenever the other person deigned to grace you with their presence. Punctuality was something I had always placed huge importance on, and in my mind, being late for a meeting was plain rude. Some of the lads would brazenly light up cigarettes between sessions and gorge themselves on rich food during the long, drawn-out lunch breaks. I came to love these quirks, but for the first few months they were a source of immense frustration.

Dan Lydiate and I spoke about the need to stay fit for Test rugby. With all the attractions France had to offer, the copious creamy cheeses and rich red wines, it would have been easy to fall off the edge of a cliff. Dan was a diligent professional, and as much as I liked to party and burn the candle at both ends, so was I. Every Tuesday, we'd meet to do top-ups: an extra half an hour a week to keep our fitness levels where they needed to be. On the other side of the country, down on the Mediterranean Coast, Gethin Jenkins had received a brand-new Wattbike indoor trainer, courtesy of the WRU, so concerned were they at his loss of conditioning during his time at Toulon.

Back home, I'd become used to short, sharp, high-intensity sessions, whereas French training was based around endless repetition. We'd rarely spend more than forty minutes on the field with Wales, and everything was done at high speed to replicate the feel of a match. In France, we'd often spend an hour and a half in the gym alone, doing multiple sets of the same exercises. Take squats as an example. In Wales, we'd do three sets of six and move on. That's eighteen squats in total. In France, we'd be doing five sets of fifteen. It was overkill, and I couldn't see the benefit. Rugby is an explosive, anaerobic sport, where everything happens in short, sharp bursts. Grunting and groaning your way through upwards of sixty squats seemed a waste of everyone's time and energy. And if you put your back out doing them, good luck finding a physio. There was one to a squad of forty, which meant if you didn't race off for treatment the minute training finished, you'd have to join a queue about nine or ten deep. In Cardiff, there were at least three physios, and a couple of extra masseurs on top.

So the first few months, when the culture shock was at its most acute, were really hard, and then I got injured during my third game for the club. We were at home to Perpignan when I went over on my ankle and ended up in hospital needing surgery. It led to a terrifying episode where I woke up unable to feel anything below my belly button. Apparently, it had been explained to me in French that I'd be sedated in order to receive spinal anaesthesia, which would render me numb from the waist down. The surgery would then be carried out while I was fully conscious. But because my French wasn't up to it, when I came round in the recovery room I thought I was paralysed. Even when I understood what had happened, I was so emotionally on edge that when François van der Merwe and Bernard Le Roux brought a few of the other Racing boys to see me in hospital, I burst into tears. The twelve weeks post-surgery was a tough and lonely time. I was living alone in the centre of Paris with no friends nearby, and I was having to get in and out of my fifth-floor flat on crutches. There were a few nights when I'd lie on my bed, look up at the impossibly high ceilings and wonder if I'd made a mistake moving there.

It was a big leap to have made, and it had ruffled a few feathers. Peter Thomas, the Cardiff Blues chairman, had publicly bad-mouthed me when I announced my departure for Paris, saying he'd felt betrayed that I'd abandoned the club, considering how much they'd invested in me as a youngster. That had left a bitter taste. I'd been offered the chance to live in one of the world's greatest cities on a big-money contract, surrounded by world-class talent. To expect me to turn that down due to some misplaced sense of loyalty was unrealistic in the extreme. I'd agonised over the decision. Was it right for me? How would it be perceived? Would I be seen as a traitor? I'd always been portrayed as something of a golden boy, and had enjoyed a decent relationship with the press, but the move had engendered some negative headlines which I'd struggled to understand. What did it matter what other people thought, what the WRU or the chairman of my rugby club thought? Leaving home and seeing the world through a different lens ultimately proved to be one of the best decisions I ever made.

Rob Howley and Warren Gatland had stressed the importance of having full release in my contract. That was non-negotiable. We had a clause drawn up guaranteeing that I'd be released for all Wales training sessions and matches, whether or not they fell in the sanctioned Test rugby window. It was imperative that the move didn't jeopardise my international career. Warren was very opinionated about the need to have his players for the build-up to campaigns, but he knew I was going to play for a strong team in a strong league, so was more than happy to rubber-stamp the move. Paris and Cardiff may have been worlds away culturally speaking, but geographically speaking it amounted to a two-hour commute on the Orly–Cardiff flight.

Before making the move across the Channel, I'd been invited for coffee with WRU CEO Roger Lewis to explore the option of keeping me in Wales on some sort of dual contract. We'd chewed the fat for more than an hour before getting down to business. He basically wanted to know how much they were offering to pay me, and when I told him, he just chuckled to himself and brought the meeting to a swift end.

There are few things I feel as strongly about in Welsh rugby as the sixty-cap rule that was introduced in an attempt to slow the 'player drain' to richer rugby countries like England and France. It didn't exist when I moved to Paris, but at that point there were a number of us playing on the Continent, and others would follow. Luke Charteris, Leigh Halfpenny, Gethin Jenkins, Jonathan Davies, Dan Lydiate, Mike Phillips and myself were among the higher-profile 'exiles' looking to expand our horizons. Panicking about the loss of their prime assets, the WRU declared that moving out of Wales would render you ineligible for international rugby unless you'd won sixty caps or more.

It's a monumentally short-sighted and reactionary approach. I understand the need to protect your own domestic league, which becomes a less attractive product if its star players are playing elsewhere, but the notion of a 'player drain' is little more than fearmongering. Only the very best players, who've proved themselves at the top level, are going to get a lucrative overseas contract. To deny them an opportunity to play abroad is to deny them the joy and adventure that travel brings. And sixty caps seems an entirely arbitrary number, one that fails to take into account length of service at either domestic or international level. What about those players who've sat on the international bench for years or turned out hundreds of times for their region? Is that not sufficient service to satisfy the bureaucrats?

As a union we can't complain about not producing legions of confident, outgoing players when we deliberately limit the scope of their horizon. You can't tar everyone with the same brush, but the Welsh are generally a shy bunch. Having played in England, where a lot of players come through the public-school system, I've witnessed a size-able gulf between the confidence levels of those players and many of the Welsh boys I've played with. As a nation we're more cowed, less confident and less inclined to question authority. Insisting players should not be allowed to play outside their own country is only going to exacerbate that. Who is your employer to tell you that you can't take those opportunities? It's insular, narrow-minded and, more importantly, a restriction of trade.

My life and career have been enhanced immeasurably by my experiences outside Wales. I feel I'm more tactically astute having been exposed to different environments, coaches, players and ways of thinking. I'm a stronger, more rounded bloke as a result, as are many of my colleagues who've done the same. Those benefits can surely only enhance Wales and our national side. In fact, I feel the WRU should *encourage* players to experience life beyond the country and their comfort zone.

I do understand the rationale behind the counter-argument. Aside from the devaluing of the domestic competition, it's argued that over-seas-based players won't be looked after the way they are in Wales. They'll be treated more like workhorses than racehorses. But while it's true that Welsh internationals play fewer games for their clubs than their English and French counterparts, I'm yet to be convinced that that directly translates to domestic and international success, or even enhanced player welfare.

Would I have allowed my life to be dictated by the national coach saying I *had* to live in the country I was born in? *No way.* How dare they prevent you from following your dreams and exploiting the opportunities that present themselves *because* of your talent. It runs totally contrary to my philosophy about seizing every moment and living your life to its fullest. Travel is one of my biggest passions, and to combine it with rugby was a dream come true. To have that door to the wider world slammed in your face in the name of narrow-minded bureaucracy is as absurd as it is infuriating.

Starting afresh somewhere new, as I did in Paris, gives you the chance to regenerate, to reignite your passion for the game. Conversely, staying somewhere too long can lead to stagnation, and that's what had happened to me at the Blues. My final few years there weren't remotely as enjoyable. Dai Young had left, a lot of the senior players retired or moved on, and I felt that the standard of coaching had plummeted, leaving a big leadership vacuum. About eight or nine of our best players left in one fell swoop, and it felt like the heart had been ripped out of the team. Martyn Williams, Xavier Rush, Gethin Jenkins: genuine titans of the game. Even more depressingly, the jersey presentation to mark their departure was held at a near-empty Cardiff City Stadium. Those guys should have been given a rousing ovation at a packed-out Arms Park. The whole thing stank of decay.

The Blues' move to the City Stadium in 2009 had been a disaster. A sterile, soulless modern arena less than a quarter full, versus a sold-out Arms Park dripping with history and heritage. I was astonished that people in senior positions had made such a bone-headed decision. I wasn't alone in thinking that: most of the players agreed. Ironically, I was roped into doing a BBC Wales campaign promoting the move, in which I was filmed running from the Arms Park to the Cardiff City Stadium, with a gaggle of excited kids following me. I went along with it, but I was dying inside.

In the 2012–13 campaign, I only played about six games for the Blues. I was in a horrible cycle of getting injured at the end of an international campaign, and recovering just in time for the next one. Understandably, some of the fans started to see me as a prima donna who cared more about Wales than the Blues, and that feeling extended to some of my playing colleagues as well. No one said anything to my face, but I sensed a growing resentment. I was drifting towards the periphery, subconsciously looking for an escape hatch.

That lack of buzz was the main factor in my decision to move to France. Don't get me wrong, the astronomical sums of money and the chance to live in Paris as a single bloke were obvious bonuses, but the truth was I'd fallen out of love with the Cardiff Blues. It's often said that your club is where you develop your strongest bonds and make your fondest memories. This was true of my early years at the Blues, but as time moved on, Wales began to feel more like my club than Cardiff did. In the final reckoning, I played 87 games for the Blues over six years; fewer than I played for Wales.

While I'm up here on my soapbox, allow me to address another bugbear of mine: regional rugby. It hasn't worked, and it's time it was abandoned. The seven years I spent playing outside Wales for grand old clubs with centuries of history made me realise how soulless the regions look and feel in comparison.

We've had regional rugby for twenty years, and the number of trophies won by the Welsh teams has been pitifully small. Victories have been isolated incidents rather than long-lasting dynasties. These teams have seen their average gates decrease while enthusiasm and passion amongst the fans has dwindled. We've reached a tipping point where we either maintain the status quo and watch our domestic scene slide further into ignominy, or we grasp the nettle and reconnect with history. We should resurrect the old club identities. Bin the Blues, Ospreys, Dragons and Scarlets, and welcome back Cardiff, Swansea, Newport and Llanelli. The game has become unmoored from its foundations and is drifting. As much as we feel for the Pontypridds and the Neaths of this world, they don't have the infrastructure or the population base to be professional.

I'd actually argue that the sixty-cap rule is weakening regional rugby. The regions now know that their best assets won't leave because of the threat of losing their international jersey, which allows the clubs to exist in a constant state of mediocrity. An open market, on the other hand, would drive standards, leading to a different mindset: *We might lose this guy, so we've got to do our best to keep him.* How do you keep top players interested? By constantly evolving and improving coaching, facilities and the level of players around them. Believe it or not, from a player's perspective it's not all about the money. At present, with no relegation and little threat of players leaving, there's no incentive to get better. Put simply, there is no jeopardy. Finishing fourth and missing out on the Champions Cup is often greeted with a shrug of the shoulders. We're perpetually talking about regions being 'long-term projects' or being in 'development cycles', celebrating one-off wins and occasional scalps as if we should be grateful for such scraps. If you apply that rationale to the next decade, Wales will cease to be competitive. Something needs to change.

I know the counter-argument is that allowing your players to go and play elsewhere will weaken the regions further, but with the current restriction on non-English or non-French qualified players in their respective leagues, you'd be able to count on the fingers of one hand the number of Welsh players who'd get signed up on big contracts abroad. During my time in Paris, the so-called 'flood' of Welsh players to France only amounted to about five or six, and that was only because we'd reached a World Cup semi-final and caught the attention of some ambitious club owners with deep pockets.

The reality is that many players are being held hostage. Some are staying purely so they can carry on playing for Wales, rather than because they're loyal and committed to their region. For them, it's a case of stay fit and play a handful of games for your region in order to play for Wales. From experience, England internationals playing in the Premiership *want* to play for their clubs week-in-week-out. For some, it's more important than representing their country. That level of affinity doesn't seem so apparent in regional rugby in Wales. Look at someone like Tomas Francis, who was effectively forced to leave the then European champions, Exeter, to come 'home' and be allowed to continue his international career. He'd never even played in Wales to begin with, and is now going to be turning out for an Ospreys side which, with respect, are nowhere near the level of Exeter Chiefs. Had he continued to play for Exeter he'd arrive in Wales camp full of confidence and at the top of his game, having been involved with a trophy-winning side.

I'm not naive. I know how important the national side is to the WRU. Wales playing at the Principality Stadium is the cash cow that feeds the rest of the game, and it means everything to the supporters as well, but I think we've lost sight of the foundation of the Welsh game, and that's club rugby. The game has to move forward, but it can't disconnect from its glorious past. Look around the Blues clubhouse and you see Gareth Edwards, Barry John, Gerald Davies, Jack Matthews, Bleddyn Williams, Martyn Williams and Neil Jenkins. You *feel* the history pulsating within its walls. It's lunacy to abandon that. Hopefully, their recent rebrand as Cardiff Rugby is the first step on a path back to an authentic club identity.

The clubs need to be independent, autonomous entities in control of their own destinies. At the moment, it feels as though they're just subsidiaries of the Welsh Rugby Union. If they're cast loose as fully functioning independent businesses, they need the right people at the helm, quality people involved at board level from business *and* rugby backgrounds. Often the blazers who sit on boards have little experience of high-performance environments, and decisions tend to be with just commercial interests in mind, the move to Cardiff City Stadium being a prime example. As things stand, the WRU has full control. You have a national coach who basically decides players' salaries, according to where they fit into an arbitrary and subjective banding system. What is that about? Players want to be in an open market. If you play well, have a good injury history, develop a profile and perform consistently, you should earn more money. It's as simple as that. When you have the head coach of your national team dictating your value, the model is broken. Your value should always be based on how much a club is willing to pay.

The 2014 Six Nations was a topsy-turvy affair for Wales, and despite a 51–3 thrashing of Scotland on the final day, we weren't good enough to pull off the 'three-peat'. The wheels nearly came off in round two when we got spanked by the Irish in Dublin, and a few of us got unwittingly papped looking the worse for wear at a popular Dublin nightspot. Alan 'Thumper' Phillips gleefully projected the article onto the screen in the team room the following Monday, and my heart sank when I saw the headlines naming me, Alex Cuthbert and Toby Faletau as the main offenders. Our crime, it seemed, was going out 'celebrating' after we'd been subjected to a humiliating loss. We hadn't been told to stay in, but it was clearly a bad look after the hammering we'd suffered.

Mike Phillips escaped censure on that occasion, but I swear he was still under the influence on the Sunday, the way he was winding up Gethin Jenkins. The forwards had been taken to the cleaners by the Irish pack. Whether it was in the driving mauls, the scrums or the line-outs, they had been thoroughly beaten. Melon was in the team room studiously going through the tape, while Mike hovered over his shoulder taunting him relentlessly. 'Another penalty, is it? Jeez. Just watching your missed tackles from yesterday, are you? Could be there a while, pal. What's that? Another Ireland driving-maul try, is it? Yep.' Every utterance was dripping with sarcasm, and Mike couldn't help himself. Depending on your mood, you could either find it hilarious or infuriating. Melon was in the latter camp that day, and did well not to swing for him.

When he was sober, Mike thought he was the best scrum-half in the world. When he'd had a drink, he thought he was the best sports-man in the universe, not to mention the best-looking bloke, and the hardest. He once tried to start a fight with Jerry Collins on a night out and had to be dragged away by his team-mates, who knew it wouldn't have ended well for him. Mike may be useful in a brawl, but Jerry was built from granite and wouldn't have had too much trouble putting him in his place. Mike not only has no fear, but genuinely believes he can win a fight against anyone. But as testing as he can sometimes be, you *need* people like that on the field. If you're in the trenches against the Boks or the All Blacks, you know you've got a guy on your side who bows to no one.

Sometimes I wonder if people on the outside think we're all best mates, but if you consider it, we're a bunch of different blokes from pretty disparate backgrounds thrown together because we happen to be decent at rugby. You have to find common ground, but there are inevitably cliques, fall-outs and flare-ups. For someone who plays an aggressive brand of in-your-face rugby, I'm usually quite reserved, but I've had my share of confrontations with my team-mates. On one occasion, Alun Wyn Jones and I squared up to one another in training after a disagreement. I'd muttered something trivial about him being on the wrong side of a ruck, and he thundered towards me from about 10 metres away, getting right up in my face. I was aware that his dad was ill at the time and he was emotionally volatile. I sensed that he wanted it to come to blows, that he needed to let the aggression come to the surface. That's just one isolated incident, but there have been many occasions over the years when I've been wound up so tightly that I've been ready to go. Thankfully, because of my temperament, things rarely ever boiled over. It doesn't take a psychologist to figure out that it's the forwards who have the shortest fuses. Ultimately, though, regardless of what happens on the training paddock, rare was the session when you didn't hug it out at the end.

We redeemed ourselves with big wins over France and Scotland, but the Ireland defeat and another to England left us in third place. If I was going to win any silverware that season, it would have to be with my club in France. We reached the semi-finals of the Top 14, the French league, but I sensed our chances slipping away during a night out on the Thursday before the match against Toulon. Mike Phillips and I were dining in a swanky Parisian restaurant with the rest of the squad, and the beer was flowing steadily. At least a quarter of the Racing boys were casual smokers, and they were regularly disappearing between courses for a puff. They must have all sunk seven or eight pints before I turned to Mike and said, 'Christ, we've got a semi-final in two days.' Mike has never shied away from a drinking session – he was sacked by Bayonne for turning up to a video session drunk – but even he seemed surprised by the amount being guzzled that close to a big game. Unsurprisingly, we lost down in Lille on the Saturday against a Wilkinson-inspired Toulon, with Matt Giteau among our chief tormentors that day.

A week later, I experienced my most vivid near-death experience to date. Since my arrival, I'd fully immersed myself in the Parisian lifestyle, riding my Vespa absolutely everywhere. I felt like I'd joined a tribe: every time you pulled up at traffic lights, there'd be another twenty riders alongside you, and a silent acknowledgement would pass between you all. My little two-wheeler signified freedom and adventure. You could take it anywhere and never have to worry about parking or being snarled up in traffic. It was the perfect way to navigate the city, weaving in and out of traffic, and absorbing the sights and sounds without being trapped in the confines of a metal box.

The Manics were touring Europe that May, and James Dean Bradfield had put me on the guest list for their gig at the Bataclan. It was a beautiful afternoon that day, and I arranged to meet Mike Phillips and François van der Merwe at the venue. The Manics were superb as always, and we hung out backstage for a while, toasting their performance with a few beers. Eventually bidding farewell to James and the boys, François, Phillsy and I agreed to reconvene at a late-night burger joint in Saint-Germain. It had poured with rain during the gig and the previously sun-drenched streets were now glistening with rain. My minimalist attire of jeans and T-shirt seemed a little optimistic in retrospect.

The rain continued to fall in a steady drizzle as I meandered towards the river, heading south and crossing over to the Left Bank by Notre-Dame. As I went over the junction by Place Saint-Michel, cruising pleasantly at around 30 mph, I suddenly found myself lying sideways and sliding rapidly into the path of oncoming traffic. My wheel had buckled and lost its grip. Before I could process what had happened, I'd been thrown to the deck and continued to slide alongside the bike for about 20 metres, bracing myself for a collision. By some minor miracle, I avoided a crash, eventually slowing to a complete stop, before curling into a ball and waiting for the pain to kick in. I was convinced all the skin had been stripped off the side of my body, especially my arm, which had been entirely exposed.

A crowd of people swarmed around, frantically asking if I was OK. It felt like a strange out-of-body experience, and it took me a moment to realise they were talking to me. The pain I was anticipating didn't arrive. I held up the arm that had been dragged at speed over an abrasive concrete surface and saw nothing but a minor graze on my elbow. No cuts or bruises, no sprains, no broken bones.

Because it was raining so much, I had aquaplaned, gliding harmlessly along the road's shiny surface and completely avoiding serious injury. While the rain had caused the accident, it had also saved me from a far more grisly fate. I looked across at the bike, and it was a write-off. The front wheel was completely buckled and the chassis was bent out of shape. Once I'd recovered my senses, my brain started to whirr. I'd had three beers. If the police arrived soon, as they surely would, I could be in trouble. It was only a few weeks after the England scrum-half Danny Care had been done for drink-driving. I went into panic mode, dragging the bike to the side of the road and chaining it to a lamppost before sprinting away, much to the bemusement of the concerned throng of onlookers.

I couldn't face going to collect the bike the next day. I gave the key to the guy at the spares shop I used, and paid him to unlock it and take it to the scrapyard. I never saw it again. I'm not proud of what I did, and not about to make excuses, but I'd fallen into that French way of life where you go out for a few drinks and happily get back on the bike. It was idiotic, and could have turned out far worse. I have never got behind the controls of a vehicle after drinking since.

There was more disappointment in a Wales jersey in that summer of 2014 when we came closer than we had in fifteen years to beating South Africa. We lost the first Test in Durban fair and square, but a week later in Nelspruit we found ourselves 17-0 ahead and cruising after half an hour. But the Boks, as they so often do, ground their way back, tightening things up and using their brawn and ballast to blast holes in our defence. A series of driving mauls saw them over the line and resulted in Luke Charteris and Dan Biggar being despatched to the sin bin. They exploited the two-man advantage ruthlessly by going the length from the kick-off and scoring another. That hiccup aside, we regrouped and came back strongly to build a commanding 30-17 lead with nine minutes to play.

Then came the heartbreak. Willie le Roux danced over to bring it back to 30-24, and with less than three minutes to play, he created an opening for Cornal Hendricks in the corner. Hendricks evaded George North's despairing tackle and appeared to have made the line before full-back Liam Williams arrived like an Exocet missile and smashed him into the advertising hoardings. At that stage in his career, Liam's long locks and insouciant swagger recalled a certain JPR Williams, and on first view the tackle was an act of heroism straight out of the JPR playbook. The referee, Steve Walsh, wasn't so sure, and television replays revealed that his elbow had hit Hendricks in the face. JPR might have got away with something similar, but in 2014, it was a clear act of foul play. After the briefest of consultations with his TMO, Walsh sin-binned Liam and awarded a penalty try. The conversion, which would have been from the most dastardly of angles, was now directly in front of the posts, giving them victory by a solitary point.

Liam suffered a barrage of hate mail after that, but it wasn't his fault. He was a young, hot-headed player who lived on the edge, and it had been a costly mistake made in the heat of the moment. A lot of players would have sunk without trace after that, but I'd argue it was the making of him. It was a harsh lesson, but he absorbed it, bouncing back to become one of the world's best full-backs.

It was a heartbreaking loss to suffer, especially given the way it had unfolded. Twice we'd built a sizeable lead, and twice we'd seen it wiped out. Despite all the success we'd enjoyed under Gatland, the old demons reared their heads once more. We could not beat the southern-hemisphere big three. Since Gatland took over we'd played them a combined twenty-five times, winning once. The most infuriating thing was we didn't know why. Were we less skilful? Less driven? Less mentally strong? Were we psychologically damaged by the succession of defeats? Did we not have the same level of mental fortitude? It was different from the early days of professionalism when Wales would routinely get pummelled due to inferior fitness and preparation. We were as fit, as powerful and as talented as these sides, but we couldn't get over the line. It was a riddle that couldn't be solved, until we eventually shook the monkey from our backs that autumn when the Boks came to our backyard. It was a dull, turgid, try-less affair in Cardiff at the end of November, but we couldn't have cared less. It was the first time we'd beaten them since 1999, and it brought that miserable sixteen-game losing sequence to an end. We hoped it would prove a catalyst for better times against southern-hemisphere opposition, and we rightly celebrated with a good old-fashioned lock-in in the Under Armour box that evening.

During my second year at Racing, 2014–15, we were unbeaten in the pool stages of the Champions Cup, as the Heineken Cup was now known, and set our sights on a maiden European title, only to be dumped out in the quarter-finals by Saracens. Marcelo Bosch kicked a last-minute penalty to guide them to a 12–11 victory. It had been my best chance of European glory since the penalty-shoot-out drama of 2009. What hurt most was the fact that for most of the second half I was watching the defeat from the sidelines. I had been feeling fit and strong and was playing well when my number came up after fifty minutes. They brought on Alexandre Dumoulin, who was a good, skilful player but didn't have my big-game experience. It seemed a senseless decision, and one I couldn't help but take personally.

There was good reason for that. A month earlier, we'd secured our home quarter-final with a thumping win over Northampton at Franklin's Gardens, and I'd weighed in with a Man of the Match display. With the 2015 Six Nations approaching and a genuine chance of European glory, I was feeling on top of the world when my agent called me a few days later. With a slightly uneasy tone, he explained that Jacky Lorenzetti wanted to terminate my contract. I was stunned. I was midway through the second year of a three-year deal. I had established myself as a first-choice midfielder and had literally just been voted Man of the Match in a high-stakes European Cup clash. Now they wanted to write me a cheque and usher me out of the door. I couldn't make any sense of it, and it absolutely slayed me. This was the same Jacky Lorenzetti who, two years earlier, had flown on his private jet to Cardiff airport to personally hand me the contract on my birthday.

My agent did his best to take the emotion out of it, saying it was a business decision based on the fact I was likely to be away with Wales at the 2015 World Cup, and that they wouldn't be getting value for money. But they'd known that when they signed me. They signed me *because* I was an experienced international. Whatever kind of gloss he tried to put on it, I felt rejected and betrayed. It felt like a punishment. Or worse, that they'd decided, on reflection, that I wasn't as good as they thought I'd be. It was impossible not to take it personally. Before that, I'd had idle thoughts of settling in Paris, of seeking a contract extension and laying down some roots. Now it was a case of 'pack your bags and sling your hook'.

I was genuinely shocked and gutted. It later transpired that they'd signed Dan Carter and were probably just trying to finesse the finances to cover his million-euro salary. I refused to go quietly, and fought my corner. I was enjoying Paris, my French had improved, I was playing well and bringing my influence to bear. I wanted to convince them of my dedication, but I was also anxious not to come across as a desperate ex trying to curry favour with a former partner that's already moved on. My overtures were in vain, though, and they were adamant my time was up.

Towards the tail end of the 2015 Six Nations, I had a conversation with Cambridge University rugby legend Tony Rodgers. I'd first met him in 2009 after my mate Will Jones had played in that year's Varsity Match. Every year since, Tony had dropped me a text asking when I was going to come and study at Cambridge. It was always tongue-in-cheek, but it had planted a seed. During that Six Nations, the usual text came through, and that year it really resonated. I'd been out of medicine for two years and was missing the academic side of life. I'd also been having conversations with Harlequins, and a plan started to formulate in my mind. I'd done Cardiff and Paris. Why not London? I loved London. Was there a way I could manoeuvre things so that I could play in the World Cup, get my teeth back into a university degree, play in the fabled Varsity Match *and* join one of English rugby's biggest clubs? I looked at the calendar and persuaded myself it could be done. It may have appeared insane to most of my friends, but to a hyperactive, multi-tasker like me it was the perfect confluence of events. There's no doubt it wouldn't have happened had Racing not shown me the door. My road ahead had suddenly become broader, and the horizon much sunnier. The disappointment had led to a whole new world of opportunity.

After a lengthy trawl through the Cambridge University website, I applied for a research-based Master's degree in Medical Science, which didn't require me to physically be in Cambridge all the time. That would allow me the flexibility I'd need, but one of the archaic rules that govern involvement in the Varsity Match is that you have to be living within ten miles of the church in the centre of Cambridge during the Michaelmas term. The plan seemed feasible. The World Cup ran until the end of October, so even if Wales made it to the final, I'd still be in a position to move into university accommodation and be eligible for the Varsity Match. I'd worn the iconic Barbarians and

Lions jerseys. To add the fabled pale blue hoops of Cambridge University to my private collection would be a dream come true, the perfect marriage of my twin passions of rugby and academia.

I negotiated a December start date with Harlequins and got all my ducks in a row. Years earlier, during the 2009 Lions tour, I'd shared a hot tub with Ugo Monye and he'd predicted then that I'd end up at Quins one day. It was my kind of club. I liked their philosophy, the way they attacked and threw the ball around. I'd had a few conversations with the Cardiff Blues too, but I wasn't ready to come home. At that time in my life, London appealed enormously. I bought a flat in Wandsworth Town with my best mate Rhys, who was already living and working in London as a criminal barrister.

I also made sure I had exactly the same side contract I'd had with Racing, allowing me full release to train and play with Wales. It was all a bit clandestine. Quins didn't want it made public because it contravened the PRL (Premiership Rugby Limited) player-release policy. International fixtures happen in an approved World Rugby 'window', during which clubs are obliged to release their international players. But Wales always plays an extra autumn international outside the window, for which there is no obligation for release. On the contrary, English clubs could be subject to heavy fines and points deductions for doing so. By agreeing to my terms, Quins were risking sanctions from their own governing body and agreeing to meet the cost of any fine, which is why I needed the guarantee written down in black and white in case there was a change of heart at some point in the future. A gentleman's agreement wasn't sufficient when my international career was at stake. I didn't know it then, but that bit of paper would become a major source of angst further down the line.

17

BROKEN BONES

The idea that you can go through your career without getting injured is pure fantasy. I broke my collarbone playing for Rumney at the age of fifteen when Lloyd Barrett's hip smashed straight into it, virtually snapping it in half. Three years later, before I'd even played a game of senior rugby, I went under the knife for a complete shoulder reconstruction. These were early reminders that injuries are an occupational hazard. Broken bones, snapped ligaments, torn tendons and concussions are all part of the deal. Take away the sport, the drama, the theatre and the passion, and you may as well strap yourself to a pole and let someone beat you with a baseball bat. The outcome would be similar.

I fractured my skull in 2008 and had wrist surgery in 2010 after playing a whole season with a damaged tendon. A patellar-tendon operation before the 2011 World Cup fixed a recurring knee issue that had made it painful to even walk. In 2012, I completely blew out the other knee, rupturing my anterior cruciate ligament. In 2013, I tore my hamstring, nearly putting paid to my Lions dream. A nasty ankle injury during my first month in Paris put me back in the operating theatre and kept me sidelined for three months. A facial injury sustained while playing for Bath left my eye socket fractured in three places. In 2020, after multiple breaks, I had my nose restraightened under general anaesthetic. There are countless niggles that could fill another page and highlight just how much stress we expose our bodies to. If you add these injuries together, I've missed out on two full years of rugby. Imagine being in a job where your employer would accept you being on sick leave for two years.

The earlier you can accept that it's an unavoidable part of playing, the less frustrated you'll be. Unless you're Martyn Williams. He was some kind of rubbery freak who didn't have an injury-related op until he was thirty-five. It almost beggars belief that a guy who played in his position, with such an unhealthy disregard for his own welfare, could reach his mid-thirties relatively unscathed. A tackle-shy winger maybe, but an open-side flanker who spent half his career with his head buried in rucks? It's fair to say that Nugget was the exception.

Injury tests you in a way nothing else does. Time waits for no man, the sport continues apace, and someone else comes in and takes your place. Since that first operation, my approach has always been to seek distraction and avoid tumbling into the vortex of depression that can accompany a long-term injury. Can I get away on trips? Can I go on holiday? Can I go and experience different things in life? I never wanted to be that guy who turns up to training, does his rehab and then hangs around all day until three o'clock. When you're given a window of rehab, it's healthy to get away from rugby and break up your schedule, so it doesn't become your sole focus. It's the only real break you'll get from playing the game. Without disrespecting the club that's paying your wages, if you take the emotion out of it, it's not a bad deal. You're not playing, but you're still getting paid.

As I've mentioned, I used to gobble down pain-relief and anti-inflammatory tablets like sweets, and before every Test match I'd drop my pants for Prof John to ram a syringeful of diclofenac into my backside. It was to stop me suffering the discomfort of all the persistent niggles in my joints. I wanted to be at my single-minded best and eliminate any distractions during games. If you couldn't feel the pain, it was far easier to dismiss those niggles from your mind. When you play for your country, you need to be 100 per cent focused.

Concussion has become one of the game's most pressing issues, and as a medical graduate, people expect me to have a strong opinion on it. I'll come to that, but my biggest fear is that I've either done damage to my gastrointestinal tract or will be vulnerable to long-term cardiac damage because of all the drugs I've taken. They don't get rid of the pain, they just disguise it, and there's a good chance it will catch up with me at some stage.

Pain exists for a reason. It alerts you to the fact that something's wrong. By masking it you're almost certainly exacerbating the problems. I never took omeprazole with my anti-inflammatories, and as a result I used to get really bad guts. As a medic, I was more aware than most of the side effects of taking so many drugs, but I continued to do so, which arguably makes me more stupid than someone without any medical insight who blindly follows the doctor's orders.

It's frightening how accepting we've become of the damage we willingly do to ourselves. As rugby has accelerated forward into professionalism, the players have become bigger, faster and stronger, which means collisions are much harder and the damage they cause more acute. Dan Baugh, one of Wales's former conditioning coaches, once told me that when he played for Canada, several of the players would have anti-inflammatory drips set up on the bus. The doc would hang them from the parcel shelf, so the drugs could be intravenously fed into the players' arms as they travelled home. I've heard stories about players injecting local anaesthetic into joints before games which, while morally questionable, is perhaps the inevitable end point of the slippery slope we're on. It's not performance-enhancing as such, but it would certainly help you play better because you'd have no fear of pain. While you're numbing the pain, you're massively raising the risk of permanent joint damage. It's not happened in an environment I've been in, but it's a line rugby could conceivably cross. We saw during the Harlequins 'bloodgate' scandal that teams are prepared to drift into ethical grey areas in the pursuit of success. It would be naive to think that other questionable practices aren't taking place.

I used to look at the way Neil Jenkins shuffled around in Wales camp. To be fair, he never had the most graceful of gaits, but he can barely bend his knees any more. He wasn't a big physical player who enjoyed the rough and tumble; he was a kicker and a distributor, generally avoiding contact as much as he could. Considering I've spent more than a decade *looking* for contact, I'm likely to end up in a far worse state. Since my mid-twenties, I've felt virtually incapacitated every morning after a game. I have to waddle across the landing and grip the banister as I struggle down the stairs. In a perverse way, I love it. I'm possibly a bit addicted to that feeling of throbbing swollen joints and tired aching muscles. It's like a drug. During the off season, I crave not only the gladiatorial aspect of rugby – the bangs and the collisions – but also the soreness the following day. It's an outwardly unpleasant sensation, but it's the physical manifestation of your achievements the day before. It's evidence that you've given your all to the cause. Add a night out and a hangover to the equation, and it's even better. In a strange way, that stumble across the landing into a steaming hot shower, followed by the stinging sensation as the water hits your sore, wounded body, is almost as big a buzz for me as running out in front of thousands of fans. I realise this probably sounds a bit demented, but I wouldn't mind betting if you asked a fair few rugby players, they'd agree. The more you've put your body on the line and the harder you've worked, the more pain you'll suffer the next day and the prouder you'll feel. On the rare occasion I'm not in pain after a game, I'll start to question myself: *Did I carry as much as I could have? Did I tackle with sufficient force? Did I dominate my opposite number?*

I fear for my mobility in my forties and fifties, and now I'm a father, I worry about not being able to have an active lifestyle with my children. I'm hopeful that modern medicine is going to improve over the next decade, and that there will be ways of repairing or reversing the damage. But when all's said and done, I have no regrets. Living with pain and reduced mobility later in life is a price I'm willing to pay for all that rugby has given me.

As for concussion, I think it's important to stress that rugby is one of the most brutal contact sports you can play, and brings with it a huge risk of head injury. That's a fact. When I played as a kid, I was constantly whacking my head on other players' hips and knees, and accepted those knocks as inevitable consequences of playing the sport. We were given precious little information about the dangers of concussion. If you got knocked out, as I did several times in youth rugby, you were expected to get back up and carry on. It was a macho environment, and leaving the field was seen as a sign of weakness. I also inadvertently knocked out a few people myself. My head is abnormally big and hard, and my tendency to tackle high would often lead to accidental head clashes in which the other guy would come off far worse. Most of these tackles would be red-card offences in the modern game.

When I was sixteen, I genuinely feared I might have killed someone during a trial match at Taff's Well. The opposition fly-half chipped over our defensive line and I started steaming in from full-back to claim the bouncing ball. My team-mate Michael Press was haring towards it from the other direction. He hadn't seen me coming, and the two of us clattered into one another, cracking heads. He collapsed to the floor like a bag of bones. It was the first time I'd been involved in a head-on-head collision like that, and I felt fine. He'd hit me square in my head, and it hadn't hurt. It was a frightening realisation of the damage I could cause. As he lay there motionless, I started to panic. His limp body was bundled onto a stretcher and he was rushed to hospital in an ambulance.

When the game was over, word filtered back that he still hadn't woken up. I felt sick with worry. His mum and sister had been keeping a bedside vigil, but the doctors hadn't been able to offer them much in the way of reassurance. After two hours they'd started to fear the worst. Then, with little warning, he woke up, saw them weeping and bellowed, 'ADRIAAANN!', in homage to Rocky Balboa. His face was a pulpy mess, much like Rocky's after he'd been the distance with Apollo Creed. His cheekbone was fractured in three places, and he'd had fifteen stitches to seal the wound. That weekend, I was playing in a sevens tournament in Lisvane and saw him there with his parents. His face was still painfully swollen and deformed. I was relieved to see him up and about, but horrified at how bad he looked. I didn't even have so much as a graze. He told me he'd been up most of the night vomiting as he'd swallowed so much blood. To his credit, he was remarkably calm about the whole episode and bore me no grudge. Ironically, it brought us much closer together and we've been good mates ever since.

I've been knocked out seven or eight times in my senior career. In 2012, Gonzalo Tiesi's head hit my jaw, and I was helped off the field looking like a giant smurf with blue paint from the sponsor's logo plastered all over my face. In 2018, James Haskell went high on me during a Wasps–Quins match, knocking me clean out before I'd hit the floor. If you watch the incident back, you'll see me adopting the 'tonic posture' usually associated with seizures as I start unconsciously burrowing my head into the ground. The fractured skull I suffered in 2008 after my clash of heads with Stirling Mortlock is the one most people remember, but it didn't knock me clean out like those two did. Medically speaking, a concussion occurs when your brain comes into contact with the wall of your skull, and that can happen regardless of whether you lose consciousness or not. Indeed, your head doesn't even need to come into contact with anything for you to suffer a concussion. The whiplash effect of a big tackle can be sufficient.

The incidents I've mentioned are the ones I recall most vividly, but I've suffered countless other 'wobbles' which are arguably of more concern. Up until around 2014, when the game started taking concussion more seriously, I suffered more of these in-game wobbles than I'd care to remember, sometimes three or four in the same game. Thankfully we now have independent match-day doctors on the lookout for such incidents who have the power to take players off the field. This gets around the issue of domineering coaches overruling a medic's opinion because they don't want to lose a key player.

So, as someone who's suffered more than his fair share of concussions, I'm in no doubt that rugby puts you in harm's way. But, as a medic and a scientist, I'm yet to be convinced that rugby definitely *causes* long-term damage to people's brains. There is no doubt there is an increased risk, but until causation is firmly established, I won't truly believe there are long-term consequences to brain health from playing rugby. I readily accept that there are such consequences to my joints, in particular my knees and ankles, because causation has been established, but as much as I devour all the research on concussion, and much as I sympathise enormously with those who have been diagnosed with early-onset dementia, I've not seen compelling evidence that rugby is definitely to blame.

There are so many other factors at play – genetic factors, dietary factors, environmental factors, alcohol and drug consumption – all of which can contribute to ill health later in life. In fact, one of the main risk factors for early-onset dementia is depression, which is something a lot of sportsmen and women have to wrestle with after retirement. What's to say a higher prevalence of depression in elite athletes doesn't lead to a higher prevalence of early-onset dementia? Blaming it all on rugby is like picking the lowest-hanging fruit. While it's tragic that a number of former players have been diagnosed with early-onset dementia, it's important to keep in mind that the majority haven't. Saying rugby union *may* cause early-onset dementia is a very different thing from saying rugby union *does* cause early-onset dementia, and it's difficult for me to give weight to something that's not evidence-based.

That doesn't mean rugby isn't a contributing factor, but it's unlikely to be the sole factor. Unfortunately, I doubt that any definitive evidence will emerge until the first generation of professional rugby players have died and donated their brains to medical science, as has happened in the NFL, and that could be decades away. Admittedly, instances of chronic traumatic encephalopathy have been found in the brains of former American football players, but the comparisons are erroneous. The helmets and body armour they wear give them a feeling of invulnerability. They're encouraged to lead with their heads, in the mistaken belief that the helmets protect them from brain injuries. In rugby, whenever a clash of heads occurs, it's *always* accidental, never intentional, so the two can't meaningfully be compared.

Let me be clear: it's brilliant that the issue is being discussed sensibly and maturely, and that more research is being undertaken into rugby and long-term brain health. I'm proud to play a sport that has shown it can be agile and progressive when dealing with such issues, and it already feels like a significantly different sport from the one I played when I fractured my skull in 2008. The advent of the Head Injury Assessment (HIA) and the return-to-play protocols are making the game much safer, and the macho culture around 'digging in' when you've taken a knock has all but disappeared, particularly at elite level. I know some players have claimed that it's easy to cheat the tests by deliberately setting a low baseline at the start of the season, by pretending your reaction times are slower than they are, but more fool the person who does that. You ultimately have to take responsibility for your own health. One thing I think will change is the six-day turnaround. At the moment, you're able to play again six days after an HIA, assuming you pass every return-to-play protocol. That feels too short to me, and seems to be based on the fixture schedule rather than any sound medical evidence. Think about it: a six-day recovery period ensures a coach doesn't lose a player for the next game.

I'm not claiming to be an expert on any of this, but I'll retain my right to be sceptical until the evidence is unequivocal. If proof ever does materialise, I can say with some confidence that I wouldn't regret a thing. What I've gained through rugby has far outweighed the risks I may have exposed myself to. And that's the fundamental point: it *is* risky. It's not an office job; it's an environment where the dangers are real. You *are* more likely to break a leg, tear a ligament or get concussed on the rugby field than in almost any other profession. It's something you sign up to. George Orwell famously said that sport is war minus the shooting. In the case of rugby, he wasn't far wrong.

18

THE BURGESS AFFAIR

Back on 3 December 2012, in the cavernous surrounds of London's Tate Modern gallery, we discovered that Wales's seven-match losing run would have consequences. Against a striking backdrop of modern art, the draw was made for the 2015 World Cup. Our slide down the world rankings had seen us drop to ninth, and into the third group of seeds, which meant we were destined for a fiendishly difficult pool. Once the draw had been completed, the scale of the task ahead couldn't have been clearer. If we were to progress to the knockout stages, we'd have to emerge from the toughest group Wales had ever found themselves in. We'd been drawn alongside our long-term nemesis, Australia, and our biggest rivals, England, who also happened to be hosting the tournament. And so commenced a three-year build-up to a fixture that had never needed any extra spice. England versus Wales would be the second match in Pool A or, as it had already been labelled by a salivating press pack, the Pool of Death.

The summer training camps in 2015 didn't have the element of surprise of the Polish ones of 2011. This time we knew what was coming, and in a strange way I'd been looking forward to it. The semi-final defeat of 2011 still stung, and if we were to stand a chance of winning the World Cup this time, we had to be fitter and stronger than we'd ever been. Like a boxer preparing for a fight, you know your preparation time is finite. You have a window, and once it's opened, you do everything in your power to reach your absolute physical peak. The countdown began in a small town nestled in the Swiss Alps.

If our destination of Fiesch felt isolated, it was a bustling metropolis compared to where we actually ended up. On arrival in the town, we were driven immediately to the cable-car station and transported hundreds of metres further up the distant slopes. Living high and training low was the concept, although it was all relative, because even the low bits were breathtakingly high. That first cable-car ride was a jaw-dropping experience, as a landscape of almost indescribable majesty revealed itself. The pristine training pitches receded from view as we glided up through jagged snow-capped peaks towards our mountain base. These views would become something of a tonic during the week as we were slogged to the point of exhaustion and collapse.

There was precious little to do in the evenings, so we had to conjure up our own amusement. As a senior member of the entertainments committee, I came up with the idea of a one-minute introduction ceremony, in which every new squad member had to stand up for a minute and talk exclusively about themselves. A minute is longer than you think, and some of the boys absolutely hated it. I'd barely heard prop Samson Lee say a word since his debut two years earlier, so the idea of him squirming his way through an uninterrupted monologue was hilarious. I've heard some toe-curling intros down the years, but Cory Hill's was one of the best, beginning with a brilliantly droll, 'Hi, lads. My name is Cory Hill, and I've won a competition to come and train with Wales for the week.' The boys all collapsed in laughter, and the ice was well and truly broken. It's great to know this tradition is still alive and well in the Wales camp.

The strength-and-conditioning staff realised the importance of variety and continually mixed things up so it didn't feel like an endless, relentless slog. We did a lot of lung-busting cardiovascular stuff, including sprinting drills set to different times and repetitions each day. One day it would be four sets of six sprints, thirty seconds on, and thirty seconds off. The next day, it would be four sets of twelve sprints, fifteen seconds on, fifteen seconds off. The day after we'd do four sets of eighteen, ten seconds on, ten seconds off. Those shorter shuttles were the toughest, and as a big guy I really struggled, because there's so much more movement involved. Instead of running in a straight line, you're constantly twisting and turning. You're supposed to run to the cone and back in ten seconds, but it was taking me twenty every time. Towards the end, I was lumbering between them like a heavy-legged shire horse, and Dan Biggar was laughing so hard that he collapsed, ensuring his times were as underwhelming as mine. All the while, the likes of Gareth Davies and Lloyd Williams were sprinting up and down like lithe greyhounds, swivelling round the cones with ease and putting the rest of us to shame.

Switzerland was brutal, but the climate was perfect. There was snow on the mountaintops, but it was pleasantly warm during the day. The same couldn't be said of our next camp in Qatar, where the heat was so intense, we could only train before sunrise and after sundown. If the Swiss altitude training had been about oxygen starvation and the stimulation of red blood cells, Qatar's warm-weather training was about increasing the volume of plasma in our bloodstreams. More plasma allows you to carry more red blood cells, which helps boost overall fitness levels. I'm not sure how much comfort the alleged health benefits gave Tomas Francis at the end of the first session, when he found himself swaddled in ice blankets and breathing through a tube. The Exeter prop had arrived in camp a shade over 21 stone and looking every bit the tubby student he'd been a few years earlier while turning out for Doncaster in the English second tier. Warren Gatland had identified him as a rough diamond in need of chiselling into shape. Poor old Tomas had struggled manfully in the soporific heat, before eventually collapsing in a sweaty heap and passing out. Fortunately we were based at a medical centre and help was at hand. An ambulance was summoned and when he came round several minutes later, he was gasping through an oxygen mask and surrounded by team-mates torn between the need to show concern and a desperate urge to rip the piss.

To foster competition between us, our daily times would be pinned to the board outside the team room. It was always an extra incentive for me to beat my fellow midfielders, to see it written in black and white that I was still the boss. Towards the end of the week, we had a scheduled 'runways' session, a brutal sprint-based fitness workout which always provoked a sense of dread. The forwards went first, and by the time the backs arrived for their turn it looked like a war zone. Almost all the big lads were splayed out on their backs, grunting, wheezing and inhaling huge draughts of desert air into their crisp-packet lungs. Those that weren't were hunched over on their knees vomiting theatrically.

Although I knew it would leave me in a similar state, I *had* to beat my fellow centres Scott Williams, Cory Allen and Tyler Morgan. Over the next few minutes, I absolutely emptied myself, pushing myself to the very edge of my physical capability, before sinking to the deck feeling sick and exhausted. As I was contemplating a very long rest, Rob Howley blew his whistle and hollered, 'OK, boys, quick rest before we get into the running. See you on the try line in two minutes.' What the . . .?! Naively, I'd assumed it was just going to be runways and done, but I should have known better, given the absolutely ruined state of the forwards. I must have looked like a lame horse during that running session, stumbling around, leaning clumsily forward and hoping my legs would follow, while resisting the constant urge to be sick. On several occasions, my vision clouded over and I came close to passing out, but somehow I dug in and managed, against all the odds, to complete it. At the end of such a torturous session, your only real concern is whether you're still breathing.

The tournament began in September 2015 and we warmed up with two games against Ireland in August, losing at home with a largely second-string side, before winning in Dublin with our first-choice XV. The third warm-up match, in early September, was against Italy, and I watched helplessly from the BBC commentary box as we lost two of our best players in the blink of an eye. Rhys Webb and Leigh Halfpenny suffered horrible injuries that would rule them both out of the World Cup. With Jonathan Davies already sidelined, our World Cup chances had been dealt a serious blow. As I was leaving the stadium that day, I bumped into Leigh's girlfriend, Jess, who was in floods of tears. She asked if I had any news, and I did my best to console her, knowing full well Leigh had done his cruciate ligament. You expect to pick up injuries during campaigns, but to lose three of our seven starting backs before the tournament had even begun was devastating.

In stark contrast to New Zealand in 2011, which had felt like an odyssey to the other side of the world, the 2015 World Cup felt strangely sterile. England were hosts, but the WRU had wangled a few home games, meaning we'd be shuttling back and forth between

Cardiff and the quiet, nondescript town of Weybridge in London's commuter belt. It lacked the sense of mystery and adventure that had so enlivened our campaign four years earlier. At times, it was easy to forget we were involved in a World Cup at all. It had been Alan Phillips's decision to hide away in Weybridge, but it won't surprise you to learn that I'd have preferred to be in the mix in south-west London, soaking up the atmosphere and mingling with the fans.

Our first opponents in the tournament, Uruguay, were despatched with ease at the Millennium Stadium, where Cory Allen experienced both the agony and ecstasy of Test rugby in the space of fifty-five minutes. Within moments of scoring a hat-trick, he was limping off with a torn hamstring. Another man down.

And then, finally, our date with destiny was upon us. After nearly three years of feverish anticipation, the England fixture had arrived. One of rugby's oldest, fiercest and most keenly contested rivalries reimagined through the prism of a World Cup. Both teams knew that defeat was unthinkable. England and Australia had already beaten Fiji, essentially reducing the pool to a three-horse race. The fact England were the hosts heaped extra pressure on their shoulders, but it also cemented their status as favourites. I knew that if we produced our best and were in the game after seventy minutes, we had a chance, but wins at Twickenham are rarer than hen's teeth. We'd beaten them there in 2012, but this was on another level, and recent history was in their favour: England were the only side we'd lost to in that year's Six Nations.

The atmosphere at the quaint, supposedly haunted Oatlands Park Hotel in Weybridge became noticeably more frenetic that week. The world's press descended on our leafy corner of Surrey, and the hype levels were ratcheted up significantly. The mere mention of England v Wales was usually enough to get supporters salivating, but that week the media was busy concocting extra subplots to help stoke the fires. Sam Burgess was a rugby league legend. He'd played for Great Britain and England, and was a hero to the fans of South Sydney Rabbitohs, with whom he won the National Rugby League Premiership in 2014.

He'd been named Man of the Match in the Grand Final, and his star couldn't have been higher when he chose to switch codes. Nine months after making his debut for Bath, he'd been fast-tracked into the England squad. In league, he was a big, powerful, musclebound forward, and Bath had seen him as a blindside flanker. But when Stuart Lancaster named him in his World Cup squad, it was as an inside centre. He'd made a brief cameo there during England's opening win against Fiji, but hadn't been on the field long enough for his performance to be properly assessed.

As the game loomed, rumours began to circulate that Burgess would be starting again at inside centre. It was a huge call to pick a union novice in a position that required such technical expertise, and it seemed to me a reckless and unnecessary gamble. The press had latched on to the rumours, and a Burgess v Roberts storyline began to take shape. The clash of the titans. The irresistible force meets the immovable object. Two, hulking, bristling slabs of muscle going head to head in a midfield duel of heavyweight proportions. It was a headline writer's dream, and my phone was soon clogged up with messages from mates who were forwarding articles about the imminent battle. Rarely did I give anything away size-wise to my opposite number, but this guy was big. We were of a similar height, but he was probably packing a few more pounds. I was big and lean; he was more dense and muscular.

The rumours proved true, and Burgess was named to start. Not long after lunch, as I was returning to my room, Rob Howley and I crossed paths in the hotel corridor. He was grinning from ear to ear. 'Seen the team, then?' I asked. 'Happy days,' he said, and continued on his way. I felt the same. As decorated as Burgess was as a rugby league player, I knew we could expose him. I was amazed that England coach Stuart Lancaster was willing to put so much blind faith in one man. It was also a tacit acknowledgement of our strength and power: an indication that they were thinking as much about us as they were about themselves. It had echoes of the Joe Worsley game in 2009. They were worried about me marauding down that channel and had deliberately picked a big lump to block my path.

Following the bewildering Howard Marks episode in 2012, Alan Phillips raised his game for the 2015 World Cup, managing to get Tom

Jones to come and present our jerseys before the England match. Every man, woman and child in Wales knows who Tom Jones is, and at least one of his records can be found in every Welsh household, but we discovered that day that his fame hadn't necessarily stretched to all corners of New Zealand. Once the last jersey had been presented, and the last hand had been shaken, Warren Gatland stood to encourage a round of applause for 'Tom James'. Thumper's face turned crimson red as Sir Tom politely declined to correct him. A few days earlier, we'd been presented with our World Cup caps by Prince William, who'd said, 'The doc is in the house,' when he handed me mine. I'd wanted to laugh out loud, but didn't know whether that would be acceptable royal protocol. Either way, it was an improvement on our first meeting, when I'd been tapped on the shoulder in the changing room and had turned round stark naked to shake hands with the future king. Not the kind of crown jewels he was accustomed to.

As he had been against England in 2012, Sam Warburton was teetering right on the edge before the game, prowling round the dressing room in a state of barely controlled fury. It was hot and stuffy in there and he'd convinced himself the RFU had deliberately cranked up the heat to try to unsettle us. By the time we emerged onto the pitch, he was ready to explode. The game erupted spectacularly around the twenty-minute mark when Dan Lydiate chopped Tom Wood down with one of his trademark low tackles. Within seconds all thirty players had swarmed in, anticipating a mass brawl, as the referee struggled to maintain order. Voices were raised, jerseys pulled and threats issued, and I found myself having to separate an enraged-looking Warby from Mike Brown, who was unwisely spoiling for a fight. Both of them are intensely competitive animals, and I was about to become Browny's team-mate at Quins, but there was only ever one winner there. While no shots connected and order was soon restored, it was a good psychological marker to have laid down. It showed that we weren't going to stand on ceremony for anyone. It may have been Twickenham, and it may have been their party, but we were the unwanted house guests who'd come to trash the joint.

They seized the initiative after that, breaching our defence with a clever move involving Billy Vunipola and Sam Burgess running decoy lines to disguise an intricate play behind the gain line. Within a few phases, Jonny May had sneaked down the touchline for the opening try, and we were ten points down with half-time approaching. We had to respond, and when we were awarded a line-out just inside our half, I decided it was time to put Burgess's defence to the test. He was unlikely to be too adept at reading strike plays, so Dan Biggar and I called one that could expose him. Lock Bradley Davies won the ball cleanly and I ran a hard line between Owen Farrell and Burgess, with winger Hallam Amos tucked in tight behind me. As I suspected he might, Burgess took the bait and turned in, leaving a gaping hole outside him. Bigs threaded a tunnel ball perfectly into the waiting hands of Scotty Williams, who accelerated into the hole, gobbling up the yards all the way to the 22. We won a penalty and narrowed the gap to seven points. As we jogged into the changing rooms, Bigs and I exchanged a knowing look. We had Burgess's number. He didn't have a clue. Scotty would have loved that too, after Burgess had insulted him during the week, saying, when asked about Scott in a press conference, 'Who's that?' Earlier in the half, Scott had piled into Burgess, smashing him to the deck and dislodging the ball. As they'd returned to their feet, Scotty had looked him in the eye and said, 'You know who I am now.'

The third quarter was tense and cagey, with Farrell and Bigs taking it in turns to knock over three-pointers. Every time England widened the margin, we pegged them back, and it was developing into a battle of wills between the two kickers, both of whom were world-class marksmen. As we entered the final quarter, the margin was four points in their favour, but we were starting to make inroads into their tiring defence. Momentum appeared to be shifting in our direction when the twisted hand of fate intervened. In the space of five bewildering minutes, we lost three of our backs. It felt like some maleficent sporting god was vengefully stabbing voodoo dolls of our players as they started tumbling to the turf in agony.

Scotty was the first to fall, rupturing his anterior cruciate ligament, and Hallam Amos followed shortly after, dislocating his shoulder in the act of handing off Farrell. They say these things come in threes, and sure enough Liam Williams completed the set, taking a stray boot to the head and being forced off with concussion. It was absolute carnage, and I was beginning to feel like the last man standing. Add in Rhys Webb, Jonathan Davies and Leigh Halfpenny, who'd not even made it to the tournament, and we were down to the bare bones. Forced into a desperate reshuffle, we moved George North to outside centre and stuck Lloyd Williams – a scrum-half – on the right wing. Rhys Priestland stepped in at fly-half, with Bigs filling in at full-back. It was one of the most important games of our lives, and we suddenly had three players playing in positions they were completely unfamiliar with. The four-point deficit, which moments earlier had seemed within reach, suddenly seemed insurmountable.

When Farrell kicked them into a 25–18 lead, a team with a weaker mental constitution might have rolled over. That wasn't in our make-up. We knew how to beat England, and knew we still could. It was at this point that Burgess was subbed off for George Ford, with Farrell shifting out to inside centre. The big brute had left the stage, to be replaced by a smaller, more elusive playmaker. As we trotted towards the next line-out, I said to Priest, 'What's the craic?' He looked me in the eye and said, 'I'm going to give you the ball, and you're going to run as hard as you can over that f***er,' pointing to Ford.

Rob Howley had always been obsessed with our work rate off the ball. After a carry, we were expected to work back into position immediately, to get deep enough and wide enough for the next wave of attack. Shortly after my none-too-subtle charge into Ford, I found myself in a ruck on the right-hand side of the field. The pattern we used involved sweeping from one side of the pitch to the other, stretching the opposition defence in search of space in the tramlines. As I emerged from the ruck, I felt knackered, but I could see the other backs had already worked back in position and were preparing to move the ball towards the left-hand touchline. Rhys Priestland and Dan Biggar were in the line, so I started running behind them towards the far 15-metre channel. Priest passed to Bigs, and Dan, noting Brad Barritt was defending tightly, lobbed a floated pass over the top. I vividly remember it coming towards me, wobbling slightly in flight, before landing in my arms. Anthony Watson was in front of me, and my split-second calculation told me he would drift towards the touchline to shut down my space. But just as I was processing that thought, he bit in ever so slightly, committing to an early tackle. It was just enough to create a sliver of space outside me, into which came Lloyd Williams on the charge. I got the offload away and Lloyd pinned his ears back, burning down the touchline. I was trying my best to keep up, half expecting a return pass, when I heard myself yelling, 'NOOOOOOO!'

He'd kicked it away.

I was fuming, cursing him out loud for squandering such precious possession, when a galloping Gareth Davies surged into my eyeline. Demonstrating the same fast-twitch speed that had put us all to shame during the sprint drills in Qatar, he cruised effortlessly towards the bouncing ball, leaving several back-pedalling English defenders trailing in his wake. Could this really be happening? The ball bounced up invitingly just short of the try line and, gripping it with the tips of his fingers, he triumphantly dived over. All is forgiven, Lloyd, you stone-cold genius. My emotions had swung from despair to ecstasy in five thrilling seconds.

For a guy to come on, out of position, in a game of that magnitude and deliver that moment was phenomenal. Lloyd is a superb player who has achieved a lot in the game, but that will forever be his defining moment. Make no mistake, that try would not have been scored if we hadn't had those injuries. Kicking the ball into space was a very 'scrum-half' thing to do. Lloyd would have known subconsciously that Gareth would be tracking inside. It was a wonderful bit of telepathy between one scrum-half and another. Our patched-up backline had conjured a bit of magic that our first-choice line-up simply couldn't have. And full credit to Gareth for finishing the way he did. He still had a few defenders to beat, and the calm and poise he demonstrated under the circumstances was remarkable.

The conversion levelled the scores and brought with it a surge of optimism. We were back from the brink, and England were shell-shocked. With eight minutes left, Bigs launched a high, hanging Garryowen, which was gathered by an onrushing Mike Brown. As he launched a counter-attack, he was consumed by a swarm of red jerseys, and Warby did what he'd done so many times before: he buried his head in the ruck and clamped his forearms over the ball. The shrill blast from Jérôme Garcès's whistle signalled a penalty to Wales. It was just shy of 50 metres out.

Bigs is a confident guy, and he'd always wanted to be Wales's first-choice goal-kicker. Leigh Halfpenny's absence had given him that chance. Here lay the ultimate test. The kick was at the very edge of his range, and his legs would have been trembling from a combination of nerves and exhaustion. He went through his increasingly lengthy 'Macarena' routine, which had been the subject of countless memes and gifs throughout the World Cup. I'm convinced he invented it to garner a little extra publicity for himself. A sweep of the hair, a twitch of the neck, a shuffle and a quick tap on each shoulder, before focusing his steely-eyed glare at the posts. I always imagine that that's the moment things could fall apart. Like a tightrope-walker resisting the urge to look down, that's when you need to block out all the noise. He swung his right leg at the ball and connected beautifully, watching as it sailed majestically between the uprights. England 25 Wales 28. A strange silence momentarily descended over Twickenham. Up in the cheap seats, the Welsh fans went wild.

Seeing their World Cup dream evaporate before their eyes, England rallied for one last maniacal surge, hurling themselves at our defensive wall, desperate to find a chink or a dent. I was convinced Warby had won the game for us when he got into the same clamp position over a prone Mike Brown. It was a virtually identical jackal to the one he'd pulled off moments earlier, but this time the penalty went the other way. Those are the vagaries of the rugby law book. One man's textbook turnover is another man's failure to release.

It was inside our 22, well within kicking range, and my heart sank as I realised they'd managed to salvage a draw from the wreckage. But as I was processing that thought, their captain, Chris Robshaw, pointed to the corner. Apparently a draw wasn't good enough for England: they wanted the victory and were prepared to throw the dice. Even in the heat of the moment it seemed an astonishing decision.

As England were discussing their calls, Warby was skulking up and down the line-out bellowing at his forwards, 'Don't you f***ing *dare* let them score.' He was a man possessed, trying to intimidate the

English pack as much as he was trying to rouse ours. I was behind the try line, thinking, *They're coming at us. I've got to be on the money. Don't be that guy who f***s up in defence.* I stared across at my opposite number, Owen Farrell, and checked the gap between George and me at outside centre. Keep it simple. Come off the line square and smash whatever comes into your channel. Lloyd approached me, asking what he needed to do. He'd never defended as a blind-side winger and was paranoid he'd get caught out of position. I made sure he was clear on his role. Plug the side of the maul. Get ready to slide under the ball if they drop over the line. There was no time for negative thoughts. It had all come down to this.

They took the conservative option and threw to the front, which seemed at odds with the decision to go for the win. The longer the throw, the greater the chance of it being picked off, but if you're going to gamble you might as well go big. It's harder to launch a strike play from front ball. They were going to tuck it up the jumper and attempt to drive us over the line, which was manna from heaven for our fired-up forwards. As soon as England secured the ball, our pack aligned as one and mowed through the England eight like a tank through a plasterboard wall. I've seen some amazing tries, and played my part in many, but that was one of the best things I've ever witnessed on a rugby field. In its own bloody-minded way, it was as graceful as a Shane Williams sidestep. In one brisk, brutal moment, it encapsulated the level of heart and desire we had. Luke Charteris, with his octopus-like tentacles, was one of the best maul defenders in the world, and once he'd swum through and isolated the ball-carrier, it just took an almighty collective thrust from the rest to decimate England's crumbling pack. Their forward power had always been an immense source of pride for them, and the driving maul one of their most potent weapons. They were used to trampling teams into the turf that close to the try line. Not Wales. Not that day.

They threw everything into the last scrum of the game, trying their best to shove us off the ball and make it messy. The ball squirted out and I ran towards the ensuing ruck thinking, *Above all else, keep that ball.* If that meant we only had one back on his feet, then so be it. Just get in there, add your weight and secure the ball. We did so, and when

Bigs booted it high into the stand we knew we'd done it. I embraced Alun Wyn and Gethin Jenkins, and the three of us started leaping around like big kids. When you've worked that hard and absorbed that many punches, there's no feeling like it. The icing on the cake was seeing my brother during our lap of honour. We couldn't hug each other because he was busy operating his camera, but the look and the smile we shared was enough.

In the chaos and euphoria that followed, Gethin Jenkins asked Lloyd if he could have his left boot. Not realising the significance, Lloyd panicked and agreed. Melon isn't much of a sentimental bloke and, unsurprisingly, the 'boot that sank England' appeared later as a pretty lucrative auction lot during his testimonial year. Cold hard cash is never far from Melon's mind. As we were heading to the team bus, weaving our way through the thousands of fans streaming out of the stadium, I bumped into a bunch of my best mates from school. Tommy, Blummy, Rhys and Dyfrig. They came bounding over with tears in their eyes, and we started spontaneously jumping up and down like the overgrown schoolboys that we were.

It was then that I noticed how many other people were crying. Dozens of Wales supporters wandering in a dreamlike state shedding actual tears. Grizzled, craggy-faced old men with damp eyes and quivering lips. That was when I realised the significance of what we'd done. The post-match chat had been fairly restrained, with Gats reminding us not to go overboard; it was just a group game, after all. But for these supporters it meant *everything*. Any England-Wales game is of monumental significance, but this was on a different level.

During the journey back, the coaches were up front enjoying a beer, while we were slumped in our seats nursing our battered bodies and tired minds. Every so often, a supporters' minibus would overtake us and there would be a sudden cacophony of beeping horns, waving flags and bursts of song. It seemed like the whole of Wales was pouring back over the border in a state of heightened euphoria. Some of the boys had received WhatsApp clips of Mike Brown's post-match interview in which he could barely contain his anger, answering mainly in monosyllables. It raised a few chuckles among us, but I also felt a good deal of empathy for those England lads. I'd suffered big losses in my career and knew how devastated they'd be feeling.

We arrived back at the Vale at 1.30 in the morning, but rather than heading to reception, the driver took a left towards the training barn at the top of the car park. A grinning Warren Gatland turned round and said, 'Cryotherapy time, boys.' We were due to face Fiji in five days, and recovery was of paramount importance. From the white-hot Twickenham cauldron and the sweeping elation of a historic victory, to a dark, gloomy ice chamber in the space of a few hours. It's not all glamour.

The physical and mental exhaustion from the England game lingered for a few days, and Gats saw no sense in beasting us before we faced Fiji. It turned out to be one of the toughest Test matches I've ever played in. They're the worst side to play when you're tired, and they sensed the possibility of a scalp. They're not the most structured, but they're all, to a man, skilful, powerful and outrageously gifted rugby players. Normally when a back-row forward is running full tilt at you, you just have to worry about getting them down. With the Fijians, you have to stop them *and* stop the offload. A good number of them had been exposed to a higher level of rugby in the French domestic league, and they were a different prospect from the Fiji we'd faced four years earlier. Despite their reputation as crowd-pleasing magicians, they hit as hard as anyone in world rugby. At one point, stepping infield from the left wing, I was poleaxed with such ferocity, it felt like I'd been thrown into an industrial tumble dryer. My body turned inside out and upside down. It was easily one of the biggest collisions I've ever been involved in. It was a really difficult Test, but we had the class and confidence to navigate our way to victory. By the time we'd returned to Weybridge, someone had scaled the side of the Oatlands Park Hotel and replaced the 'O' with a 'G'. No one owned up to it, but I have a feeling it might have been Thumper.

The next game in our group, England against Australia, was now a knockout match for the hosts. Lose that and they were dust. The boys were keen to watch it as a team at the hotel, but I was feeling increasingly claustrophobic in Weybridge, and ventured out to Rosslyn Park Rugby Club to watch it with a mate. I'm fairly certain I was the only Welshman in there, and as much as I wanted to keep a low profile, my gleeful outbursts whenever Australia scored drew obvious attention to me. I couldn't help myself. I'm not one of those jingoistic Welshmen who always delight in seeing England fail, but I'd be lying if I said I didn't feel a touch smug when they were dumped out of their own World Cup.

Australia's win secured our passage through to the last eight, meaning our match with them would determine who'd top the Pool of Death. The winners would face Scotland in the quarter-final, while the runners-up would take on the Springboks. Although we'd ended our fifteen-year losing streak against the Boks the previous autumn, we hadn't lost to the Scots for the best part of a decade. It was an almighty incentive.

The Aussies had ripped England to pieces and racked up 33 points. If we were to beat them, we'd *have* to score tries. Attempting to squeeze the life out of them while knocking over penalties wouldn't be enough. As I was boarding the bus for training that week, Gats sidled up to me and asked, 'Doc, in the last World Cup cycle, how many times have we run the same play off the line-out, with the nine passing directly to you?' It had been a go-to play for us for years, a sure-fire way of putting us on the front foot.

I shrugged and said, 'I dunno. Fifty?'

'Seventy,' he replied. 'And how many times have you offloaded?'

Again, I shrugged. It was clearly a loaded question. 'Ten times?' I ventured, hopefully.

'Twice,' he said. 'Have a think about that.'

The message was clear, and it resurrected all those old ghosts about my supposed limitations. For years, Gats had based his entire game plan around me running hard and direct into contact, and here he was suggesting I'd become predictable and one-dimensional. As I was walking to the back of the bus pondering such things, Ken Owens bellowed 'Oooh, check out Doc in the *Daily Mail*.' Grinning inanely, he showed me his phone, which displayed the classic tabloid-style head-line 'Wales star Jamie Roberts steps out with mystery blonde'. It was my girlfriend, Nicole. I'd gone to Chelsea to grab a bite to eat with her on my day off, and we'd apparently been 'papped'. It felt surreal, and a little disturbing, knowing that when I was wandering down the King's Road, someone had had a long lens trained on me from behind a bush somewhere. I was used to being in the press back home, and had a good relationship with most of the Welsh journalists, but this felt intrusive. It was a reminder that we were taking part in a global tournament, and the world was watching.

It felt intrusive to Nicole too, especially as we'd only been on a handful of dates at that point. Our relationship had begun, in the modern way, on Instagram. I'd been scrolling absent-mindedly through my feed while sipping a flat white in a Parisian café, and I was given pause by an image of a striking blonde woman drinking champagne at St Pancras station. I assumed she must have been heading to Paris, so I sent her a completely unsolicited message along the lines of 'clear skies here in the French capital', with a photo of a cloudless blue sky attached. I hoped it was suitably mysterious to arouse her curiosity, while acknowledging that as chat-up lines go, it was pretty unimaginative. She replied with a curt 'I'm going to Lille, actually', but crucially a connection had been made. Over the next few weeks our correspondence continued, until I plucked up the courage to ask her out. Our first date was in a Soho drag club (her choice), and while she had an inkling that I was a professional rugby player, she was completely perplexed when the drag queen – who happened to be from Neath – recognised me, and called out my name. Fortunately, our relationship has survived these inauspicious beginnings.

We dominated the first half of the Australia game, keeping them pinned in their own half and denying them the time and space they'd enjoyed against England. The 12–6 lead they'd built up early in the second half was a result of their superiority in the scrum, and the penalties they'd milked from it. At some point, though, their discipline deserted them, and scrum-half Will Genia and second row Dean Mumm were despatched to the sin bin in quick succession. This was our chance to show our killer instinct: seven minutes with a two-man advantage. Unfortunately, we didn't, and the hackneyed old argument about us lacking the nous to bury a southern-hemisphere side reared its head once more. Even with Warren's critical words ringing in my ears, I found myself carrying again and again into an unyielding wall of Wallaby defenders. We were camped on their line for most of that seven-minute period, but repeatedly ignored the space out wide.

A two-man advantage is bound to deliver overlaps, but we kept running hard and straight, and kept being hit backwards. We were incapable of making the right call at the right time. The times we should have gone wide, we punched short, and the one time we should have punched short, we went out the back. It was off a five-metre scrum, and I knew I'd have the angle to get over the line. It was the right decision to go 'route one'. I told Gareth Davies, 'Mate, I'm coming. Hit me,' knowing the momentum would carry me over the line. Instead, he played it out the back, and Adam Ashley-Cooper made a great defensive read, which led to a turnover and the end of a fruitless attacking sequence. It was so frustrating, and as a senior player, I had to shoulder a good deal of responsibility for our failure to score. In fairness to Australia, their defence was incredible. They played smart rugby, choosing not to contest for the ball and keeping as many men on their feet as possible. Three times we should have scored; three times they snuffed us out. George North, Liam Williams and Toby Faletau all got within millimetres. All three were denied.

After the game I was sharing a quiet beer with Gats in the hotel when Nicole – who's Australian – came bounding in wearing a green-and-gold scarf, an Australia jersey and two gold Wallabies daubed on either cheek. She'd been at the game and had had a few drinks. Kiwis hate Aussies at the best of times, and given the circumstances, Warren struggled even to raise a smile when I introduced them. Nicole didn't have a clue who he was and hadn't picked up on the sombre tone. I had to take her to one side and ask her politely but firmly to go to my room and wipe those bloody Wallabies off her cheeks.

The next day, Rob Howley was absolutely furious. At the start of what proved a painful debrief, he just looked at us incredulously and said, 'Lads. Thirteen men,' before pressing Play and forcing us to watch the entire seven-minute period in all its gut-wrenching misery.

Other than a few tuts and derisory shakes of the head, he stayed silent. The press was on our back again, reheating the same old lines about a lack of imagination, about a team conditioned to play one way and one way only, unable to expand the limits of its horizon. The fact is, we'd backed ourselves to run over the top of them. When you've got me and George in the midfield, it's an obvious tactic, but to continue with that approach against thirteen men was bone-headed. We only had ourselves to blame.

Alex Cuthbert had been given a yellow card in the dying moments of the match and the social-media trolls were out in force again. Cuthy was the kind of guy that couldn't ignore it, and it was really getting him down. The negativity seeped from every pore and his body language was starting to betray his gloomy outlook. His shoulders were hunched, his face etched in a permanent frown, and he was beginning to moan about everything. During training, every dropped ball or overthrown pass would see him throw his hands up in exasperation. I called the lads into a huddle and confronted it head on. I didn't want to embarrass him, but it needed to be addressed.

I said, 'Cuthy, come on, mate, let's get rid of this negative body language, this attitude. You're a world-class player: just back your ability and don't worry about all the other s***.'

I don't know how well it went down, but I wanted to give him a bum-tap in front of the lads because I could see how much pressure he was under. In hindsight it may have been presumptuous to call him out that way. I didn't realise quite how insidious an influence it had become in his life. I hated seeing him like that. He'd lost his vitality, his zest for life, and had become a shrunken imitation of his former self. I discovered later that he was on the verge of quitting the game altogether.

Positivity was the name of the game leading into the quarter-final. The Australia game was to be parked, and our injury crisis was not to be used as an excuse. The message from management centred on belief and desire. We had a week to sharpen our attack, and could use the England game as inspiration. We'd had our backs to the wall then, and had come out fighting. Gatland was forced into another backline reshuffle, with Gareth Anscombe, normally a fly-half, starting out of position at full-back, and twenty-year-old rookie Tyler Morgan partnering me in the midfield. James Hook had been the other option at 13, someone Tyler coyly admitted he'd worshipped as a kid, growing up with Hooky's poster on his bedroom wall. I did wonder if Mike Phillips might have been in with a shout for selection. His abrasive style was perfect for taking on the Boks, but he'd fallen from favour and ended the campaign without playing a single minute. It was a limp exit for one of Wales's greatest players of all time. He remains forever marooned on 99 international caps.

The first half against South Africa was all blood and thunder, and we steamrollered into them. George was denied over the line for the second week running, and if Melon's wayward pass had found Tyler we could have been a few scores clear by the interval. As it was, we entered the sheds a solitary point ahead thanks to a superb display from Dan Biggar. He'd sent one of his trademark up-and-unders skyward, and out-jumped Willie le Roux to claim it and put Gareth Davies away for a fantastic try. Then, in injury time, he'd coolly slotted the drop goal that nudged us ahead.

It remained tight and nervy all the way through, and with seven minutes to go, we were clinging on to a slender one-point lead. What happened next haunts me to this day. The Boks were awarded an attacking scrum in our 22 and managed to get a bit of a shove on, but our pack refused to buckle, forcing them to play. Their burly No 8, Duane Vermeulen, picked up from the base and charged into Lloyd Williams, who did a decent initial job of slowing his momentum. There was no South African winger in the blind-side channel, so Cuthy ran in to help Lloyd out and stop Vermeulen building up a head of steam. It was at that point that Fourie du Preez set off on an arcing run around the back of the scrum, from the open side to the blind side. Vermeulen popped the ball out of the back with a delicacy that belied his giant stature, and du Preez scampered over untouched. Game over. It was utterly heartbreaking.

Predictably, Cuthbert copped a load of criticism for what happened, but I'd wager the Boks would have scored that against any team in the world. It was the right call to come off his wing and put the double shot on Vermeulen. Fourie du Preez appeared like some sort of apparition, and would have ghosted through any defence. It was a brilliant play from a genius of a scrum-half, a sprinkle of stardust on a display otherwise built on brute force and defiance. *No one* saw du Preez coming.

When the whistle blew I sank to my knees, and my overwhelming thought was *That's it. I'll probably never get a chance to win a World Cup again.* Three weeks earlier, on the same pitch, in front of the same stand, we had experienced the ultimate joy. Now, we had slid all the way to the other end of the emotional scale. Bereft, hollow and empty. Not many had given us a chance, given the injuries we'd suffered, and in many ways the closeness of the result made it worse. We'd still been on our feet, slugging it out, when a sucker punch had knocked us to the canvas. It was only the third try we'd conceded in the entire tournament, but it was the one that sent us home. The next morning we packed our bags.

Three years later, my phone buzzed with an Australian number. Not recognising it, I didn't answer, letting it go straight to voicemail. There followed a long, rambling sequence of text messages from someone referring to themselves as 'the greatest' and imploring me to pick up. It took me a while to figure out it was Sam Burgess. He may have been under the influence, going on to describe himself as 'the guy who shut me down' before England had apparently 'bottled it' and replaced him with George Ford. When the English press combed through the wreckage of their failed campaign, they'd been desperate to find a scapegoat, and Burgess – the outsider from rugby league – had proved a convenient one. The public opprobrium had clearly left its mark, and all those years later it obviously still hurt.

19

THE BEGINNING OF THE END?

Within a few weeks of playing in front of 80,000 fans in a World Cup quarter-final at Twickenham, I was standing with my hands tied behind my back, eating food off a naked man's belly. Welcome back to university life. The man in question was nicknamed 'the plate', and insisted this ritual was an essential part of the post-match initiation. It was proper private-schoolboy stuff.

The quarter-final was on 17 October 2015. By the 26th, I was wandering up Grange Road on a wet Monday evening to meet the rugby lads for my first Cambridge University training session. My body was absolutely battered. I'd been playing Test rugby non-stop since 2008, and this was just what I needed. Because of the World Cup, there were no autumn internationals, so it was a perfect chance to decompress and take a break from the professional game. For the next few months, I'd be strictly an amateur player. My salary at Quins wouldn't kick in until the new year. It was like going back in time.

I'd gone from the most professional, regimented environment imaginable, to running around a muddy field with a bunch of amateurs wearing a mishmash of kits, who were more used to post-match pints than protein shakes and lean steaks. From the bowling-green surfaces of Cardiff and Edinburgh, and the unyielding glare of public scrutiny, to the spongy turf of Grange Road and anonymity in Cambridge. All of a sudden I was playing for completely different reasons. The pressure, the match fees, the expectant crowds, the constant carping of the press – all these things were gone. The only thing that mattered was messing about and having a laugh. I felt completely free and unencumbered.

Cambridge University is stunning. The setting, the architecture, the almost tangible presence of history at every turn. You genuinely feel as though you're walking in the footsteps of giants. The influence that place has had around the world is awe-inspiring. The discovery of

DNA; Alan Turing and the creation of artificial intelligence; Isaac Newton and gravity; Darwin and natural selection. It's humbling just to be there and soak it all in.

As much as I felt out of place – I was too long for my bed and ten years older than most of my colleagues – I loved being there. It was a unique and inspiring setting, and I distinctly remember thinking how fortunate I was that I was able to do this at this point in my life. It also allowed me a degree of anonymity that I wasn't able to enjoy in Cardiff. While sport forms an important part of the university's identity, particularly through its rivalry with Oxford, it remains a frivolous distraction compared to the more serious business of study. The presence of an international rugby player barely raised an eyebrow among the college's academically minded intake.

If I was in any doubt about the calibre of student in Cambridge, it was made clear during my first morning in the breakfast hall. I fell into conversation with an eighteen-year-old girl from Gonville and Caius college whose tutor was Stephen Hawking. She was convinced that one of his theories was flawed, and patiently explained how she planned to disprove it.

My choice of an MPhil (Master of Philosophy) gave me a great degree of flexibility. It was research-based, as opposed to a taught course, so once I'd sat down with my supervisor and formulated a plan, I could devise my own timetable. I chose to research methods of measuring knee-cartilage thickness using magnetic resonance imaging. It was an area that fascinated me, and it had an obvious connection with my day job, in which knee injuries are an occupational hazard. I'm under no illusions that my knees will start to buckle and crack once I've retired, and the thought of contributing even a tiny amount of research to potential treatment in this area was highly appealing. I also had easy access to reams of data given my status as a pro rugby player. I was able to distribute surveys and questionnaires among my Harlequins colleagues, and use their experiences as a rich seam of information. It was the perfect way to combine my backgrounds in medical science and sport.

The Varsity Match is one of the oldest fixtures in rugby union history. The first contest between Oxford and Cambridge took place in

1872, nine years before Wales played its first international. In fact, the man who captained Wales that day in 1881, James Bevan, was a Cambridge University student at the time of his selection. This historic connection was irresistible. I'd grown up watching the Varsity Match on television, and was intrigued and seduced by the age-old rivalry; by its uniqueness and exclusivity. It was a surreal experience preparing for it with warm-up games in places like Durham University, where opposition players would spend eighty minutes trying to take your head off, and then politely ask for a selfie.

Things had changed since the amateur era, when it wasn't uncommon for the Oxford and Cambridge university sides to contain international players. In the professional era, I was definitely a curio in this regard. Compared to what I'd been used to, the standard was distinctly average, but the commitment was absolute. The lads were giving it everything. It took me a while to recalibrate, and I must have been a bit of a pillock initially, bellowing orders and berating team-mates for making silly mistakes. After a few sessions, the skipper had to take me aside for a quiet word, explaining patiently that these guys weren't at my level, that they weren't getting paid and I couldn't get angry every time they dropped the ball. My win-at-all-costs mentality didn't translate well to an amateur setting. I had to seriously chill out.

The traditions in the build-up to the Varsity Match are brilliant. Port and Nuts Night does exactly what it says on the tin. The team convenes at the captain's college to drink vintage port, eat nuts and take it in turns to tell stories. A few days out from the match, there's a procession up Castle Hill, the one crinkle in an otherwise pancake-flat landscape, which affords an arresting view over the whole of Cambridge. After a few foaming pints of ale in one of the cosy, wood-panelled pubs, we meandered up the hill to find a lone piper playing at its summit. The route was lined with former Cambridge Blues, dressed in their old university scarves and blazers.

The stars looked amazing that night as the clouds drifted lazily across a darkening sky and former Cambridge captain Angus Innes delivered a rousing speech about how special the place is, how many Nobel prizes the university and its alumni had won, how influential this small corner of Britain had been, and how privileged we all were to be wearing that jersey. I thought of the Welshmen who'd worn the famous blue-and-white hoops before me – Gerald Davies, Eddie Butler and James Bevan among them – and felt immensely proud to be joining such a select group. I'd worn the Lions shirt and the Barbarians shirt, and while this one wasn't quite as coveted, it was equally iconic in its own way.

After all the build-up and the media hype about a British Lion playing in the Varsity Match, the game itself was really disappointing. During my first purposeful carry, my opposite number mistimed his tackle and caught his head right on the sweet spot of my quad. Although it knocked him clean out and ended his involvement, it gave me a dead leg which bled into my knee as the half progressed, severely hampering my ability to run. The hole in my quad remains to this day. I watched the second half from the bench with my hood pulled up and a TV camera trained permanently on me, hoping for some kind of reaction. After all the anticipation, it was an entirely underwhelming experience and, to make matters worse, we lost, 12–6. The lads were devastated. That was their World Cup final, and in their way, they felt as crestfallen as I had been on that same Twickenham turf a few months earlier. It was the first tryless Varsity Match in fourteen years, and Cambridge's sixth loss to Oxford in a row. It wasn't meant to unfold like that.

I moved out of college accommodation at the end of 2015, and started with Quins a week later. Chris Robshaw, Mike Brown, Danny Care and Joe Marler were among my new team-mates, all of whom had been involved in that fateful World Cup match, and it gave me great pleasure to bring it up constantly during my first few weeks at the Stoop. As much as I felt for them, particularly Chris Robshaw, whose decision it had been to kick to the corner, I couldn't call myself a proper Welshman if I didn't rub their noses in it just a little. It was also the first time I'd seen the Aussie lock James Horwill since the Lions tour in 2013, when he'd escaped punishment for allegedly stamping on Alun Wyn Jones. He'd become something of a pantomime villain among the Lions fans but, as I was to discover, he was a gentle giant of a bloke and someone who became a great friend over the next few years. Tim Visser, the Scottish-Dutch winger, had signed on that season too, and the two of us became thick as thieves. We're still good friends to this day.

The Stoop is a great venue when it's full and bouncing, and Harlequins is a club that appreciates the value of entertainment. It's written into the club's DNA to throw the ball around, and we did so with abandon that season, encouraged by the attack-minded head coach, Conor O'Shea. We went well in Europe, reaching the final of the Challenge Cup in Lyon, where I experienced yet another last-minute defeat, this time against Montpellier. The circumstances were bizarre. We had the ball in injury time, and were about to launch one final attack, when our fly-half, Ben Botica, inexplicably booted possession away. Montpellier gratefully gathered up the ball and kicked it dead. The conspiracy theorists on social media were convinced there was something sinister at play, as Botica had signed for Montpellier next season. From our point of view, we were just gutted we couldn't send the outgoing Conor off with a trophy. A group of us drowned our sorrows with a ludicrously extravagant trip on a private jet to Nice the following morning to take in the Monaco Grand Prix during what turned out to be a memorably debauched weekend. A food fight at Anjuna Beach Club and a helicopter ride to Cannes for the film festival were particular highlights.

Messrs Brown, Marler and Robshaw had managed to get their own back during the 2016 Six Nations. Stuart Lancaster had fallen on his sword after the World Cup, and the brash Aussie Eddie Jones had been appointed as his successor. They beat us narrowly at Twickenham en route to a first Grand Slam since 2003. I didn't play well. At one stage we had a clear overlap to score and, for no good reason, I kicked the ball. I'm not the most accomplished footballer, but this was comfortably the worst kick of my career. I fed through a harmless little grubber, which Anthony Watson picked up gratefully, dabbing it down for a 22-metre dropout. On another occasion, we worked another overlap and just needed to put the ball through the hands, but Dan Biggar and I ran into one another and ended up knocking it on. I used to pride myself on being powerful and precise every time I pulled on the red jersey, but that day I felt clumsy and ineffective. I came off the field knowing I'd delivered a below-par performance. England had claimed revenge for their World Cup defeat, and it was another Quins colleague, Danny Care, who kicked the ball out at full time to seal the victory. I was sure my performance was just an aberration, but it bothered me for days afterwards.

Wales's tour to New Zealand in the summer of 2016 was a dry run for the Lions the following year. Warren would be leading them again, and this was an extended recce in his eyes. Gats knew that winning Lions tours were based on a squad's ability to thrive in hostile environments. He made no secret of the fact that this was a trial for all of us who had ambitions to return in the Lions jersey a year later. I was excited and eager to prove I still had it. We'd be up against a fiendishly strong All Blacks side, but if there was one area in which we might have had an advantage it was the midfield. Foxy had returned in incredible nick, and the two of us were back in the saddle. We were the incumbent Lions midfield, and there was no better audition for resuming our partnership than a three-Test series against the same opposition in their backyard. The pressure was on.

The first Test at Eden Park – where the All Blacks hadn't lost since 1994 – was a hell of a match. Toby Faletau scored a peach of a try in the left-hand corner, and we were leading after an hour. But as is so often the case, New Zealand raised the tempo in the final quarter and pulled away. Their last try was scored after the hooter had sounded, and while the 18-point margin flattered them, it was a familiar, depressing story. High hopes dashed by the ruthless black tide.

The second Test was in Wellington, and I can't help thinking that a decision I made in the first minute led to the end of my Wales career. Their centre Malakai Fekitoa received the ball off the top of a line-out and ran straight at me, his knees pumping. I planted my feet and set myself for the tackle, and then, *crack*, our heads collided. For a brief moment, everything went blurry. It was a horrible, disorienting sensation, like an out-of-body experience. Play continued and I hauled myself gingerly to my feet, unsure which direction I was meant to be facing. My vision was still blurred and I could see two of everything. Every player had a watery outline like a strange hologram shadow surrounding them. My legs felt as if they weren't connected to my brain: dead and unresponsive, like a pair of heavy logs being dragged beneath me. I was struggling to retain my balance or support my weight, expecting to collapse at any moment. After what seemed like a minute, I was gripped by the opposite sensation. I felt lighter than air; like a feather floating on the breeze. I was running, but as in one of those terrifying fever dreams, I wasn't getting anywhere. I had no power left. The whistle blew and it sounded unusually piercing. I felt a trickle of blood dribbling over my cheekbone. The doc appeared alongside me with the magic sponge and started dabbing at the cut that had now started bleeding profusely.

I was spaced out, but lucid enough to know I was experiencing all the classic symptoms of concussion. As a qualified doctor, I knew more than anyone what the dangers were, but as an international rugby player I stupidly chose to ignore them. The match-day doctor hadn't seen the collision, and I lied to my physio, saying that I was cut and nothing more. It was a reckless, bone-headed decision. The doctor in me was screaming, *Get off, get yourself out of harm's way*, but the warrior within was saying, *Stay put. You're playing the All Blacks; you can't look weak.* We'd frightened them for an hour the previous week, and I desperately wanted to be part of a Welsh victory in New Zealand, whatever the cost. After what had happened to me in 2008 when I collided with Australia's Stirling Mortlock, the decision to stay on was even more witless, but in the white-hot cauldron of Test rugby, heart overrules head and passion trumps common sense. In a classic case of hubris, I thought I'd be letting the team down by leaving the field. The fact is, I was letting them down by staying on.

I had a very poor game. I was off the pace, my judgement was skewed and I made a succession of amateur mistakes that belied my status as a big-game player. One missed tackle on Beauden Barrett led to a try that turned the tide in their favour. We battled bravely and never gave in, but I will forever remember that game as the one where I betrayed my principles. I regret it to this day, because staying on tarnished my reputation, undermined my team's chances and – most importantly – seriously risked my health.

A few days later, I seriously upset our medical team by claiming during a press conference that I couldn't remember half the game. It was true. I'd watched the match back during the debrief, and entire chunks had seemingly been erased from my memory. I normally have a forensic recall of every moment the day after a game, but I'd watched that one back like a fan catching up on the highlights. It was an unsettling experience. Back at the hotel, Prav Mathema called me out on it, angry not only that I'd said such a thing publicly, but that I'd hidden it from him in the first place. He was absolutely right, and I issued a retraction the following day. I said that the comments had been throwaway, and that I was exaggerating. My official line was that symptoms of concussion had only become apparent after the game, but I was covering my tracks. I knew the truth.

With the series already lost, we rolled over in the third Test and suffered a spirit-sapping 46–6 defeat. Later that night, the Brexit vote filtered through, which, as a passionate European, did little to lift my mood.

I needed to escape after such a depressing end to the tour, and another trip to Monaco was just the tonic. After the World Cup, I'd been invited to a Rolls-Royce event in London and had been offered the use of one of their Wraith sports cars for a week. The price tag on one of those is a cool quarter of a million. That month, I'd twice had the wheels nicked off my Mercedes in Wandsworth Town, and didn't want to be in the embarrassing situation of returning a £250,000 car to Rolls-Royce minus its wheels, so I cheekily asked if I could have it in Monaco instead. They agreed and a week or so after the New Zealand tour, I was picking it up from a dealership on the French Riviera.

My old Monaco acquaintance Mark Thomas had invited me to a barbecue and a spot of paddle tennis at Prince Albert's private mountain palace in Roc Agel. I realise as I write this how ridiculous that sentence sounds. My companion for this trip was Michael Press, the same guy I'd accidentally put in a coma back when we were kids.

Michael hails from Gabalfa, one of the less genteel suburbs of Cardiff, and his brusque response to my invitation was 'What the f*** is paddle tennis?' It was a good question, and one I put to Mark. 'Don't worry,' he said, 'just pack shorts and trainers.'

Roc Agel is Prince Albert's summer retreat atop Mont Agel, and is accessed via a steep, treacherous mountain road; the same windy track that Albert's mother, Grace Kelly, was driving down when her car plunged over the side of the cliff in 1982. The palace was on the upper slopes, surrounded by security guards and miles from anywhere. I'd been to Albert's 'driver's cocktails' the night before the Grand Prix at his main residence a number of times, but this felt significantly more exclusive. There were probably only twenty people there, and Mike and I felt like total charlatans.

We had a few beers and some food and I fell into conversation with this demure American girl whose voluminous hair was hidden beneath a baseball cap. She had a certain detached presence about her, but was refreshingly down to earth. After half an hour of easy-going chat, I went to grab a few more drinks when Mark approached me, asking, 'You know who that is, don't you?' I had no idea. 'It's Lana Del Rey.' I felt like a right idiot. Her song 'Summertime Sadness' had been on my summer playlist, and had most probably been playing in the Wraith as we wound our way up the mountain road. As I was digesting that, Bono walked in, strode to the bar, ordered a beer and introduced himself. We chewed the fat over rugby and he asked how Brian O'Driscoll was, then he announced he was off to watch the paddle tennis. Things were getting increasingly surreal.

It was my cue to get changed and discover what on earth this game was. It turns out it's very similar to actual tennis but with stringless racquets, and you're allowed to hit the ball off the walls like in squash. Michael and I were up against Prince Albert and his mate, who'd been an Olympic pole vaulter. Unsurprisingly, we were no match for those two, and we suffered the indignity of being aggressively heckled by Bono and Lana Del Rey as we slipped and stumbled our way around the court. It didn't help that we'd sunk several beers before attempting to play a game we'd never heard of until a week earlier. Halfway through the first set, a flustered Mike turned to Bono and said, as if he'd known him his whole life, 'Oi, Bono. Either go and get your kit on and 'ave a go yourself, or pipe down.' You can take the boy out of Gabalfa, but you can't take Gabalfa out of the boy.

The next day, we arranged to have lunch with our new friends and drove to the unbelievably palatial Hermitage Hotel in Monte Carlo to pick up Lana and her Australian publicist, Stella. What we'd forgotten was that our mate Rhys was flying out to meet us that day, meaning there'd now be five of us in a four-seater car. Pressy relied on his charm to come up with a solution. When the girls emerged from the hotel, he greeted them in his broadest Cardiff accent: 'All right, Lan, we've got a little problem, but I've sorted it.' Lana was eyeing him suspiciously. 'There's five of us, but only four seats, so I'll squeeze in the middle and you girls can go either side.' Lana looked at him with the most withering expression, and said, 'That's *not* happening.' Instead, she and Stella agreed to share a seat while Pressy had one to himself.

And so it transpired that we cruised around five miles down the coast to Èze-sur-Mer with Lana Del Rey and her publicist squished up in the back seat of the Wraith. We hung out all afternoon at Anjuna Beach Club trying, with no success, to initiate the two of them into the world of rugby drinking games. Needless to say, those two sophisticates were far from impressed by our antics. Later, I had a glimpse into what real fame felt like when we took a stroll around the town and swarms of delirious fans began flocking around Lana, begging for selfies. I found myself acting like her private bouncer, physically restraining the more eager ones who were desperate to get close to their idol.

She politely refused every photo because her publicist said the minute she agreed to one, it would be posted on social media, then word would get out she was in Èze-sur-Mer and she'd be even further swamped. Also, her image is one of cool detachment. There's always been a strong air of mystery about her, and a flood of gurning selfies would somewhat undermine that. For the record, she was a lovely girl. I'm not sure I'll ever persuade her to come and see Wales play, though, especially as Pressy tried his hardest to get her to agree to a date, claiming repeatedly that he was 'in LA a lot for business', which is as hilarious as it is untrue.

Those couple of days had set the bar really high, and we were never going to sustain that for the remainder of our road trip. We went from a palace in Monaco to a succession of basic three-star hotels and a few hairy moments parking the pristine Wraith in grimy multi-storey car parks. But the company was good, the sun continued to shine and we had an absolute ball.

20

DISAPPOINTMENT
AND OPPORTUNITY

I had always had this notion that if I was still playing Test rugby at thirty, it would be a miracle. The uncompromising way I approached the game was almost certainly unsustainable in the long term. On my thirtieth birthday, in November 2016, I was dropped for the first time in more than seven years. Not counting the first time after my debut, because that had been the plan all along, it was only the second time it had happened. This time it was unquestionably because of a bad performance. Three days earlier, I'd played really poorly in a humbling defeat to Australia. Unlike recent encounters with the Wallabies, this one was done and dusted by half-time. We'd been slow, ponderous and uninspired, and my individual contribution had been way below my usual standard.

Everything about the game felt off. The stadium was half-empty, the roof was open and it had been an early-afternoon kick-off. Previous encounters against the Wallabies had been under a closed roof at night in front of a capacity crowd. As the game unfolded, I made a litany of errors: poor reads, mistimed tackles, dropped balls, over-cooked passes. The harder I tried, the worse it got. Everyone makes the occasional mistake, but I'd never delivered such a consistently poor performance. They tore us to shreds, playing at a lightning speed we couldn't live with and carving gaping holes in our defence at will. It wasn't even a particularly strong Aussie vintage.

There are many character traits the Welsh are renowned for, and honesty ranks among the highest. As I was walking down Castle Street later that night for a few quiet beers, someone hollered, 'Oi, Roberts. You were f***ing average today, boy.' My mates all started laughing and, despite myself, so did I. I knew I'd played poorly and so did most of the fans. As perverse as it sounds, I appreciate that brutal honesty. It's better than feeling paranoid that people are saying these things behind your back. As big or as famous as you get in Wales, you're never allowed to rise above your station. When you accept the responsibility of playing for Wales, the public owns a part of you. It's an unwritten part of the job description. My encounters with Harlequins fans in leafy Richmond were always ultra-polite and deferential by nature. 'Excuse me, Jamie, I'm really sorry to bother you, but would you mind awfully if we got a quick photo with you and our son Jonny. He's a big fan.' There's no such decorum back home. I've had fans get me in headlocks and tell me how badly I've played, while simultaneously asking me to smile for a selfie.

There's something unique about the Welsh and their ability to wrap up an insult in a joke. It's so disarming, you often don't realise you've been criticised until they've disappeared into the night. Others have lectured me earnestly and at length about how to improve my game. It can get annoying sometimes, but it's a reminder that it's the people's game. Without their passion, enthusiasm and commitment, none of us could make a living out of it. I've been on nights out with Welsh players who've refused photographs with people, and it's really annoyed me. They spend their hard-earned wages watching you play, so giving them a bit of your time after the game is part of the deal.

My thirtieth was safely the most miserable birthday I'd had to date. Donald Trump was elected US president in the morning, and in the afternoon I was given the 'tap of death' from Rob Howley. He ushered me into the Trecastell Suite at the Vale Hotel, opened his laptop and talked me through a succession of my most glaring errors from the Saturday before. Rob had been my coach for the best part of a decade, so when he turned to me and said, 'Mate, it was a really poor performance,' it cut deep. I'd been a starting player for eight years, and a foundation stone of the Welsh team during one its most successful periods. Now it felt like I was discarded goods. As was the case in 2012, Howley was in sole charge, with Gats away on Lions sabbatical, and he could see history repeating itself. He had no room for loyalty when his own job was on the line. It was a tough conversation, but I had no qualms. I'd played poorly and had to pay the price.

Much as I wanted to dismiss it as an anomaly, the fact was I'd played badly for three games in a row. That head knock against Fekitoa had precipitated a marked decline in my performance. It may have been a coincidence, but my decision to stay on the field had harmed my reputation, possibly terminally. The time for Howley to give an old stalwart the benefit of the doubt was up. Had my prediction about not playing into my thirties become a self-fulfilling prophecy? For the rest of the autumn campaign, I became a bit-part player, spending most of it picking splinters out of my backside on the replacements' bench. I didn't know it then, but my days as a starting player were over.

When the 2017 Six Nations rolled around, Rob was honest with me, confirming that Scott Williams had usurped me as first-choice 12. I'd started every Six Nations match since 2010, and they considered it only fair to give Scott the benefit of an extended run and an opportunity for him to stake a claim for a Lions jersey. I couldn't argue with that. I'd been afforded the same luxury. They'd let me grow in that 12 jersey, even when it wasn't my natural position, and now it was Scott's turn. As much as it hurt, I respected it. I wasn't jettisoned from the squad completely, but after so long as a starting player, the bench felt a long way from the action. While the coaches assured me that they 'knew what I could do', the thought of not being in the shop window ahead of the Lions tour was deeply concerning.

I had seven minutes against Italy, then came on with ten minutes left against England. We were ahead, having bullied them for much of the game, but in the dying moments, Foxy failed to find touch with a clearing kick and England scored the winning try from the resulting counter-attack. Although it wasn't my fault personally, I couldn't help but feel responsible. We'd been leading when I came on, and we ended up losing.

I met Tim Visser for coffee on George Street the day before the Scotland game, and taunted him mercilessly about Scotland's miserable record against Wales. I told him I'd never lost to Scotland and wasn't about to break the habit. The Dutch are a confident bunch, and he told me I might end up eating my words as well as the chocolate flapjack we'd just shared. I laughed sarcastically and wished him all the best. By the time I came off the bench, Scotland were well in control and Visser was having the game of his life. He'd denied Rhys Webb a try with a heroic tackle, and eventually went over for the winning try.

The Ireland game was my only positive experience of the campaign. I came off the bench at around the same time I had against Scotland, with Wales clinging on to a one-score lead. With three minutes left, Toby charged down a Johnny Sexton clearance and the ball bounced kindly into my hands. If ever a surge to the line encapsulated eight months' worth of frustration, it was that one. Sexton pretty much leapt on my back en route to the whitewash, but nobody and nothing was going to stop me from scoring. It was a genuine Roy of the Rovers moment, and I thought it might have earned me a start in the final round against France. It didn't. They went with Scotty again, and while I made my usual second-half cameo, it was in another losing cause. After thirty-five Six Nations starts in a row, I'd now been a sub for an entire campaign. And if that wasn't bad enough, we ended up in fifth place, our worst Six Nations finish for a decade. The Lions dream was receding fast in the rear-view mirror.

After the Six Nations, I received the letter that the Lions routinely send out to around seventy of the top players in Britain and Ireland. It always gives you that same frisson of excitement, even though you know far more people receive it than end up getting picked. My former Quins colleague Danny Care has had four of them in his career and has never made the final cut, so I wasn't about to get ahead of myself. The coaches knew me well, and I had a good deal of credit in the bank, but my performances in New Zealand in 2016 were bound to count against me, not to mention that stinker of a game against Australia. Add to that the fact I'd spent the entire Six Nations on the bench, and my case for inclusion seemed increasingly weak.

The day before the squad was due to be announced, I was boarding the train at Marylebone station when my phone buzzed. It was a message of congratulations from a friend of mine, the first of many after it emerged that Sky Sports News had declared that I was going to be named in the squad. There's always a flurry of speculation leading up to a Lions squad announcement, but it's rare that a news organisation declares unequivocally that someone is in. My story was newsworthy because of the fact I'd been dropped as a front-line player for

Wales, and there's rarely smoke without fire. While I tried with every fibre of my being to ignore it, I knew that their information must have come from a reliable source. The flame of possibility had flickered into life again.

I didn't sleep that night, and morning training at Quins was torturous. We had a team meeting scheduled at the exact time the squad was going to be announced live on television. I couldn't concentrate and paid no attention to what was being said. My phone was in the changing room, because it would have been unbearable had it started vibrating in my pocket during director of rugby John Kingston's interminably long briefing. Once it was finally over, I made a beeline for the changing rooms, taking care not to catch anyone's eye. Fumbling around for my phone, I saw that I'd received dozens of texts and voicemails. Congratulations or commiserations?

With a deep breath, I opened the first. It was from my brother: 'Unlucky Bro – difficult to know what to say to someone but I'm feeling your disappointment. You've had a hell of a run up till now and have a few years left. The sun will still come up in the morning and the knock-backs will only strengthen you kid.'

I scrolled through the rest of the messages in a kind of silent stupor. They were all of a similar sentiment. It was the hope that had killed me. My clubmates Joe Marler and Kyle Sinckler had been selected, so I sought them out to offer my congratulations, through barely suppressed tears. I wandered into the physio room feeling utterly deflated, only for the ever-loud and brash Tim Visser to bellow from a nearby bed, 'F***ing hell, Doc. I thought you were a dead cert yesterday.' He was trying to lighten the mood, but I wasn't ready for jokey banter. Graham Rowntree, our forwards coach, grabbed my arm and told me how unfair the past twenty-four hours had been. He was also the Lions forwards coach and would have known that the rumours were baseless, but he hadn't been in a position to tell me. I couldn't even say thanks, because I knew my voice would crack. Sometimes emotions are so overwhelming, you have to surrender to them, so I slipped off the bed, climbed the stairs and shut myself in one of the empty offices.

Once the door handle clicked shut, my defences dropped and I burst into tears. Not just token tears, but full chest-heaving sobs. I was mortified when John Kingston walked in, but to his credit he pulled up a chair and listened to me pour my heart out for twenty minutes, eulogising about the Lions and how it had changed my career, my perspective and the entire course of my life. Even now, when I cast my mind back to that April morning, I feel myself welling up. It was completely soul-destroying. The training session that followed was awful. My emotions were so raw and tender, I couldn't even begin to concentrate. I loved the Lions with a passion, and after touring South Africa and Australia, this had been my chance to complete the set. I spent the rest of the afternoon curled up on my sofa, crying and feeling sorry for myself.

I called Rob Howley the next day. I'm not sure why. I always want an answer, but sometimes there isn't one. I probably cared too much. He told me I'd been in the conversation until the very end, but they'd decided Ben Te'o was in better form and could add a bit more power. He assured me I was on the stand-by list and told me to stay fit.

A few weeks later, I was in Valletta, sinking a few beers and watching my mate Dom win his fiftieth cap for Malta against Israel – at rugby, believe it or not – when I received a call from Robin McBryde, the Wales caretaker coach. He came straight to the point in his gruff North-Walian accent: 'Jamie, how do you fancy being captain on the summer tour?' It was a wonderful surprise. He told me to think about it, but I didn't need to. Without hesitation, I told him I'd be honoured to lead my country. It had been a long-held ambition of mine, and one I thought would go unfulfilled because Warren had always preferred forwards as leaders. The press tried to frame it as a conso-lation prize – *you've missed out on the Lions so here, take this to soften the blow* – but I didn't see it that way at all. Granted, the opportunity wouldn't have arisen had I been selected for the Lions, but this was a different team and a different challenge, and one I was ready to confront wholeheartedly.

It was unique in every way. Our destination was the South Pacific, and the mission was to uncover the next generation of Welsh talent. It was all about the kids, and there was a duty on me to help. It was a sharp switch in mindset. Up until then, my overriding focus had been me, the present and my personal ambitions. This was all about the new breed and the future. I was going as a player, but as a mentor too. There was a smattering of senior players like Alex Cuthbert and Scott Williams named to accompany me, but it was largely young fresh talent taking their first steps in international rugby. Guys like Ellis Jenkins, Cory Hill and Tomos Williams.

The Pacific Islands nations produce a quarter of all the world's professional rugby players. Let that sink in. It's an astonishing statistic, and one which illustrates just how deep and well-stocked their talent pool is. Despite this, they remain unloved and underfunded by rugby's authorities, and are resigned to having their best players pilfered by bigger, richer unions able to entice them with bumper salaries and a supposed better quality of life. Though New Zealand is by far the biggest beneficiary, it took them ninety-one years to deign to play a Test on the islands, when they eventually faced Samoa in 2015.

Considering their invaluable contribution to world rugby, the islands have been criminally neglected, and it was a major point of pride for me that Wales were travelling there to take on Tonga and Samoa. It was the first time we'd been there since 1994, and I emphasised to the boys how lucky they were, and how special an opportunity this was. I wanted them to understand this was an epic adventure to a remote, far-off land, and not just a sterile rugby trip. We went out with the intention of winning both Tests, but I wanted us to travel with our eyes open. I'd seen enough of the academy generation and their mobile-phone addiction to realise they had to be dragged rather than teased out of their comfort zones. This was going to be a tour like no other, and I wanted to ensure we embraced the South Pacific in all its palm-fringed, sun-drenched glory.

Unfortunately, the match against Tonga had to be moved to New Zealand because Tonga's ground wasn't up to scratch. Though disappointing, it did mean that my parents, who were following the Lions tour in New Zealand, could come and see me lead Wales out in the flesh. It also means I can claim the rather unique honour of being the only Welshman to lead his side to victory at Eden Park. I'll leave that on the CV, and bury the name of the opposition in the small print. It wasn't the most fluent of performances, given the number of new caps and combinations, not to mention the driving wind and rain, but it was a comfortable enough victory. During my post-match TV interview, I said conditions would be considerably better in Samoa, optimistically predicting a feast of running rugby. Little did I know what would await us there.

On arrival, the weather was as warm as the reception we received. The Samoan people couldn't have been more welcoming. Nothing was too much trouble, and wherever we went we were greeted with beaming smiles. I'd never been to Samoa, and the reality far exceeded even my lofty expectations. It was an absolute paradise. Our hotel, Aggie Grey's, where Wales had stayed during their first ever South Seas tour, was right on the ocean, affording incredible views. Turquoise lagoons lapped gently onto the powdery white sand, and the beach was framed by palm trees.

It didn't take me long to appreciate the concept of 'island time'. The humidity is so oppressive that everything operates at a snail's pace. Punctuality isn't a concept the Samoans are too familiar with, and when a bus Thumper had ordered still hadn't arrived fifteen minutes after the agreed pick-up time, I started getting twitchy. We'd booked it for a visit to the To Sua Ocean Trench as part of my mission to see as much of the island beyond the hotel as we could. I felt like an aggressive teacher on a school trip, until someone with a beaming smile approached me and explained in the most calming way that 'it'll come when it'll come.'

To Sua, which translates as 'giant swimming hole', was the most picturesque place I'd ever taken a dip. The aquamarine pool was surrounded by huge leafy green tropical plants, and only accessible via a rickety wooden ladder. The water was impossibly clear, and shoals of luminous fish would dart about as you drifted languidly in its depths. After several hours in this multi-coloured paradise, I was a firm advocate of 'island time'.

The beautiful weather didn't last, and as the week progressed, the humidity levels crept up towards 100 per cent, a sure sign a storm was coming. On game day we woke up to an overwhelming tropical downpour. Huge, fat drops of rain were hammering relentlessly on the tin roofs of the villagers' huts, and cascading through the over-flowing drains. Water was everywhere, and we feared that the stadium pitch might flood. We'd trained there earlier in the week and it was spongy enough when dry. As well as having the weather to contend with, a sickness bug had taken hold in the camp, and a few of the lads had been ill with vomiting and diarrhoea. We'd also lost four of our best players to the Lions, with Gats calling up Cory Hill, Tomas Francis, Gareth Davies and Kristian Dacey in a direct echo of four years earlier, when Shane et al. were summoned to make up the numbers. As in 2013, it caused an almighty stink and the old arguments about devaluing the jersey were reheated. So my second match as Wales captain would be played in monsoonal conditions, and with a team depleted by illness and absence.

Samoa were looking to redeem themselves after a humbling by the All Blacks the previous week, and they started strongly, handling the conditions well as they built a 10–9 lead. My most vivid memory of the first half is sprinting off at the end of it, fearing that my bowels were about to erupt. I'd had the runs all week, and clearly hadn't fully flushed the bug out of my system. I made it to the cubicle in the nick of time, before emerging to find a queue of around ten ashen-faced colleagues waiting their turn. We were pretty much all in the same boat. The coaches were patiently waiting for us to congregate for the team talk, amid a cacophony of belching, groaning and dramatic chundering. It was what Larry David might have described as an 'olfactory nightmare'. When the rap on the door came for our two-minute warning, any notion of a team talk had to be abandoned.

We changed out of our sopping wet jerseys and got into a huddle. All I had time to say was 'Boys, whatever it takes.' Ellis Jenkins and I locked eyes. He'd been among the spewers, and looked as pale as a ghost, but there was a grim determination in his expression. The half-backs, Aled and Sam Davies, were our saviours in the second half, keeping Samoa at arm's length with some really smart tactical kick-ing. As the half progressed, the sickness continued to tighten its grip, though not on the bowels of one of our forwards, who I'm convinced had a little 'accident' on the pitch. The conditions were so awful that you couldn't tell for sure amongst all the mud and rain, but if I had to put money on it . . .

It was the very antithesis of running out to a capacity crowd under the lights at the Principality Stadium, but part of me treasures that experience as much as any other. It was a horrible escapade to endure, but to push beyond the pain barrier in howling wind and rain and come away with a battling victory was an incredible feeling. I couldn't have been more proud of the lads. If you'd seen the state of the changing rooms at half-time, you wouldn't have thought that group of pale, green, sickly players had a chance in hell, but no one was willing to give up and roll over. Everyone just dug in and – for want of a better expression – gutsed it out. For that, I was immensely proud. Shaun Edwards, who's won more than fifty trophies in his remarkable career, told me afterwards that it was one of the best wins he'd been involved with. That says it all.

On reflection, the tour felt like a bit of a parting gift. It hadn't been presented to me as such, but it was the equivalent of my carriage clock. *Thanks for your service, all the best.* A more cynical person might have considered it beneath them to go on tour with a bunch of kids after being spurned by the Lions, but I considered it an amazing privilege. I didn't know it then, but I think Gats had already cast me adrift. He was a pretty stubborn bloke once he'd made his mind up, as I'd witnessed in the past when the likes of Phillsy and Bomb had been jettisoned. Looking back, the South Seas tour was an attempt to smooth my exit. I was allowed a controlled descent with a parachute rather than being booted out of the plane.

That realisation didn't come until later, though, and when Rob Howley called to tell me I hadn't been included in the squad for the 2017 autumn internationals, it came as a genuine bolt from the blue. I knew I'd lost my place to Scotty during the Six Nations, but that had been solely to give him a run in the shirt. I didn't think he'd played that well, and he'd been overlooked for the Lions too, so I saw the autumns as a clean slate. Because I was caught off guard, I started waffling about how well I was playing for Harlequins and how disappointed I was at the snub. Rob insisted it was nothing personal, explaining that they wanted to experiment with two 'playmakers' in the 10–12 axis. After losing the first Lions Test in New Zealand, when Ben Te'o had been picked to perform the same role I had in 2013, they'd switched tack and picked two fly-halves, in Johnny Sexton and Owen Farrell.

It's a southern-hemisphere approach, one that relies on unpicking defences with guile rather than blasting through them with brute force. I'd seemingly become an anachronism overnight, a victim of changing trends, like someone stubbornly wearing boot-cuts when everyone else was wearing skinny jeans. They'd picked five centres in total, two of whom were uncapped and one, Owen Williams, who'd played for Wales once. If Foxy went down, the four remaining centres would have five caps between them. It seemed a big gamble, but they were looking ahead to the next World Cup. When the conversation had run its course, I told Rob that I wanted to speak to Gats as well. I wanted to hear it from the horse's mouth.

He called me a few days later while I was relaxing in the Ned rooftop bar in London, where he repeated Rob Howley's explanation about wanting to try something different. He was understanding, saying he knew how difficult it must be to take, especially when I'd given as much to Welsh rugby as I had. His tone was generally sympathetic, but he said one thing that jarred. He claimed he was sick to death of the constant references to 'Warrenball' and wanted to get the press off his back. There was still a vocal minority of critics who craved a bit of flair and panache over Gatland's blood-and-thunder approach, and as much as he liked to dismiss it as water off a duck's back, the carping clearly bothered him. I'm not sure how he expected me to interpret that, but it felt like I was being thrown to the wolves just to appease the critics. 'With respect, I couldn't give a damn what the press thought.' That's what I wish I'd said, but I chose to keep my counsel, biting my lip rather than making my real feelings known.

The narrative about Wales being a one-dimensional side without a plan B had been playing in the background throughout Gatland's tenure. Our championship wins and World Cup runs had helped mute some of the critics, but they were never entirely silenced. We were only ever one defeat away from the argument rearing its head again. There's no doubt it gnawed away at Gats, and however much it grated, we had to acknowledge that there was more than a grain of truth to it. We'd repeatedly come up short against the southern-hemisphere sides and were less effective against teams that could match us physically.

I agreed that we needed to evolve, but I couldn't understand why I couldn't be part of that. Again, I wished I'd asked him that question directly, instead of becoming consumed by insecurity. All those doubts about whether I had the skillset or was versatile enough came bubbling back to the surface. I wasn't built to be a silky second play-maker; that's not my game. I'm a power athlete, and a physical force, but I can also put people into space. I may not be able to perform conjuror's tricks in the vein of a Matt Giteau or a Quade Cooper, but I can unlock defences using decoy lines, running angles and my passing game. I felt like I still had a lot more to offer.

Nicole and I watched the first November international against the Wallabies in a Covent Garden pub, and I felt completely detached as we fell to our thirteenth consecutive defeat against them. Foxy was stretchered off towards the end with a nasty-looking ankle injury, which was a bittersweet moment for me. I was naturally gutted for Jon, who'd had some real bad luck with injuries, but this one had nudged the door ajar for a possible recall for me.

Sure enough, the following morning, Thumper rang to invite me back into camp. It wasn't over yet; this was my chance. I trained really well, determined to prove I wasn't a fading force, and Gats rewarded me with a place on the bench against the All Blacks. I came on for Scotty with the game still in the balance, but my only contribution of note was a defensive error that gifted them a try. As they attacked off a scrum, I rushed up to close down Sonny Bill Williams and slipped in the act of making a tackle. It left a hole in the midfield for Rieko Ioane to glide through and put the game beyond reach. In many ways, it's a fool's errand being thrown on in the last quarter when your team's already trailing the world champions, but I was absolutely furious with myself. There was one more game of the autumn series remaining. It was against South Africa, and it would offer me a chance at redemption.

Then came the bombshell. My agent called and said we had an issue. Harlequins had been in touch to say that if I played in that final game, I wouldn't be a Quins employee by the weekend. I couldn't understand it. I'd reported for Wales duty with their blessing, and had been gearing up for the final week of the autumn when the ultimatum arrived. I was to report for training on Thursday morning or they'd tear up my contract. Their position was that the South Africa game fell outside the international window, and they weren't obliged to release me for it. This was exactly the situation I'd sought to avoid. I had signed a side letter to my contract on the understanding it gave me *full* release. What exactly had changed, and why had their tone become so bullish and impersonal? As far as I could see, they were the ones reneging on the terms of our deal, not me.

A few years earlier, Northampton had released George North in similar circumstances and been fined £60,000 by Premiership Rugby Limited for breaching its policy. I could only assume Harlequins had now been threatened with a similar sanction. It was precisely because of George's situation that I had made sure I had the appropriate clause in my contract. Within that side letter was an explicit guarantee that Harlequins would deal with any potential conflict with PRL, and cover the costs of any fines.

It was a horrible position to be in: forced to make a choice between my Wales career and my life in London. One more shot at international glory versus my job, my livelihood and the roots I'd laid down in Wandsworth Town. Playing for Wales had always been my absolute priority, and with that in mind, I assured Warren I'd do everything in my power to play if he wanted me involved. He was straight with me, saying they wanted to give the newly qualified Hadleigh Parkes an opportunity at 12, but were fully intending to pick me on the bench. That was the affirmation I needed, and with my hackles well and truly raised, I pledged to fight Harlequins over the issue.

Things escalated pretty quickly, and when they appeared intransi-
gent, we got in touch with Blackrock Solicitors in London for a legal
opinion. We were prepared to go to court over this, and wanted to send
a message to the Quins board that we weren't going to roll over the
minute they started flexing their muscles. The offer of an olive branch
followed when the Harlequins CEO, David Ellis, proposed a rendezvous
on the Wednesday. My agent and I met him at a hotel off the motorway
near Swindon, where he looked me in the eye and told me I'd breached
a confidentiality clause in our agreement, rendering it void.

I had no idea what he was talking about. They were saying I'd
blabbed about the clause, which was patently untrue. The only people
that knew about it, other than me and my agent, were the Wales
coaches, and that was kind of the point. They were acting like it was
some clandestine, under-the-table deal when the letter explicitly said
that they'd log the issue with PRL and cover any penalty costs that
may arise. The exact quote read as follows: 'The club intends to fully
disclose to Premiership Rugby our intent to release you, but wish to
keep this matter private and confidential between the parties.' We'd
always been really discreet about my Wales involvement during 'out-
of-window' periods, to the extent that the team photographer would
ensure I wasn't in any training photos released to the media.

Ellis said they had evidence I'd told people other than Gatland, but
they weren't willing to say who I was supposed to have told, or how
they'd found out. I was beginning to feel like a character in a Kafka
novel. My hunch is that Premiership Rugby had decided to police the
policy more strictly, and had perhaps threatened them with a points
deduction as well as a fine. If that was the case, I was simply the fall
guy, an unwitting pawn in an elaborate game of rugby politics.

That brought with it a certain guilt complex. If I stuck to my guns
and won the legal argument, Quins might lose league points, which
could impact on their prospects and therefore the prospects of my
colleagues. They were mid-table at the time, so depending on the
penalty, my 'selfishness' could contribute to them either being rele-
gated or missing out on a top-four finish and a shot at the title. They
said they were happy to write me a cheque there and then for £130,000
to buy me out of my contract. That was more than double the amount

Northampton had been fined over the George North incident, which confirmed my suspicions they were facing a bigger punishment.

I was livid. My life was in London, I was still studying at Cambridge, I'd bought a flat, and Nicole lived down the road. I'd been offered an enormously lucrative deal in Japan the year before which would have eclipsed the money I'd been on even in Paris, but I'd stuck with Quins out of loyalty. I wanted to honour my contract with them, and I wanted to reach an ultimate goal of a hundred caps for Wales. This was the year I was hoping to do that and Quins, in a heartless bureaucratic way, were looking to trample all over it.

Ellis was cordial enough, even offering me a future role at the club if I was willing to walk away from Wales. God knows what that meant. It was difficult to embrace such an offer when the bloke making it was also threatening to sack you in the same breath. We stood up, shook hands, and I told him I'd decide within twenty-four hours.

I didn't sleep a wink that night as I wrestled with a maelstrom of conflicting emotions. When the sun eventually came up and the fog of twilight began to dissipate, I thought, *It has to be Wales. My club has always been Wales; it's the team I've played for the longest, the jersey I've worn the most. Wales is my country, and that's where my loyalty should lie.*

A text from my agent said that the lawyers from Blackrock had reviewed the paperwork and thought I had a 50–50 chance of winning a tribunal. It was a significant gamble. As the day progressed, the conviction I'd felt in the morning had begun to weaken, and all the same doubts returned to crowd my thoughts. Going back to the hotel after afternoon training, I bumped into Shaun Edwards, who could sense how conflicted I was. I opened up to him, saying it felt reckless to walk away from my life in London for the sake of one last cap. Shaun's never been one for big emotional gestures, but he's always been good at taking the emotional temperature. After listening patiently, he looked me in the eye, and said, 'Lad, if you go home now, Gats won't pick you again.' He understood my dilemma, but he also understood the way Warren Gatland conducted his business.

After dinner, with a sense of resignation, I had a conversation with Warren I never imagined I would. I turned down the chance to play for

Wales while suspecting, with Shaun's words echoing in my mind, that it would be the last time I'd ever have such an opportunity. No grand farewell. No hundredth cap. No dream finish. No final chance to gulp down that intoxicating cocktail of emotions that comes with a match day in Cardiff. I really hoped he could see that my hand had been forced, and that Quins had me over a barrel. He shook my hand firmly and told me he understood, but on some level I'm sure he thought I was turning my back on Wales.

I walked out of the team room on the verge of breaking down when Leigh Halfpenny intercepted me, and took me to the bar for a coffee. Pence listened patiently as I poured my heart out, nodding in all the right places and saying all the right things, but I was inconsolable. Once I'd drained my mug, I wandered out in a daze, nearly bumping into Alun Wyn Jones, who was coming the other way. He'd witnessed my emotional exchange with Warren Gatland and asked what was happening. I explained the situation, told him about the choice I'd made and apologised to him. As much as I had to view this decision as an individual one, I couldn't shake the feeling I was letting my comrades down. He enveloped me in a big man-hug and wished me all the best.

It was my last interaction with a Welsh colleague in a Wales camp, before I trudged through the car park and clambered into my car. I cried all the way down the M4 on my journey back to London. Crossing the Severn Bridge seemed symbolic, like an imaginary drawbridge had been pulled up, slamming the door on my Wales career. I still couldn't understand why it had come to this. Why were Quins being so hard-hearted? I couldn't decide whether they wanted to keep me, and were using these bully-boy tactics to do so, or whether they actually wanted rid of me and were using the clause as a convenient excuse to hide behind. Paranoia jostled with all the other emotions that were crowding my brain: sadness, betrayal, regret, despondency.

I didn't sleep again that night, and turned up to training looking gaunt and exhausted. John Kingston seemed astonished to see me. It was obvious from his reaction that David Ellis had already put the wheels in motion to get me sacked. I'll never forgive Ellis or the Quins board for railroading me into that decision. I'd signed the contract in good faith, but when push came to shove it wasn't worth the paper it was written on. It pains me to this day that I buckled and gave in. To make matters worse, Hadleigh Parkes had an absolute stormer, scoring a brace of tries on his debut, while I watched on helplessly from my distant London flat.

The following March, I sat in John Kingston's office listening to him explain the reasons why Quins weren't going to re-sign me. They'd signed the All Blacks centre Francis Saili and had little room left in the budget. His exact words were 'If I told you what we could offer you you'd be insulted, so I'm not going to bother.' I'd declined a big-money move to Kobe Steelers in Japan, and turned my back on my country, and for what? Nothing. If time is a healer, a good deal of water is yet to pass under this bridge. The animosity runs deep to this day. It was always impossible to make a rational, clear-headed decision in a situation like the one I faced, but I know now that I made the wrong one. I should have stayed with Wales.

21

SOUTH AFRICAN SUNSET

Every muscle in my body is tensed as the Alpha Jet scorches a path through the Austrian alps at 600 mph. I'm pinned to my tiny seat by the g-force when I hear the pilot's crackly voice over the roar of the jet engine. 'Jamie, are you ready?' Before I have time to respond, he lifts his hands off the controls and says, 'All yours.' For ten terrifying seconds, I'm in control of 3,500 kg of metal, flying at face-melting speeds through the jagged peaks of Austria. I loosen my sweaty palms as the pilot reclaims the controls and starts doing loop-the-loops, flipping the plane upside down. It was simultaneously the most frightening and the most exhilarating experience I've ever had, a genuine once-in-a-lifetime thing, and it wouldn't have happened were it not for rugby. I mention it because I want to make clear that however crushed I felt at the way my Test career ended, rugby on the whole has given me access to a whole world I could never have dreamed of. That flight happened during one of my Red Bull trips, and all I'd been told in advance was that I was heading to Austria for two nights to film a cinema advert. Treasured experiences such as these, the tours I've been on, the countries I've seen, the amazing people I've met – all were made possible because I happened to be half decent at rugby. When I look back, the countless fond memories will easily eclipse the disappointments and low moments.

That's not to say I didn't plumb the depths of despair after the Harlequins saga. For the next two years, every time a Wales squad was announced and I wasn't in it, my heart would sink and I'd feel a little less like me. I'd always text Rob Howley and badger him for answers. I'm not sure why, but I think I was looking for closure. I almost wanted to hear him say, 'Thanks, mate, your time's up,' but he never did, allowing me to cling to the hope of an unlikely recall. I was locked in a perpetual cycle of hope and disappointment. There wasn't a day that went by when I didn't think about it, and at times it was *all*

I thought about. I'd lie awake pondering how I might get back into favour. Did I need to change my approach, like a golfer remodelling his swing, or should I stick to what I knew best, and hope that ball-carrying inside centres would come back into fashion?

I was earning less at my new club, Bath, which I'd joined in August 2018, than I had been at Quins, which was another, literal, reminder of my declining value. I'm not quite sure if I've ever suffered with depression or not, but for nearly two years I lost my zest for life, spending endless hours moping around Bath, nursing a sense of grievance. I enrolled on an MBA course at Loughborough University, hoping to fill the empty space and manufacture a degree of pressure that I knew I needed to feel alive. At times, though, I felt physically shrunken, as though a vital part of my identity had been stripped away. My Test jersey had been like a suit of armour; without it I felt smaller, less imposing, more vulnerable. I understand the nature of professional sport – careers are finite, and selection is often based on the whims and vagaries of one person – but I'd been in favour for so long that when the end arrived so abruptly, I felt unmoored and disoriented.

I was glad to be outside Wales. Bath is a wonderful city with picture-postcard views around every corner, and a fantastic, authentic rugby club and ground in the Rec, so there are worse places to be when you're feeling a bit down about life. Running out in front of 12,000 Bath fans didn't replace the international buzz, but it was a damn sight better than running out in front of half-empty stadiums back home and being around boys who were involved in the Wales squad. As frustrating as it was being overlooked for Test selection, it would have been much worse if I'd been playing in Wales. Gatland often picked players in the national squad to groom them for eventual selection. They weren't necessarily ready, but they'd probably grow into Test players at some point in the future. They were part of the overall jigsaw in a way that I no longer was. To have been in that environment, and to be rejected in favour of someone not yet at my level, would have been even harder to swallow. When I reflected on those phone calls with Gats and Rob in which they said the door was still open, I realised they may have been white lies. It was more than likely a straight 'thanks and goodbye', and I'd been naive to think otherwise.

The 2018 Six Nations was the first I hadn't been involved in since 2008. I'd planned to go for a long walk on the beach during the opening match against Scotland and pretend it wasn't happening. I didn't feel ready to watch a Wales team I wasn't part of. I hope that doesn't come across as self-centred; it's just that after a decade of the Six Nations being a defining pillar in my life, I couldn't bear the thought of merely being a spectator. As game day dawned, though, I realised I *had* to be there. I had to confront it head on. Pushing it to the margins would just amplify my state of denial; the equivalent of sticking your fingers in your ears when someone's trying to talk to you. I had to accept that I was no longer a Welsh international, and physically going to the match was the way to do that: to don a shirt and jacket instead of my rugby kit, to watch from a distance rather than feeling the searing heat of battle.

I arranged to meet up in the Cardiff Blues box with Peter Thomas and Richard Holland, the chairman and CEO of the Blues, as well as my good friend Rhys Blumberg, and made my way there on foot, wandering down Westgate Street amid the red-shirted hordes. I was an actor in the scene I'd been so accustomed to watching from the air-conditioned comfort of the team bus. I was now right amongst it all – the whiff of spilt beer, the clamour of broken conversation, the rousing bursts of song and the excited ramblings of thousands of fans. It was a kaleidoscope of noise and colour: women in daffodil hats, children in baggy jerseys with red dragons painted on their cheeks, pensioners in blazers and club ties skirting the more rambunctious youngsters crowding the pavements outside the City Arms. It felt strangely liberating. These were people just like me: passionate, proud Welsh rugby fans, excited about what lay ahead. My heart was racing as I walked through the Cardiff Arms Park entrance. I'm not sure why, but I felt nervous and on edge, less in control of my emotions than I'd been for every match day I'd experienced in the previous ten years.

On my way to the box, I bumped into Foxy, who was injured and on corporate duty. He'd not made plans to watch the game itself, so I dragged him into the Blues box with me. From there, we watched Wales take Scotland apart in a one-sided drubbing. Most neutral observers had predicted a Scotland victory, so it was an extremely satisfying result from a Welsh perspective. From a personal point of view, it just increased my feelings of redundancy. Not only was I discarded goods; my absence had been barely noted. Hadleigh Parkes played well again, and it felt as though the torch had been passed on. As much as it felt like spying on an ex having a whale of a time with her new lover, it was an important part of letting go. Seeing the tries rack up and hearing the exultant cries reverberate around the packed stadium was a strangely melancholy experience. I felt completely detached, watching from a sealed box high up in the third tier while down below my friends and comrades were at the mud-stained, sweat-soaked coalface. But it was a necessary catharsis. I needed to close the door and move on. I was an ex-international.

I'm conscious that there's a perception of me in certain quarters as a privileged bloke who's had everything handed to him on a plate. It's true that I've never quite conformed to the stereotype of a Welsh rugby player, and it's coloured some people's opinions of me. Whether it's my education, my comfort being in the public eye or my love of travel and some of the finer things in life, I've always felt something of a square peg in a round hole. Throughout my career, I've suffered jibes about being 'Mr Perfect': whispered comments and sly digs when I've left training early to go and work on the wards, taunts about me living the life of a student or travelling the globe in my free time, enjoying the best of all worlds. They were almost always meant in jest, but there were times when it got wearing, when it felt more like jealousy or resentment, and it certainly played on my insecurities. It has all contributed to what I feel is a misplaced perception of me as being cocky and arrogant, whereas all I've ever wanted to do is maximise every opportunity that came my way. That's the attitude I've always had, probably a product of my upbringing, but it's often perceived in Wales as getting above your station. Classic tall poppy syndrome.

The idea of people sniping from the sidelines gnawed at me for years and played on my insecurities. *Look at Roberts, that big-headed bastard who's got it all.* I'd worked so hard to achieve what I had and enjoy the opportunities that came my way. Of course I'd soaked it all up and enjoyed every second, but I was always conscious of how my attitude and approach might be perceived by others. When I was young, I worried incessantly about what other people thought, reading everything that was written about me in the newspapers and taking the criticism to heart. There were times when I was so sketchy after a night out, I'd search my own name on Twitter, dreading what I might find out; what people might have seen or what they thought about me. It wasn't until I moved to France that I was able to rise above all that, to realise how suffocating the goldfish bowl had become.

In October of 2019, after fifteen months at Bath, I received a WhatsApp message from a Welshman called Jonathan Gardner, who was working as an analyst for the Canterbury Crusaders in New Zealand. Their coach, Scott 'Razor' Robertson – a former All Black with a penchant for break-dancing – had apparently dropped my name into the conversation when discussing midfield options. After nearly two years of feeling my career was on an inexorable slide downwards, this was a fizzing jolt to the ego. The Crusaders were the best club side in the world. Needless to say, I was keen. After a few conversations with Razor, I was offered a provisional contract for the following Super Rugby season, which was scheduled to run from January through to June 2020. Nicole, being an avid traveller, was all for it. I broached it with my coach at Bath, Stuart Hooper, who was happy to release me early. All my ducks were in a row.

Little did I know that the England rugby team was about to scupper my dream move. While I was awaiting official confirmation from the Crusaders, England shocked the rugby world by dumping New Zealand out of the World Cup in a one-sided semi-final. Within days, the New Zealand Rugby Union had vetoed my transfer to Canterbury. The nation had gone into paroxysms of panic following the defeat, and the powers that be had decreed that the signing of an ageing Welsh centre to their country's premier club team would block the progress of a home-grown youngster. The Crusaders were as shocked as I was, and were forced to tear up the contract. I was absolutely gutted.

I returned to Bath the following day in the pouring rain struggling to summon any enthusiasm for a bone-on-bone tackling drill with the forwards. Despite the grandeur of their Farleigh House training base, the rain-sodden fields of the West Country suddenly seemed infinitely less appealing, and Stuart Hooper had already put the feelers out for a replacement. After showering off and returning to my flat through the increasingly heavy downpour, I picked up the phone to my agent and told him to work his contacts abroad. The seed had been sown and my wanderlust had returned.

A few weeks later, I was at the gym when he called back and asked, 'How do you fancy Cape Town?' The Stormers were looking for a 12 with Test experience. With respect to Christchurch and the Crusaders, this was even better. The prospect of basking under warm South African skies as the winter gloom was deepening here in England was immensely uplifting. I'd had a love affair with South Africa ever since I toured there as a schoolboy. The Stormers coach, John Dobson, happened to be in London on business, so I jumped on a train from Bath to meet him. Over a couple of pints in an Oxford Circus pub, we shook hands on the deal.

On New Year's Day 2020, I woke up to a text from John saying that the deal had been rubber-stamped and they were ready to welcome me in Cape Town. I was told the visa might take a while to process, but the Stormers' skipper, Siya Kolisi, who'd just captained South Africa to World Cup glory, was able to pull a few strings and speed things along. Nicole and I were enjoying a mid-morning ice cream on the King's Road when I had a phone call confirming my visa had been approved and two seats had been booked on a BA flight that night. I jumped in a taxi to collect my visa while Nicole returned home and hurriedly packed our cases.

We essentially had about four hours before we had to leave for the airport; just enough time, I reckoned, to fit in a marriage proposal. I'd bought the ring a month earlier and it had been burning a hole in my pocket ever since. Her family were all in London, living in an apartment by Albert Bridge, so I seized the moment and called her dad. Thankfully, permission was granted and they hastily booked a table at George Best's favourite London haunt, the Phene, for us to enjoy the briefest of celebrations. After dragging an unenthusiastic Nicole away from the last-minute packing to 'take the dog for a last London walk', I dropped to one knee on a beautifully illuminated Albert Bridge, and popped the question. Fortunately, she said yes, because her mum, dad and sister were waiting round the corner with a bottle of champagne on ice. We had time for a glass each before we had to jump in the taxi and head for the airport. We were in Cape Town by morning.

We landed on our feet with an apartment on top of the Fifteen on Orange hotel with panoramic views of Table Mountain and Lion's Head. Life was amazing. The stunning beaches of Camps Bay and the vineyards of Stellenbosch were all a Vespa ride away, and Cape Town itself was a sparkling place to live, fringed as it is by craggy mountains and overflowing with gourmet restaurants, hip bars, amazing galleries and cosy coffee shops. It was everything you could dream of in a city. As career swansongs go, our South African sojourn was going to be difficult to beat.

On the night of our arrival, I was summoned to a drag club for my Stormers initiation. Bleary-eyed and exhausted after our night flight, I was hauled up on stage and ordered to neck three pints. Dillyn Leyds was their social secretary, and although I'd never met him, he'd already come up with a chant for me. To the tune of 'Bread of Heaven', he started singing, 'Jamie Roberts, Jamie Ro-oberts, feeeeed him now and he will score, feed him no-ow and he will score.' Within seconds, the entire bar had joined in. It was quite the welcome.

The rugby was fantastic too. I made my debut at Newlands against the Hurricanes in front of 30,000 vocal, passionate fans. The atmosphere was buzzing, not just inside the stadiums, but across the entire country. Two months earlier, in a moment of enormous symbolic significance, Siya Kolisi had become the first black South African captain to lift the World Cup. The Springboks had made a mockery of England's favourites' status, blowing them away with a powerful performance that lifted the entire Rainbow Nation. And here I was playing alongside Kolisi and several other world champions, including Pieter-Steph du Toit, Herschel Jantjies and Steven Kitshoff. After a few years of feeling unloved and off the radar, I was back at the epicentre of world rugby and loving it.

It was a wonderful trip down memory lane, too, as I revisited many of the iconic venues I'd played at with the Lions back in 2009. Ahead of the game against the Lions (the South African version), I delivered a tongue-in-cheek presentation to the lads, using footage from the 2009 game in which I'd scored two tries and been Man of the Match. I explained that I had fond memories of Ellis Park and a proud winning record against the Lions. It came back to bite me because I can honestly say I've never been so exhausted as I was in that game. On my previous visit, I'd been ten years younger and we'd played in cooler night-time temperatures. A decade on, in the searing midday sun, I was reduced to a wobbly wreck. After an 80-metre sprint to attempt to prevent a try, I collapsed on my hands and knees, sucking huge draughts of air into my lungs like an emphysemic pensioner.

Although Nicole and I were exposed to the very best that Cape Town had to offer, reminders of the seedier side of life I'd witnessed on previous tours were never far from the surface. Drugs and prostitution were rife, and an underlying threat of violence remained. As an entitled Westerner earning good money and living in a luxury apartment, I felt continually conflicted at the obvious gulf between the richest and the poorest in South African society. Not far beyond the gleaming skyscrapers of central Cape Town lay the sprawling shanty town of Khayelitsha, home to nearly two million people living in pitiful conditions way below the poverty line. I was shocked at the indifference shown by some of the locals to the plight of poor, black South Africans, and would regularly empty my pockets for beggars and homeless people. On one occasion, I inadvertently caused a brawl between a gang of street children by buying them a bag of chocolate. Once I'd turned the corner, they all started fighting over it, scrabbling around on the floor and pushing each other into the road.

By mid-March, we'd won four of our opening five games and were hitting our straps. I was starting to think I might have another trophy in me. The memories from 2009 had also triggered an idea that was irresistible for a rugby romantic like me. The Lions were due to tour South Africa again the following summer, twelve years after our 2009 odyssey, and the first game on their schedule was against the Stormers in Cape Town. How amazing would it be if I could play *against* the Lions in the same country I'd toured with them during that life-changing adventure more than a decade ago. It was a tantalising target. After my disappointing end with Wales, what appeared to be the perfect career denouement was unfolding in front of me. And then the world changed.

*   *   *

The deadly coronavirus that had been spreading through the Far East and Europe hadn't been causing much concern in Africa. It was seen as something that was happening on distant shores, and the authorities in South Africa seemed unperturbed by the rising panic. As disturbing as the news footage of mass graves and empty, locked-down cities appeared, it was seen primarily as Europe's problem.

We played the Sharks in Kings Park, where the Lions had lost the opening Test back in 2009, and as we jogged off the pitch, the stadium PA announcer declared, in strangely apocalyptic tones, that Super Rugby was being suspended indefinitely. It came as a huge surprise to the players, who'd had no inkling up until then. In the changing room, coach John Dobson played it down, telling us to take the week off before reconvening the following Monday. It was being dismissed as a little bump in the road before normality resumed, but the scientist in me knew that it was a big deal. As an expat, I'd been following the BBC news coverage on my phone, and the sense of alarm contrasted sharply with the more sanguine tone of the South African broadcasters.

Unsure what to do, Nicole and I treated it like a holiday. A mate of mine, Tim Swiel, who I'd played with at Quins, lent us a car for the week and we travelled up the Garden Route, through Knysna, Plettenberg Bay and Hermanus, where we stayed with my ex-Bath team-mate Francois Louw's parents. No restrictions had been imposed at this point. Bars and restaurants were open and people were mixing freely. The South Africans didn't seem remotely bothered about the coming storm.

By the time we arrived back on the Sunday, a national lockdown had been announced. The nightmare was coming true. This was a global pandemic, and no one was safe. Nicole and I were gripped by a sudden urge to go home. Being 8,000 miles away from our families and friends when people were dying in their thousands no longer seemed so appealing. On Monday, the team reported to the High Performance Centre in Bellville and I told John Dobson I wanted to leave. He laughed it off, telling me to relax and claiming the league would be back up and running in a few weeks. I told him, 'Dobbo, mate. We ain't gonna be playing for months, potentially years.'

The gravity of the situation had well and truly sunk in with me, while the South Africans still appeared to be driving blind. The lockdown was days away from coming into force and Nicole and I started looking at villas in Camps Bay to hunker down, away from the city and the massed swarms of humanity. It had become clear that this thing was spreading fastest in highly populated urban areas, and the prognosis for the poorly sanitised, ultra-crowded shanty towns didn't look good. We went as far as viewing a couple of villas that evening, but then a further announcement was made that South African airspace would also be going into lockdown from Thursday night. We woke up on Tuesday morning, went for breakfast and decided, 'Let's get the hell out of here.'

I went on Skyscanner, as any expat Brit in South Africa would, and there were no flights available before the deadline. The only one I could find was on the Friday, so I booked two seats at £330 a pop, hoping they'd still let foreigners leave once the deadline had passed. Then on the Wednesday night, the president, Cyril Ramaphosa, announced in a sobering television address that *all* international flights would be grounded at midnight on Thursday. We were stuck. It was a horrible feeling. I went back on Skyscanner and spent hours trawling around looking for alternative options, eventually discovering an indirect flight with connections in Addis Ababa and Zurich, which took around twenty-seven hours and cost an eye-watering £3,000. Feeling desperate, I whacked two on my credit card. The following morning, I had two lots of good news: a text from BA saying they'd brought our flight forward to 10 p.m. that night to beat the travel ban, and an email from trip.com saying they'd been unable to confirm seats on the other flight and had refunded my six grand. Phew.

We had half a day to pack our lives up again. I barely had enough time to bid farewell to my new team-mates before heading to the airport. There we were confronted with a scene of total chaos and disorder. There were hundreds of people crowding the aisles, shouting, arguing and crying in frustration. Most of them didn't have tickets and were just hoping for the best. We'd been really fortunate. There were three BA flights scheduled for London, but only ours had been brought forward. There was an inevitable delay leaving and we were still stuck on the runway when midnight arrived. For a brief moment, we feared we'd have to get off, but the slot was honoured and as the wheels left the tarmac, Nicole and I clinked glasses and thanked our lucky stars we'd made it out in time.

Two weeks after returning home, my agent called and said the Stormers were happy to get me off the books. Rugby's financial security, precarious at the best of times, had fallen off a cliff. With no prospect of rugby resuming in the near future, income from paying fans and TV broadcast deals had dried up virtually overnight. UK-based players were being placed on furlough and forced to take pay cuts, and I was out of work. In the grand scheme of things, my first-world problems were a thundering irrelevance, but there was no denying that my dream career swansong had quickly and dramatically turned sour. I spent the next three months twiddling my thumbs in Chelsea, cycling round London's empty streets and contemplating life after rugby. That, it seemed, was me done. I honestly thought I'd never play professional rugby again.

After a couple of weeks of walking the dog round Battersea Park and bingeing on Netflix, I started to wonder if there was any way I could put my medical training to use. Seven years had passed since I'd been anywhere near a ward, but I knocked together a CV and sent it to Cardiff and Vale Health Board. There was no way I could have gone to work in the trenches with all the doctors and nurses, but they saw an opportunity to get some positive messages out there amid all the gloom, hiring me as a kind of 'NHS Champion'. It was a really fearful time, and the news was a constant cycle of death, illness, misery and despair. Because of my profile as a rugby player, the NHS saw me as a conduit for good news; someone who understood the clinical environment and could tell stories from the front line about all the amazing work that was being done. I visited maternity wards, palliative care wards, cancer wards, laboratories and many other environments and wrote about the incredible work being done by the most dedicated of teams under the most testing of circumstances. I also emceed the opening of the 'Dragon's Heart Hospital' in the Principality Stadium, built in a matter of weeks to accommodate the hundreds of extra patients requiring treatment. The entire experience was humbling, and a reminder of how lucky we all are to live in a country with a National Health Service like ours.

Meanwhile, the taps had been turned off to every rugby club in Britain, plunging them all into financial disarray. Player recruitment had ground to a halt because no coach knew what his budget was going to be the following season. There was no guarantee there'd even be a new season, so it was a genuine surprise when my agent called in July 2020 to say an opportunity had come up at the Dragons. They'd signed the Australian three-quarter Joe Tomane before the pandemic, but he'd decided to return home. That left a hole in their midfield, and as the money had already been allocated, their head coach, Dean Ryan, had been allowed to spend it. Part of me would have loved to finish my career back where it all began at Cardiff, but the Dragons arguably offered an equally satisfying sense of symmetry. Newport was the team I'd supported as a boy, and Dad, for one, was very happy that I'd be bringing the curtain down on my career at Rodney Parade.

My one wish, before I hang up the boots for good, is that I get to play in front of a crowd once again. Those Rodney Parade terraces don't half look windblown and lonely compared to the bustling hives of humanity they were in the late nineties when I stood amid the black-and-amber-shirted hordes, raucously cheering on my heroes. I'd give anything to run out once more and luxuriate in those sights and sounds, to feel that warm embrace that makes sport the glorious folly that it is. It's about the spectacle, the drama and the sense of shared passion. Without people watching, it soon loses its lustre. For too long, that surge of anticipation you feel when something special is about to happen on the field has been absent. That unique stirring of space and displacement of energy when a winger gets the ball, or the collective intake of breath when he gets clattered into touch – these are the things that make the pain, the toil and the struggle all worthwhile. That, and the smell of stale beer and frying onions. I really need to experience that again.

Since 'coming home', I've become a father to Tomos, and Nicole and I are making plans for our wedding. The change in our circumstances, and the arrival of our son, has led to me playing some of the best rugby of my career. As any father will testify, the responsibility of being a dad puts everything else into perspective. Things that used to bother or irritate me seem gloriously trivial through the prism of parenthood, and I'm enjoying being a senior statesman among a group of talented youngsters. With the pressure off, I can enjoy my twilight years and hopefully pass on some wisdom to my younger colleagues. I've always been a strong believer that you learn more from senior players than you do from coaches, and I'm happy to be that guy.

I came tantalisingly close to adding to my tally of international caps when the new Wales coach, Wayne Pivac, put me on standby for the 2021 Six Nations game in Murrayfield. Had my Dragons clubmate Nick Tompkins not recovered from injury, I might have had one last shot. It's ironic that it came at a time when I'd made peace with my absence from the international scene. I'd love to play for Wales again, and at the ripe old age of thirty-four, I still feel capable of doing so. But I don't expect to, and that's fine with me. The 2019 World Cup gave me the closure I needed. I was lucky enough to travel to Japan with ITV and cover the tournament from a pundit's perspective. I got to witness the boys finally beat Australia when it really mattered, and share in their heartbreak when they suffered another agonising semi-final defeat to South Africa. I even got to play with the Manics again at Tokyo's Toyosu Pit.

I used to think I'd failed by not reaching 100 caps. It was a bit like a cricketer closing in on a century, only to be caught out off a deceptive slow ball. There was no blaze of glory, no bold stride out of my crease to send the ball crashing through the pavilion. But I can live with that. When I reflect on my wonderful decade at the top, ninety-seven Test appearances isn't a bad return. I'm not sure how much longer it'll last, but at the time of writing, I'm still in the top ten most-capped Welsh players. If you'd said that to the gangly teenager running around Rumney's Riverside Park in the early noughties, I reckon he'd have taken it.

ACKNOWLEDGEMENTS

Rugby union. It's a sport I've given everything to and from which I've received everything I could have dreamed of in return.

My life has forever revolved around rugby, be it at club level, in school, as a professional player or within its varied and inclusive social circles. Its values have helped define me as a person: hard work, enjoyment, respect and teamwork, to name just a few. They've been ingrained in me by some very special coaches, mentors, friends and fellow players down the years.

As I reflect on my career, I appreciate more than ever those that helped me on my path to the pinnacle. My coaches at CRICC were adamant that enjoyment through the Welsh language was all that mattered. I'm grateful to them for helping me fall in love with rugby. My PE teachers at Glantaf school in Cardiff were the most influential in my development as a player and person. Adolescence is a time of great change and I was very fortunate to have some wonderful teachers during my time there. Dai and Gat, thank you for helping me stay on the right track and for giving everything to ensure my friends and I grew up as good people, not just good rugby players. To the late Keri Evans, you were one of a kind. From welcoming me to high school as head of year 7 to penalising me for 'dull play' on Saturday mornings, you embodied all that is great about our sport. You're forever in our thoughts.

To Trystan and Tombsy, for going out of your way to help me juggle my professional playing commitments with my university studies, I am forever grateful. To Dai Young and Bob Norster, who first welcomed me into the professional ranks at Cardiff Blues and gave me my first opportunity, thanks for believing in me and giving me the guidance I needed. To all the coaches and support staff at Racing 92, Harlequins, Bath, the Stormers and now the Dragons, thank you for your support during my time spent at your club.

I fondly remember the moment Shaun Edwards tapped me on the shoulder before the second Test at Loftus Versfeld on our Wales summer tour in 2008, telling me I'd be wearing the number 12 jersey that Saturday. It became a defining moment in my life and career. Having won my first cap on the wing and second at full-back, playing at 12 in my third Test against the current world champions in their own backyard was everything I'd dreamed of. After that day, the battle of the advantage line was a drug I couldn't get enough of. It came to define my career.

To Warren Gatland, Shaun Edwards, Rob Howley and Neil Jenkins, thanks for giving me my opportunity at Test level. Thanks for backing me through the good and the bad times, and helping me develop as a player and person. Thanks for identifying the strengths in my game that enabled me to thrive in the midfield for club and country. To all the support staff at the Welsh Rugby Union – Caz, Prav and JR, to name just a few – thank you so much for the best of times.

To the supporters, thanks for the love and praise as well as the insults. I've enjoyed both as much as each other. Our sport is all about you, your passions, and opinions. Without you, it is nothing. I've met so many brilliant people down the years on tour and in the stands, and I look forward to joining you on the terraces for a beer in the not too distant future! A huge thanks too to the members of the press I've been fortunate to work with. I respect immensely the work you do in promoting our sport to the wider public.

To the staff at Cardiff, UWIC, Cambridge and Loughborough universities, thank you for your understanding and support in helping me achieve my academic goals while pursuing my rugby career.

Ross, thanks for helping me write the book, mate. Your talent as a writer is equal to your brilliant talent as a broadcaster. I've enjoyed our long chats and getting to know you better. Your success as a broadcaster and author doesn't surprise me one bit. Long may it continue.

To my team-mates, thanks for the good times. We're fortunate to play a sport which has given us so many precious, cherished memories. I look forward to reminiscing over a beer or two in the near future. See you at the bar!

Lastly and most importantly, I'd like to thank my family. My brother, David, eighteen months older, was always the brother I was chasing, wanting to beat. It was that sibling rivalry that pushed me to greater heights and helped forge the competitive sportsman within. So, David, thanks for beating me up as a kid and being a loving older brother as we grew up together. To my parents, Jackie and Norman, thanks for providing me with a wonderful, loving family environment. You gave me all the ingredients to succeed in life and for that I'm forever grateful. Nothing was ever out of reach, every experience was maximised, no opportunity ever wasted. No doubt there have been difficult times, as there are in most families, but you both gave my brother and me all the love we could ever need. I look forward to raising my children the way you raised us.

To Nicole and Tomos, you are now my 'why'. Thanks for putting everything else in perspective and for making all those things that once seemed so important now so trivial.

I've been so fortunate to travel the world playing the sport I love. I've made lifelong friends with whom I've shared many training paddocks, stadiums, bus journeys and bars. I've experienced every emotion imaginable, from elation to utter despair and everything in between. But the one word I'll always associate with the sport is 'enjoyment'. This wild ride I've been on has brought me so much joy, and for that I'll be forever in rugby's debt.

Hope you enjoyed the read, Jamie.

PICTURE ACKNOWLEDGEMENTS

The author and publisher would like to thank the following for permission to reproduce photographs:

Section One: Allstar Picture Library Ltd/Alamy Stock Photo; Author's own; Author's own; Author's own; Author's own; Author's own; Huw Evans Agency; Reuters/Alamy Stock Photo; Author's own; Welsh Rugby Union; Welsh Rugby Union; Stu Forster/Getty Images; Jed Leicester/Shutterstock; Stu Forster/Getty Images; Stu Forster/Getty Images; David Rogers/Getty Images; Author's own; Inpho/Dan Sheridan; David Rogers/Getty Images; Ian Kington/AFP via Getty Images.

Section Two: Reuters/Alamy Stock Photo; David Rogers/Getty Images; Marty Melville/AFP via Getty Images; Tim Clayton/Corbis via Getty Images; Stu Forster/Getty Images; Welsh Rugby Union; Welsh Rugby Union; Welsh Rugby Union; Angus Jenner; Author's own; Cameron Spencer/Getty Images; David Rogers/Getty Images; Phil Walter/Getty Images; Welsh Rugby Union; Cal Sport Media/Alamy Stock Photo; Reuters/Alamy Stock Photo; David Rogers/Getty Images; Andy Hooper/ANL/Shutterstock; Nic Bothma/EPA-EFE/Shutterstock; Steve Bardens/Getty Images for Harlequins; Welsh Rugby Union; Author's own.

All other photographs are from private collections.

INDEX